From Tee to Green

Southern Alberta
Northern Montana
Southeastern British Columbia
Southwestern Saskatchewan

John Gradon

Detselig Enterprises Ltd.
Calgary, Alberta

From Tee to Green

© 1996 John Gradon
Calgary, Alberta

Canadian Cataloguing in Publication Data

Gradon, John.
  From tee to green
  Includes index.
  ISBN 1-55059-129-0
  1. Golf courses – Canada, Western – Guidebooks. 2. Golf courses – Montana – Guidebooks. 3. Canada, Western – Guidebooks. 4. Montana – Guidebooks. I. Title.
  GV985.C2G72 1996   796.352'06'8712   C96-910083-3

Detselig Enterprises Limited
1220 Kensington Road NW
Calgary, Alberta T2N 3P5

Distributed by:

Temeron Books Inc.
1220 Kensington Road NW, Unit 210
Calgary, Alberta T2N 3P5

Temeron Books Inc.
P.O. Box 896
Bellingham, Washinton 98227

Cover picture: The island 12th hole and 15th tee, Cottonwood Golf and Country Club, Calgary, Alberta. Photographs in this book by John Gradon.

All rights reserved. No part of this book may be reproduced in any form or by any means without permission in writing from the publisher.

Printed in Canada   SAN 115-0324   ISBN 1-55059-129-0

With much love

Doreen and Stuart

The finest companions a man could have
on the fairways of life

Introduction

The Fore Word

This book, a labor of love, is written with the travelling golfer, the "tour player," in mind.

It is a hole-by-hole guide to scores of courses open to public play in southern Alberta, eastern British Columbia, western Saskatchewan and northern Montana, and is meant to be a compass for adventurers charting new golfing waters.

From Tee to Green, compact and spiral bound, is designed to be carried in your golf bag or power cart, to be opened at the course you're playing, and referred to on each tee box as guidance on how best to tackle the hole.

In effect, it is a portable caddie to be used in the absence of first-hand advice from a member or regular who already knows the secrets of the course.

It is written by someone who has passed the same way before you.

It is not written by a professional golfer although many have contributed greatly to its evolution.

Rather it contains the advice of a reasonably competent, right-handed golfer with a handicap hovering around the 10 to 12 mark and hopefully improving, someone who loves the game, someone who sometimes plays it well, and someone, some have said kindly, who even understands it to a degree.

It is a genuine attempt to give fellow players the best possible advice and options to help them manoeuvre their way round the included courses with the least possible damage to their score and to have fun doing it.

To put my perspective in perspective. Assuming I connect cleanly, I strike a ball up to 240 yards with a three-wood tee shot, further with a driver I seldom use, a five-iron up to 200, an eight 150 and a full sand wedge just over the 100 mark.

I try to approach each hole as simply as possible endeavoring, sometimes unsuccessfully, not to overstretch my ability. Without being paranoid I try not to take too many chances.

It was during my summer tour of 1995 that Jack Nicklaus, inaugurating a revamped Eagle Bend at Bigfork, Montana, touched on that very topic.

He told a clinic my family and I were lucky enough to attend, "A 10-handicapper trying to play like a 6-handicapper will play like a 15-handicapper. A 10-handicapper playing within his capabilities will likely play like a 6-handicapper."

It is perhaps the best, if somewhat belated, advice I ever heard on the game.

Even in normal circumstances, I mentally file away lessons learned from each hole as I play it for the first time. This summer, during my journey of exploration and reacquaintance, those notes were physically entered in notebooks and on film as research for this book.

It had all begun with a chance remark thrown at me during a spring round in Montana that I should write a guide book. Well, I thought, I *do* write for a living and I *do* play golf . . .

The odyssey which the suggestion sparked was to end six months and nearly 15 000 kilometres later.

Needless to say there were moments on damp days on remote courses or on some lonely stretch of prairie or mountain highway that I really wondered what on earth I was doing, and about the magnitude of the task.

Something always happened, however, to reaffirm the mission I often told people had been undertaken "for the love of it, or the stupidity of it."

One such moment came on a balmy July night in Waterton.

The conversation was swinging animatedly back and forth across the dinner table. It was about The Game.

We talked of how golf in many ways is a metaphor for life itself with the holes being various stages through which we all pass, how each round in its entirety is a journey or lifetime full of challenge, adversity, recovery and, hopefully, eventual triumph.

We talked of the legends of the distant past, Bobby Jones, Walter Hagen, Gene Sarazen, Sam Snead, Byron Nelson, the era of Jack Nicklaus, Gary Player and Arnie Palmer and his Army.

We talked of today's giants, my man Nick Faldo (Please just get back to enjoying the game, Nick), Greg Norman, Nick Price, Corey Pavin, and their respective championships, personalities, swings and styles.

The banter drifted to courses, far away places with mystical names like Turnberry, Muirfield, Pebble Beach, Augusta and St. Andrews.

We talked too of Alberta courses, British Columbia courses.

We touched on what we thought made a good course good, a great one great, its architecture, its character, its philosophy, the respective problems of mountain versus desert, forest versus seaside. How to fade shots, draw shots, the advantage of flop over bump and run and vice versa.

But engrossed as we were, we eventually became conscious our enthusiastic conversation was selfishly one-dimensional and was perhaps beginning to dominate proceedings in the cosy confines of the restaurant in Waterton's fine Kilmorey Lodge.

During a rare mutual pause for breath, my sole and soul companion turned to the young American couple at the immediately-adjoining table three feet away and asked with a smile, "Is all this golf talk boring you?"

"Why no, not at all," trilled the young woman. "It's kinda wonderful to hear two friends talking about something they love so much. How long have you known each other?"

"Oh, I don't know," said Waterton Lakes' Ken Roome dryly, glancing at his watch.

"It must be all of four hours by now. I'm the head pro here and he's writing a book about golf," he said thumbing in my direction.

"That's wonderful," the vacationing Los Angeles twosome chirped in near unison. "You sound as if you'd known each other for years. What is it about golf?"

They had in fact for two hours been witness to some of what it is "about golf."

Roome and I knew that but he sat back, and with the back of his hands to the table and palms raised, pushed the subject over to me.

"I dunno, it's just being out there," I think I began.

And I continued with something like: "It's being with friends, making new ones. It's the scenery. It's the character of a golf course, the definition of its fairways, the contours of its greens. It's the course's history, its tradition, its feel. Its greenery or its wildness. It's how the course 'fits' with the mountains, the hills, the trees, the water.

"It's how pretty the sand and water look . . . or how threatening they look. It's where they are. It's the mountains, the coastline, or the desert. It's hitting the ball perfectly and seeing it arc away. It's duffing it. It's sometimes just aching to hit the ball well.

"It's the quiet excitement and uncertainty of playing a new course for the first time, or a familiar one where you've got some scores to settle.

"There's no such thing as a bad course, only some that are better than others. Each and every one has something to recommend it. It may be just one hole, one green, one fairway. It's usually a lot more than that though, maybe how you feel the course subtly applying pressure to your game, maybe a sequence of tough holes . . . or a sequence of easier ones lulling you to sleep so it can stand up and bite you."

"Or just one shot, one drive, one putt," laughed Roome. "All that's what it's all about."

"That's just wonderful," shrilled the non-golfers.

Before they departed into the night, they promised to drive up to the Waterton course the next day to have a look before leaving the national park homeward bound.

I like to think they did take time to stop and stare because that course at dawn is an awesome sight, special.

I know I did before setting off, revived, renewed and reconvinced on my own journey.

As I had tried to explain, there is, in my book – figuratively and literally – no such piece of land as a bad golf course, only some better than others.

They all have their qualities and some even exist in a state of grace, greatness.

But anywhere a ball can be placed on a tee as the fairway dew glistens in rising sunlight, or as the cloud fringes redden in the day's last rays, anywhere a perfectly-struck ball can be seen soaring forever against a verdant backdrop of trees or hills, or in the cyan of an infinite prairie sky, or over roaring surf, or against the grey mass of mountain granite . . . anywhere like that is hallowed ground.

As a youngster in Ayrshire, Scotland, I was raised near an abundance of such sacred turf.

I had the opportunity to play such courses as Turnberry, still my favorite anywhere, Troon, Barassie and Prestwick. There were rounds too at Royal Dornoch in the far north, St. Andrews and Gleneagles.

And there were rounds on courses with little or no Trans-Atlantic reputation like Bishopbriggs and Ballochmyle, but which in so many ways share the traits and calibre of their more noted brothers and sisters.

For a time I was a junior member at one such inland course. But over the years I drifted away from the game. There was a casual reunion with it about ten years ago here in Canada but in the last five years the relationship has blossomed into a more passionate, more serious, more rewarding affair without, I hope, any humor at the game being lost.

I however resist the temptation of joining a club. The reason is simple. I'm afraid of boredom and like playing a variety of courses and finding new ones.

But I do admit that when I am playing a course new to me, I'm pleased to be teamed with members or regulars who know its ins and outs.

Poor execution often makes a mockery of the information so kindly provided, but even so, it always seems so much better to at least know what I'm supposed to be doing.

And equally, if asked, I'm delighted to be able to share my local knowledge with visitors to courses with which I am familiar.

That is the philosophy of *From Tee to Green*.

I am sorry not to be teeing off with you in person. But I am with you in spirit and I have passed this way before.

If my advice prevents you unknowingly striking a seemingly "perfect" ball into a pond you had no idea existed, then it's been worthwhile.

Omission from the book in no way implies criticism of "neglected" courses. Only one course in all my travels declined my approach. That others are not included was simply a question of time, travel and space. Maybe next year.

None of the included courses made any financial contribution to be part of this book.

I have no doubt at all that some members and regulars at the various clubs included may have some alternative suggestions on how to approach certain shots or certain holes. That's fair enough. But I called it as I saw it, and isn't that a major part of the grand old game too?

I loved doing my "research." I hope you derive some pleasure and benefit from it. – J.G.

Contents

Southern Alberta

Akokiniskway Golf Club, Rosebud	17
Balmoral Golf Course, Red Deer	19
Banff Springs Golf Course, Banff	22
Bow Island Jubilee Golf Club, Bow Island	26
Brooks Golf Club, Brooks	28
Canmore Golf & Curling Club, Canmore	31
Connaught Golf Club, Medicine Hat	34
Cottonwood Coulee Golf Course, Medicine Hat.	37
Cottonwood Golf & Country Club, Calgary	40
Crowsnest Pass Golf & Country Club, Blairmore	43
D'Arcy Ranch Golf Club, Okotoks	45
Dinosaur Trail Golf & Country Club, Drumheller	48
Elbow Springs Golf Club, Calgary	51
Fort Macleod Golf Club, Fort Macleod	54
Hanna Golf & Country Club, Hanna	56
Heatherglen Golf Club, Calgary	58
Henderson Lake Golf Club, Lethbridge	61
Heritage Pointe Golf & Country Club, DeWinton	64
Highwood Golf & Country Club, High River	68
Inglewood Golf & Curling Club, Calgary	72
Innisfail Golf Club, Innisfail	75
Kananaskis Country Golf Course - Mt. Kidd	78
Kananaskis Country Golf Course - Mt. Lorette	80
Keho Park Golf Club, Nobleford	83
Lakeside Greens Golf & Country Club, Chestermere	85
Land O Lakes Golf & Country Club, Coaldale	88
Lee Creek Valley Golf & Country Club, Cardston	91
Magrath Golf Club, Magrath	93
McKenzie Meadows Golf Club, Calgary	96
Medicine Hat Golf & Country Club, Medicine Hat	99
Milk River Country Club, Milk River	102
Nanton Golf Club, Nanton	104
Oyen & District Golf Club, Oyen	107
Paradise Canyon Golf & Country Club, Lethbridge	109
Picture Butte Golf Club, Picture Butte	112
Pincher Creek Golf Club, Pincher Creek	115
Redwood Meadows Golf & Country Club, Bragg Creek	117
River Bend Golf Course, Red Deer	120
River's Edge Golf Club, Okotoks	123
Riverview Golf Club, Redcliff	125
Rolling Hills Golf & Country Club, Rolling Hills	128

Shaw-Nee Slopes Golf Course, Calgary	130
Strathmore Golf Club, Strathmore	133
Sundre Golf Club, Sundre	136
Sylvan Lake Golf & Country Club, Sylvan Lake	139
Taber Golf Club, Taber	142
Three Hills Golf Club, Three Hills	145
Water Valley Golf Club, Water Valley	147
Waterton Lakes Golf Course, Waterton Lakes National Park	150
Wintergreen Golf & Country Club, Bragg Creek	153
Woodside Golf Course, Airdrie	156

Northern Montana

Anaconda Hills Golf Club, Black Eagle, Great Falls	161
Buffalo Hill Golf Club, Kalispell	164
Eagle Bend Golf Club, Bigfork	167
Glacier View Golf Club, West Glacier	171
Marias Valley Golf & Country Club, Shelby	174
Meadow Lake Resort, Columbia Falls	176
Mission Mountain Country Club, Ronan	179
Polson Country Club, Polson	182
Signal Point Golf Club, Fort Benton	185
RO Speck Golf Course, Great Falls	187
Village Greens Golf Club, Kalispell	190
Whitefish Lake Golf Club, North Course, Whitefish	193
Whitefish Lake Golf Club, South Course, Whitefish	195

South-East British Columbia

Cranbrook Golf Club, Cranbrook	201
Creston Golf Club, Creston	204
Fairmont Hot Springs Resort, Fairmont Hot Springs	207
Fernie Golf & Country Club, Fernie	210
Golden Golf & Country Club, Golden	213
Kimberley Golf Club, Kimberley	216
Kokanee Springs Golf Resort, Crawford Bay	219
Mountain Meadows Golf Club, Elkford	222
Radium Hot Springs Resort, Radium Hot Springs	224
Riverside Golf & Country Club, Fairmont Hot Springs	227
Sparwood Golf Club, Sparwood	230
The Springs Golf & Country Club, Radium Hot Springs	232
Trickle Creek Golf Resort, Kimberley	235

South-West Saskatchewan

Chinook Golf Course, Swift Current	241
Cypress Hills Golf Course, Maple Creek	243
Elmwood Golf & Country Club, Swift Current	245
Harbor Golf Club & Resort, Elbow	248
Maple Creek Golf Club, Maple Creek	251
Riverbreaks, Riverhurst	253
Riverview Golf Club, Outlook	255

Statistical Guide   257

Detselig Enterprises Ltd. appreciates the financial support for our 1996 publishing program, provided by the Department of Canadian Heritage, Canada Council and the Alberta Foundation for the Arts, a beneficiary of the Lottery Fund of the Government of Alberta.

Appreciation is expressed to Steve Young for the drawing of the four maps in this book.

Acknowledgments

From Tee to Green would not have become a reality without the help, direct and indirect, and encouragement of many people. It would be wrong for them to go without grateful acknowledgement.

There is the Eagles Golf Society, a motley crew of inappropriately-named fairway friends, Gary Park, Tom Keyser and Don Martin. The group's often insane annual spring tour helps preserve sanity for other times and other places. In fact it was in this illustrious company during a tee-box pause in Montana that the germ of an idea first took hold.

I have been blessed, maybe cursed, with an until now at least uniquely useless talent for near-photographic recollection of golf holes I play.

Acting as tour guide on one course I'd already played, I detailed for the assembled newcomers where to put their ball, where not to, and what perils to look for next. Someone, Park I think, said: "You should write a guide book..." As a little bell went off in my head, I promptly put my drive exactly where I'd told them not to. It was later during the same trip as we wandered lost in the magnificence of Buffalo Hill in Kalispell, wishing we had a guide book, that the idea appeared to have real merit.

There's the Monday Club. This larger group consists of the Eagles plus Peter Menzies, Larry Wood, Chris Wood, Dereck Louw, Dave Pommer, Peter Brosseau, Bob Bergen, Robbie McKee, Monte Stewart, Tony Johnson and occasionally my son Stuart. I thank them all for their friendship, support, wit and abuse, both during so many rounds of this wonderful game and in life off the course.

There's Gord Jaremko, a non-golfer and therefore an endangered species. It was he who encouraged me in the enterprise and pointed me in the right direction – publisher Ted Giles – to have the end product see the light of day. To Ted, too, thanks and are we doing it again?

There are Mike Board, Mike Dempster, John Fawcett and Wendy McLean who helped me out with their members' expertise on Heritage Pointe, Redwood Meadows and Highwood.

There are, of course, all the club pros, assistants and staff who made this "tour player" feel so welcome during his odyssey of Summer '95.

Among their number I'll make particular mention of Waterton Lakes' head pro Ken Roome for his special contributions and guidance well above and beyond the call of duty.

Creston's Randy Panton, Radium's Bob Tutt, and Canmore's Darren Cooke are also due special thanks.

There was retired Calgarian Tony Valentine, marshal, player and gentleman at Fairmont's Riverside who gave me his wisdom on the game, the course and life during a guided tour. The same must apply to Trickle Creek's John Stone. Our several conversations during our respective tours of inspection on an exilharating late summer morning were a delight.

Down in Bigfork, Montana, there's Eagle Bend's John Porterfield who through several meetings, many telephone conversations and one slightly crazy round of golf, has become a friend. I wish him well in his new venture, Polar Bear Productions Explore TV in Whitefish.

And then there are the new fairway pals I made during seemingly countless rounds on seemingly countless courses during a seemingly endless summer.

There were Frank and Fran Saynor and George Smith who made a round at Innisfail a hoot even when, or was it especially when, the wheels came off bigtime for me after a hot sub-40 first nine. I was tired, okay? And Fran, ease up on Frank's game!

There was the Golden gang, Adam Marshall, Dean Nelson and Rick McCluskey who made a stranger to their group feel so welcome. Try not to hit the first tee running in future, Rick. It'll do wonders.

There was Gladys Mader and Millie Ironside at Swift Current's Elmwood who took it upon themselves to become my unofficial guides. I really believe you ladies. You just forgot to tell me about the "secret" water on the marvellous 16th. But I missed it anyway and got my par. So there!

There were the hilarious Ron and Jan Smith at Medicine Hat's Connaught layout. Too bad . . .

Thanks too to Philip Cronkite of Camera Expert at Midnapore Mall in Calgary for his expert services.

And, most important, there are of course my wife Doreen and son Stuart who gave me so such invaluable help in the production of the book and were such great company on and off the course during the Montana leg of the odyssey. Thank you Stuart for your computer know-how and for being a great kid.

And thank you Doreen for your encouragement, your advice, and your many hours of hard work, dedicated input, and editing. *From Tee to Green* wouldn't have been possible without it. Thank you both so much for all that, for much more and for being there.

John Gradon
February, 1996.

Southern Alberta

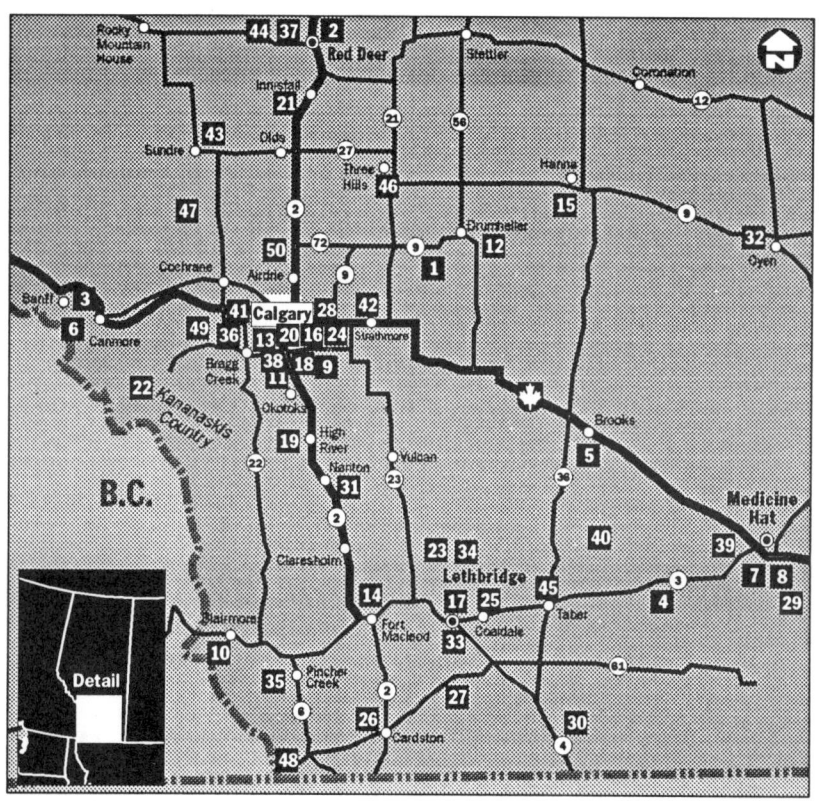

1. Akokiniskway Golf Club
2. Balmoral Golf Course
3. Banff Springs Golf Course
4. Bow Island Jubilee Golf Club
5. Brooks Golf Club
6. Canmore Golf and Curling Club
7. Connaught Golf Club
8. Cottonwood Coulee Golf Course
9. Cottonwood Golf and Country Club
10. Crowsnest Pass Golf and Country Club
11. D'Arcy Ranch Golf Club
12. Dinosaur Trail Golf and Country Club
13. Elbow Springs Golf Club
14. Fort Macleod Golf Club
15. Hanna Golf and Country Club
16. Heatherglen Golf Club
17. Henderson Lake Golf Club
18. Heritage Pointe Golf and Country Club
19. Highwood Golf and Country Club
20. Inglewood Golf and Curling Club
21. Innisfail Golf Club
22. Kananaskis Country Golf Course
23. Keho Park Golf Club
24. Lakeside Greens Golf and Country Club
25. Land O Lakes Golf and Country Club
26. Lee Creek Valley Golf and Country Club
27. Magrath Golf Club
28. McKenzie Meadows Golf Club
29. Medicine Hat Golf and Country Club
30. Milk River Country Club
31. Nanton Golf Club
32. Oyen & District Golf Club
33. Paradise Canyon Golf and Country Club
34. Picture Butte Golf Club
35. Pincher Creek Golf Club
36. Redwood Meadows Golf and Country Club
37. River Bend Golf Course
38. River's Edge Golf Club
39. Riverview Golf Club
40. Rolling Hills Golf & Country Club
41. Shaw-Nee Slopes Golf Course
42. Strathmore Golf Club
43. Sundre Golf Club
44. Sylvan Lake Golf and Country Club
45. Taber Golf Club
46. Three Hills Golf Club
47. Water Valley Golf Club
48. Waterton Lakes Golf Course
49. Wintergreen Golf and Country Club
50. Woodside Golf Course

Akokiniskway Golf Club

"By the River of Many Roses..."

Par 30/31

The Cree were here first and gave it its name. Then along came Albert Clark who, late in life, took to golf in nearby Drumheller. One day a few years ago he announced to his wife, Joan, he was going to clear some ground to practise some shots. It worked just dandy but only up to a point. So he decided to build a whole golf course, and he did, with the help of a local designer and some earth-moving equipment. Now it stands in the beautiful Rosebud River valley on the outskirts of the historic village of Rosebud. It wasn't my intention to include any par 3-type courses here but, after all, this one does have three par 4s and besides, there's not an easy par 3 to be found. It's challenging short-game golf in pristine surroundings.

#1 - Par 4.
R: 300 yards
F: 200 yards

Drive between trees into open fairway. Long hitters take note. You have as much chance of landing and sticking on this small, elevated green as you would on a dime. Play short and flop one on.

#2 - Par 3.
R: 160 yards
F: 150 yards

Only the flag top shows in a dip at the far end of a wide fairway. But beware, there's a nasty grass bunker 25 yards in front of green, and the trees backing it are merciless.

#3 - Par 3.
R: 210 yards
F: 135 yards

Simply an outstanding hole. The green is a distant target down across the valley, an old CN Rail bridge beyond, thick trees left of it and wicked shrub and bushes lining the right fairway. Be brave and play it as right as you dare. The landing area's deceptively big.

#4 - Par 4.
R: 255 yards
F: 200 yards

Another beauty. The Rosebud's on tee-box's left, and that railway track is hidden, too close for comfort, on the right. Hit onto steep 80ft. upslope to green. Practise that soft flop-shot again.

#5 - Par 3.
R: 165 yards
F: 155 yards

Start tee shot well right of flag, maybe at tall trees out there. Everything on this hole, contour, feel, look, is going to bring it back left towards the green.

#6 - Par 4.
R: 300 yards
F: 235 yards

Down by the riverside and it's picturesque beyond words. The river's right all the way up to the dogleg left about 230 yards out. But the further right the ball lands, the more open the green is for the approach.

#7 - Par 3/4.
R: 205 yards
F: 205 yards

Having fun yet? Alarming tee shot is up steep, mogulled hill to tiny green immediately backed by wall of railway ties. And adding to the lack of convention is the eight-inch ridge running diagonally across the dance floor.

#8 - Par 3.
R: 190 yards
F: 170 yards

Downhill tester. Rosebud's on the right and it curls round behind green. Bad idea to be long here.

#9 - Par 3.
R: 165 yards
F: 160 yards

Club up one more than normal for the length. Uphill finisher has the faithful Rosebud on the right, a tiny green carved into the hillside and fronted by railway ties. Ideal shot into green would be fade along left side. Doing it is something else.

Box 717
Rosebud, Alberta, T0J 2T0
Telephone: (403) 677-2250

The sixth fairway

Balmoral Golf Course

"A place for family and friends..."

Par 72/74

Manager Lesley Harder cheerfully admits that they've targeted their market and have gone for it with this charming 6 419-yard course on the northeastern fringe of Red Deer. If you like courses riddled with often-unnecessary sand and water hazards and manicured to the point of distraction, then this one isn't your bag. Instead Harden and company have concentrated on providing a fun place to play the game in surroundings maintained as naturally as possible. What you get is a pleasantly uncomplicated course ideal for the family and for beginners particularly. But that is not to say that more-seasoned campaigners won't enjoy some real challenge and lots of relaxation during a round on a course in a neighborhood named primarily to keep some homesick Scottish settlers happy.

#1 - Par 4.
R: 339 yards
F: 339 yards

A gentle, straightaway tree-lined opener. Long hitters could come close but Mr. Average will be left with a short iron or wedge onto a green with sand left and trees scattered haphazardly around it. There could be some tricky lies among them so be careful on approach.

#2 - Par 3.
R: 88 yards
F: 88 yards

Wedge time. But be careful with this ever-so-short hit across the water. There's a nasty trap front left and again the green is well-covered by attendant spruces.

#3 - Par 4/5.
R: 415 yards
F: 415 yards

A nice dogleg left where an ideal draw tee shot past the small fir tree on the inside of the turn will pay dividends for the approach. This green is well guarded by traps.

#4 - Par 5.
R: 480 yards
F: 480 yards

OB and the highway all along the left on this beautiful hole. Be straight out with the drive and then you'll have a long or mid-iron approach into a picturesque green nestling among the trees at the end.

#5 - Par 4.
R: 348 yards
F: 348 yards

Another really nice hole with a new green and traps in 1996. Best for tee shot is down centre right to open up severely-trapped approaches and well-bunkered green. There are to be traps short left and right of the green and bunkers on each side of it.

#6 - Par 3.
R: 187 yards
F: 187 yards

A charmer. This green has a sculptured hedge immediately behind and water just beyond that. The message is clear. Don't be long!

#7 - Par 4.
R: 322 yards
F: 322 yards

It's straight so long hitters can unload the cannon on this one. But there's a nasty trap on the right side and really the trees snuggle in pretty tight to the green. So look before you leap.

#8 - Par 4.
R: 404 yards
F: 304 yards

A dogleg right with the fairway narrowing in the turn. A solid centre-right tee shot should carry it easily however. A lofted approach should take the front right trap out of play but anything too left will be eaten by the trap on that side.

#9 - Par 5.
R: 564 yards
F: 476 yards

Super dogleg right where tee shot should be aimed centre right with a fade towards the small farm building in the distance. But watch OB all the way right. Your long trek will be rewarded by a tiny green with a huge tree immediately behind. Good hole!

#10 - Par 4.
R: 357 yards
F: 357 yards

A centre-right fade, maybe even with a long iron, will set up comfortable approach into a green trapped right. One thing. There's a disconcerting little dip bang in front, so make allowances for it.

#11 - Par 4.
R: 359 yards
F: 359 yards

The signature hole, best here, toughest for women, and a little gem. It's a late dogleg left. Really it's best to hit an iron about 200 yards out into the turn setting up a mid iron, short iron approach down an excruciatingly narrow funnel of trees into the green. Another complication is the dip in front. Green slopes back-left to front-right. Just an excellent golf hole.

#12 - Par 3.
R: 175 yards
F: 101 yards

What a vicious (great, that is) little par 3. Hit tee shot through or over painfully tight funnel of trees straddling the ravine. There's a hidden pond in gully left and the 'middle fairway' through the trees is in actuality rough. Green tilts back-right to front-left.

#13 - Par 4/5.
R: 415 yards
F: 405 yards

Uncomplicated straightaway hole that takes the strain off a bit. A welcome surprise on this one is a big green to make up for some others around here, particularly #9!

#14 - Par 4.
R: 430 yards
F: 366 yards

Toughest handicap hole for men. Favor the left all the way down if you can. The green is tucked away right. Anything too right could be disaster for an approach screened by trees and sand.

#15 - Par 3.
R: 152 yards
F: 152 yards

Fine par 3 across water in the gully. There's a big landing area on the other side, though, up towards a green trapped on the right.

#16 - Par 5.
R: 530 yards
F: 448 yards

Straight down the middle if you can. A slice or overfade could spell nightmares in hidden marshland right of the landing area. Further up, trees start pressing in on the right side. The green is guarded by sand on the left.

#17 - Par 4.
R: 371 yards
F: 371 yards

This latish dogleg right has a nice swing to it. Be in the centre of the fairway off the tee to best open up a small rolling green.

#18 - Par 5.
R: 483 yards
F: 483 yards

Attractive longish finisher requiring only patience and accuracy. Hit straight out towards the big rolling green which is trapped on the left.

R.R. 2, Site 10, Box 6
Red Deer, Alberta T4N 5E2
Telephone: (403) 347-6263

Banff Springs Golf Course

"Grandeur, grandeur and more grandeur..."

The vistas at this, one of the world's great golfing destinations, are endless and, needless to say, spectacular. The problem most of the time is concentrating on the game as you play any of the 27 holes now making up this course in the shadow of the Banff Springs Hotel, mighty Mount Rundle and Sulphur Mountain. The original eighteen, designed by world-renowned course architect Stanley Thompson, feature the Rundle and Sulphur nines. In a golfing world often gone berserk in design, they have stood the test of time and one can only hope, maintenance rather than alteration, will continue the tradition for decades to come. The new Tunnel nine, designed by Cornish and Robinson, opened in 1989. Golf here is not cheap, but the holes winding through the trees and providing unforgettable mountain views at every turn, plus the value of the experience, make it one of the few "must play it at least once" courses in the entire golfing world.

Par 71

Original Eighteen – (Rundle Nine)

#1 - Par 4.
C: 414 yards
R: 391 yards
F: 380 yards

Centre right is the place to shoot for off the tee on this tree-lined opener. A happy landing somewhere just beyond the traps left will leave a comfortable short-iron approach into a gently rolling green which tilts slightly right to left. Approach should favor the right avoiding the trap front left and one back right.

#2 - Par 3.
C: 174 yards
R: 164 yards
F: 129 yards

Lovely par 3 involving a tee shot up to an elevated green. Watch for pin placement here as one at the back will require an extra club. But do your best to stay below the pin on a green that slopes fairly dramatically back to front. Oh and by the way, it has seven traps.

#3 - Par 5.
C: 514 yards
R: 499 yards
F: 462 yards

Ideal drive on this challenging long hole is one centre left to land beyond fairway bunkers on the left. It can be reached in two with a long fade by long hitters but the rest of us should be content to lay up left and chip onto a green flanked left by two traps. This green is distinctly lower at the back and leans down right from centre. Tricky.

#4 - Par 3.
C: 171 yards
R: 157 yards
F: 78 yards

The world-famous Devil's Cauldron. Gorgeous and treacherous. The small green is surrounded by bunkers and is atop a sharp bank just across the lake. Go for it! But watch the wind.

#5 - Par 4. C: 424 yards R: 413 yards F: 401 yards	A tee shot centre, centre right up onto the top fairway level of this late dogleg left is the best for an approach into a very long, diagonal green with traps both sides and behind. The front end is lower than the back where putting can be a humbling experience.
#6 - Par 4. C: 351 yards R: 341 yards F: 330 yards	A fairly open fairway by Banff standards. Straight down the middle is the thing to a length you feel comfortable with for your approach into another heavily-trapped green. This one too slopes back to front so try and stay below the pin.
#7 - Par 5. C: 514 yards R: 504 yards F: 484 yards	Highest handicap hole and round these parts that's saying something. Tee shot has to be kept away from fairway sand on the left and then the second should be played into the region of more traps further along the left. Any approach landing on either edge of the long green should come down towards the centre.
#8 - Par 3. C: 138 yards R: 120 yards F: 102 yards	Check the flag for wind direction and strength. It's important to know on this one. It's usually into your face so club selection is vital. A centre ridge running from back to front splits the green with the right side running back down towards the water.
#9 - Par 5. C: 474 yards R: 455 yards F: 435 yards	The river is with us all the way right and there are sufficient gaps in the trees to spell trouble for a slicer. So centre left is best. Long hitters can sure go for it on this one. Best spot for lay up is short of the sand. This green, trapped back left and back right, flows down to the river.

(Sulphur Nine)

#10 - Par 3. C: 220 yards R: 204 yards F: 155 yards	Shot must cross loop in the water right and avoid a huge trap short left and left of the flattish green. There are more bunkers behind and right of it too. Watch out for that wind again.
#11 - Par 4. C: 398 yards R: 386 yards F: 377 yards	Sand, sand and more sand. Tee shot, however, should dice with fairway trap left to stay away from tree and gully trouble right. There's more sand both sides in the approaches too and there's another dip just in front. Green is flattish though.
#12 - Par 4. C: 420 yards R: 411 yards F: 402 yards	Tough hole and there's no doubt more fairway sand is gradually making its presence felt. The river's with you again on the right. Centre, centre left is ideal for the tee shot. The two-tiered green slopes down from the back.
#13 - Par 3. C: 230 yards R: 220 yards F: 145 yards	Long for the men. Shot has to hit another long green on which pin placement can drastically affect club selection. A three-wood is not out of the question here. One consolation is that

#14 - Par 4.
C: 429 yards
R: 415 yards
F: 401 yards

this well-bunkered green is another on which anything hitting the fringes will tend to drift down into the middle. Wow!

Best tee shot on a real challenge is centre left flirting with traps shortish left off the tee. Approach also has to dice with a fairway peppered with traps short of a well-bunkered green. Again it flows left to right towards the water and it rears upwards on the back end.

#15 - Par 4.
C: 411 yards
R: 404 yards
F: 348 yards

If the Cauldron is the signature hole, this is Banff's signature shot. Tee shot from the old elevated #1 tee box landing centre left across the creek is good for an approach into another heavily-trapped green. This one too tilts up at the back. Now, as for putting. Good luck and be prepared for anything. Par and you're laughing. That's all, folks!

#16 - Par 4.
C: 394 yards
R: 380 yards
F: 366 yards

Fly the left trap or hit right-to-left shot round it. Your choice. On approach all the trap trouble lies right, short and alongside. This green is tiered and is another where putting can be character-building.

#17 - Par 4.
C: 372 yards
R: 362 yards
F: 352 yards

Where did they find all this sand? Tee shot must be played centre right to take major trap front left of the green out of play for your, hopefully, short iron approach shot. This is definitely another green where being below the pin is a sound plan.

#18 - Par 5.
C: 578 yards
R: 565 yards
F: 451 yards

Majestic, sweeping dogleg right with OB and road right. Aim tee shot down the left steering clear of the fairway trap right. Then the centre-fairway trap is a good target to fly or lay up short of. The tiered green, trapped left, presents serious problems. Above the flag, just breathe on the ball. Below the pin, swallow a can of spinach.

Par 36

New Nine – (Tunnel Nine)

#1 - Par 4.
C: 388 yards
R: 368 yards
F: 349 yards

Tee shot needs to be hit through chute of trees onto a fairway which opens up on the right in the landing area. Drive should be hit centre right then and that will set up ideal approach line into a long, four-trap green. It's smallish and tiered but if you're on, you're in birdie territory.

#2 - Par 4.
C: 357 yards
R: 340 yards
F: 318 yards

Beautiful hole where a long iron or fairway wood is often best to land drive somewhere centre just beyond fairway trap on the right. That will set up nice mid or short iron approach to the green flanked left by water and bunkers right. Like most others here, this rolling green tilts towards the water.

#3 - Par 5.
C: 534 yards
R: 510 yards
F: 491 yards

A superb dogleg par 5 where a centre, centre right draw off the tee will produce the best results. Tricky lay up should split the bunkers on both sides of the fairway. Good one will open up green, guarded by intruding trees short left, to a short pitch on. Get the pitch as close as you can because putting on this big roller is a lottery.

#4 - Par 3.
C: 192 yards
R: 167 yards
F: 140 yards

Another short one where it pays to note the wind. The shot is across the valley to a high green which slopes from back-left to front-right. Anything short right of this one is pretty well doomed.

#5 - Par 4.
C: 384 yards
R: 365 yards
F: 358 yards

Best place to be is as close as you dare to the left side fairway bunkers. Take enough club to be there with your approach shot otherwise traps on the hill including a pot bunker immediately in front will cause you nothing but grief. Green slopes back to front and a saddle splitting it that way can roll the ball left or right.

#6 - Par 5.
C: 474 yards
R: 438 yards
F: 410 yards

Claustrophobic landing area between the major fairway trap on the left and the trees hugging the right. Finding the gap might mean a long iron or fairway wood. Then go for it in two or lay up centre short of the trap front left. The problem on this well-guarded green is a sizeable ridge crossing it causing front-end and back-end tilts.

#7 - Par 4.
C: 382 yards
R: 360 yards
F: 313 yards

Ideal drive of about 230 yards will land ball in wide landing area just before a narrowing neck alongside the fairway trap on the left. A mid-iron approach onto a tiered green has to avoid bunkers left, back left and back right. This green is another lottery with uphill, downhill and sidehill putts all part of the agenda.

#8 - Par 3.
C: 134 yards
R: 121 yards
F: 106 yards

Another short one where, surprise, surprise, the wind can be a player. And that water is tight right. The traps are threatening but it's far better on this one, with front-end slopes, to be on the front rather than deep at the back.

#9 - Par 4.
C: 424 yards
R: 404 yards
F: 366 yards

What a view! But you need to concentrate. Perfect tee shot is one of about 220-230 yards to land just short of the fairway traps closing in from both sides. To make the green, be sure you have sufficient club to fly the traps guarding the front. An exceptionally difficult putting green because of ridging and rolls.

P.O. Box 960
Banff, Alberta, T0L 0C0
Telephone: (403) 762-6801

Bow Island Jubilee Golf Club

"A Park on the Prairies..."

Par 36/37

A picturesque and worthwhile stop along Highway 3 between Lethbridge and Medicine Hat. In an area where sun-parched brown is a way of life, the splendid greenery of the fairways, greens and mature trees is heightened by the contrast of the surroundings. And the nine-hole course is as challenging as anyone would want. If ever a second nine is added, Bow Island could boast one of the finest parkland tracks in Southern Alberta. What already exists is splendid enough. A leisurely delight.

#1 - Par 5.
R: 460 yards
F: 385 yards

A worthy opener with a fairway zigzag, left then right. Aim tee shot to left side as there's a scary row of mature trees right. If you're laying up, a second towards the left will open up the trapped green nicely.

#2 - Par 4.
R: 329 yards
F: 321 yards

Beautiful hole! Major row of trees along left with sand inside the turn of a dogleg left. Stay right but not long enough to hit thick hedge 220 yards straight out.

#3 - Par 5.
R: 493 yards
F: 416 yards

Toughest on the course. Be patient. Straight drive into narrow, uphill fairway helps and then it's downhill. Long hitters could make this one in two, but the rest of us should lay up.

#4 - Par 4.
R: 315 yards
F: 299 yards

Long guys can reach. But a solid drive and wedge will give the average and patient soul a really good shot at birdie.

#5 - Par 3.
R: 138 yards
F: 133 yards

Nice par 3. Short iron shot needs careful steering through trees playing sentry on both front edges.

#6 - Par 4.
R: 375 yards
F: 346 yards

Trees and out-of-bounds all along right. Tee shot should be aimed between 150 yard markers 230 yards out. Watch sand in front and more sentry trees on approach into pretty saucered green.

#7 - Par 4.
R: 380 yards
F: 308 yards

Straight up the slope all the way. But a narrow funnel between fairway trees requires some squeezing of your approach second. Big bunker trouble right.

#8 - Par 3.
R: 187 yards
F: 167 yards

Longish hit uphill to pin set against horizon. Split those guard trees again. Club up!

#9 - Par 4/5.
R: 384 yards
F: 378 yards

OB right. Aim tee shot left of fairway tree about 170 yards out. Cleverly-positioned trees, Mother Nature's work, will also cause flutters for that short mid-iron approach into green.

Box 861
Bow Island, Alberta, T0K 0G0
Telephone: (403) 545-2718

The 384-yard, par 4, 9th hole

Brooks Golf Club

"Ups-and-downs in the Flatlands..."

Par 71/72

The board at this already-fine facility have their eyes on making the course and everything that goes with it even better. The terrain around the town is typical prairie-flat. But the people who, fifty years ago, laid down the first nine holes found some gorgeous rolling territory on which to do it. The gentle undulations on the fairways, old and new, never allow boredom. And those ups-and-downs are scaled down on the greens, particularly on the old front nine, to provide some challenging weighting and tracking decisions for the putter. The new nine, added around five years ago, has a subtly different feel about it on both fairway and green.

#1 - Par 4.
C: 337 yards
R: 337 yards
F: 319 yards

Sound opener. Aim tee shot centre left onto advancing upslope. A short iron or wedge second needs to be straight onto narrow green.

#2 - Par 4.
C: 381 yards
R: 373 yards
F: 361 yards

Downhill drive. Make use of left-to-right sloped fairway by aiming centre left to best set up approach. The green, two-tiered, is difficult to hold.

#3 - Par 4.
C: 359 yards
R: 335 yards
F: 245 yards

The challenge is bang in front. The tee shot has to carry 170 yards to make it over the lake onto upward-banking fairway. Lofted short iron, wedge needed for successful landing on two-tiered green.

#4 - Par 4/5.
C: 406 yards
R: 406 yards
F: 406 yards

Yet another fine hole. Fade tee shot through narrow chute of trees onto another welcoming uphill slope. Perhaps an uphill club-up is necessary to reach a tiered green with as much as 3 feet elevation difference front to back.

#5 - Par 3.
C: 215 yards
R: 206 yards
F: 200 yards

Whoa pardner! Track all along the left and then out of bounds in local rodeo grounds. Hole almost slides left. Ideal shot is long iron, seven wood aimed at right and drawn into a flat green.

#6 - Par 4.
C: 283 yards
R: 266 yards
F: 263 yards

A short one with plenty of character. Trees left and right all the way, and road all along the left. Longer hitters can hit this one. Narrow green with slopes every which way.

#7 - Par 5.
C: 516 yards
R: 506 yards
F: 408 yards

Good, good golf hole. Dogleg left if you want to be conventional about it. But there's plenty of room over the trees left and a big landing area before the lake comes into play. You might save some yards this way but your lie in prairie grass could be awkward. Ten-foot wide creek 10 yards in front of green makes life exciting in the final approach.

#8 - Par 3.
C: 137 yards
R: 128 yards
F: 92 yards

What a fine little hole. The tee shot has to cross the creek twice to get to the rolling green.

9 - Par 4.
C: 417 yards
R: 410 yards
F: 376 yards

Seems to play longer. Straight, but 12-foot wide creek comes into play for second shot. Green backed and sided by mounds, slopes back to front. Be below the pin. An excellent hole.

#10 - Par 5.
C: 540 yards
R: 523 yards
F: 462 yards

A cracker! Sharp dogleg right 200 yards out. Local rule states that, for safety reasons, any shortcut attempt landing on the 11th fairway allows a free drop back on 10th fairway. Be sensible. Suddenly there's sand around green, back right and side right.

#11 - Par 4.
C: 429 yards
R: 419 yards
F: 366 yards

The dogleg left starts at the end of the fence 200 yards out. Good position in the turn allows a medium or long iron into green, with a disguised trap left and two right, side and back.

#12 - Par 4.
C: 384 yards
R: 375 yards
F: 320 yards

Dogleg right. Tee shot should hug or go over trees right with about 200-yard carry. Be careful around the green. Sand left, back and right – and you don't see it from the fairway.

#13 - Par 3.
C: 198 yards
R: 175 yards
F: 140 yards

If you like a challenge, here it is. Two more traps, front right and back left.

#14 - Par 4.
C: 372 yards
R: 349 yards
F: 308 yards

Aim tee shot centre right of fairway. Now, steady with the second. The creek is 40 yards in front. There's more beach back-right of green.

#15 - Par 4.
C: 423 yards
R: 368 yards
F: 325 yards

Water, water everywhere! Creek slap in front of blue tee box, and then it winds down left side. It re-crosses fairway 125 yards in front. Sahara-time front and back-left of green.

#16 - Par 3.
C; 202 yards
R: 191 yards
F: 157 yards

Club choice can vary by three or four depending on wind direction. If that's not enough, the creek's 50 yards in front of green fringed by sand front left and right side.

#17 - Par 4.
C: 413 yards
R: 373 yards
F: 321 yards

Is there any dry land out there? Of course there is! Cross the creek with drive, but don't go too far right into pond. Oh, oh. There's that creek again in front of green. Sand right of green.

#18 - Par 5.
C: 502 yards
R: 489 yards
F: 385 yards

Great finishing hole. Creek in front of tee box. Be leftish with drive both for position and for avoiding pond right. Cross-the-creek time again on second or third – and there's another pond right in front of green. Sand left and back of green.

804 - 2nd Avenue East
Brooks, Alberta T1R 1C3
Telephone: (403) 362-2998.

The 406-yard, par 4, 4th hole

Canmore Golf and Curling Club

"A genuine jewel in the Rockies..."

Par 71

It is Canmore golf club's happy fate to be a halfway house between its much vaunted neighbors in Kananaskis Country and Banff. But if they are the bread in the sandwich, the undeservedly less-celebrated Canmore is the delicious meat in the middle. This is a fabulous golf course, its fairways natural and serene, its hazards positioned for challenge rather than "aesthetic value" and its scenery in the shadow of the Three Sisters and Chinaman's Peak nothing short of majestic. And the presence of wildlife in the form of elk, moose, deer and the occasional bear that strays across the wandering Bow River add to the delight. A day's play in this lovely alpine and nordic events centre is what mountain golf should be all about. I won't beat about the bush. It's become a favorite of mine and always will be. I defy anyone to be disappointed.

#1 - Par 5.
C: 527 yards
R: 504 yards
F: 483 yards

The forgiveness in this opener is gone with changes late in 1995. The green is now left of its former position and guarded short left by a waste bunker and mounds. Going for it in two is not such an attractive proposition now. Centre, centre right is good for the tee shot and best bet for approach is to lay up to the right of the green to chip on. Watch the back-front slope.

#2 - Par 3.
C: 159 yards
R: 150 yards
F: 131 yards

There's not much daylight in this magnificent, treed arena hole. The water extends to the front edge and the trees creep in threateningly all around. What a hole!

#3 - Par 4.
C: 389 yards
R: 370 yards
F: 335 yards

OB all the way right. Watch the grove of trees coming into play from the left. Good tee shot is down centre to set up approach into a tiered green trapped front left, right and behind. It's important on this one to try and hit the same level as the pin.

#4 - Par 5.
C: 498 yards
R: 467 yards
F: 399 yards

One of the best long holes around Calgary. The problem, especially for long hitters, is the large fairway tree – and the right fairway sand. The tree is probably 190 yards out from the green. Pick your side. But for approach its best to be right of it if the pin is back left, and left if it's right, if you know what I mean.

#5 Par 4.
C: 378 yards
R: 352 yards
F: 298 yards

Another fine hole drifting right with the Bow River right there all the way. Best place for drive most of the time is centre left into the gentle right turn. Watch the major trap front right on approach.

#6 - Par 4.
C: 440 yards
R: 422 yards
F: 400 yards

Toughest here without a doubt. Centre left is good for a difficult tee shot that has to have good length. That length sets up best chance for high approach necessary to stick a very difficult three-tiered green. Lots of players deal with this one as a par 5. Makes sense.

#7 - Par 4.
C: 339 yards
R: 321 yards
F: 300 yards

Straightaway but watch the fairway trap that comes into play around the 150-yard marker. On a hole that's usually downwind, it's important to land the tee shot somewhere down the middle to avoid trees on approach. Placement, not distance, is the thing.

#8 - Par 3.
C: 159 yards
R: 132 yards
F: 117 yards

Another picturesque par 3 involving a shot across water. This biggish green is trapped left and right, and has a marked back-front slope. There's a large bail-out area right of the green behind the trees. Watch for the wind and for the friendly neighborhood herd of elk hanging out.

#9 - Par 4.
C: 374 yards
R: 360 yards
F: 316 yards

A fine dogleg left with water left and fairway sand on the inside of the turn. Hit tee shot down the middle of the fairway to come to earth somewhere in the region of the 150-yard marker. Then pin placement will decide club selection for hit into a green with a large bunker front right and a shallow trap left. Green also dips on the right.

#10 - Par 5.
C: 505 yards
R: 468 yards
F: 426 yards

OB left and right on a hole that's not overly long. But perfect tee shot is down the left side to land close to the maintenance area on that side. That should take your approach away from two large trees that threaten the right, the first about 180 yards out and the other short of the green. Pretty straightforward green, but there's a slight back-front tilt.

#11 - Par 3.
C: 174 yards
R: 160 yards
F: 121 yards

What can I say other than beautiful? Shot has to be hit towards mountain backdrop across the water, avoiding or flying the large tree centre right. The big green is protected by a front trap and there's an immediate drop-off behind that will hurl overhit into trees.

#12 - Par 4.
C: 341 yards
R: 320 yards
F: 273 yards

Reasonably straight but wants to go left. This is one for the irons. Concentrate on hitting into the area of the 150-yard marker avoiding the trees left. There's a nasty dip front left of the green and a trap front right. It leans back to front.

#13 - Par 4.
C: 301 yards
R: 289 yards
F: 271 yards

Dogleg right where it's iron time again. Mid-iron tee shot inside the fairway traps left is ideal. Then it's another comfortable iron into a green which has water short left, left and behind, a trap front right, and slopes right to left.

#14 - Par 4.
C: 327 yards
R: 304 yards
F: 286 yards

Yet another nice hole bending away right. and it's another where the driver can get you into trouble. Be content to hit it out towards the 150-yard markers and go from there. The green is protected by two large front traps and it's tiered. Be on the correct plateau!

#15 - Par 3.
C: 181 yards
R: 172 yards
F: 164 yards

Longish and slightly downhill. Large green is guarded by a trap on the right. A well-judged tee shot landing just short and right will likely run down and on.

#16 - Par 4.
C: 444 yards
R: 356 yards
F: 273 yards

A stunning hole. A personal favorite anywhere any time. Essential to get decent length down centre left on this one to open up the green tucked behind pond infiltrating the right. The green is flattish but is slightly higher right. There are also two traps left. Wow! Double wow!

#17 - Par 3.
C: 217 yards
R: 208 yards
F: 176 yards

Tough, long hole with trees all along the right. There's a trap short right and one left of the very large green. It's stating the obvious, but make sure you have enough club to make the green.

#18 - Par 5.
C: 551 yards
R: 520 yards
F: 489 yards

They saved the longest for last. It sweeps right with trees all the way along the inside. But if you can keep it straight, tee shot centre right is best. Trees poach in on approach and there are traps front left, front right and behind. Oh, and there's also water close enough back right to threaten the over-enthusiastic.

Box 1560
Canmore Alberta T0L 0M0
Telephone: (403) 678-4784

Connaught Golf Club

"A charmer with challenge . . ."

Par 72/73

Folks down Medicine Hat way may not have quantity in public golf courses, but there's no doubt they have quality with all three championship-length courses providing locals and visitors alike with a wonderful variety of golfing. Connaught, its fairways and greens outstanding, is a bit of a hybrid and I mean that as a compliment. In its present state of maturity, it's really a cross between a parkland and links course. From hole to hole it can vary from being quite heavily treed to virtually wide open, but with an abundance of water, sand and reeds, there's potential trouble around no matter where you are in your round. The change of feel is good. And at no time does it threaten the consistently high enjoyment factor and challenge.

#1 - Par 4.
C: 404 yards
R: 379 yards
F: 367 yards

Attractive starting hole doglegging left with trees and sand lurking along the left. Tee shot from tree-shaded tee box should be hit centre left and long enough to get out towards the turn. Green ringed by large trees and sloping back to front, has major trap front left.

#2 - Par 5.
C: 500 yards
R: 485 yards
F: 471 yards

Elegant straightaway hole with big trees on both sides of a fairly generous landing area requires a straight tee shot. Then it opens up again in approaches to green which has a high-lipped trap front and a smaller one behind. Green has a marked back right-front left slope.

#3 - Par 3.
C: 142 yards
R: 131 yards
F: 122 yards

Shot from chute of trees has to avoid high-backed trap front-right, another bunker left, and a hidden trap immediately behind. With a heavy back-to-front slope it really pays to be below the pin here, but that front trap is daunting . . .

#4 - Par 4.
C: 398 yards
R: 385 yards
F: 330 yards

Maybe the toughest here. It's a dogleg right. The problem is the water starting about 220 yards out in the landing area left and continuing all the way up to the green. The dilemma is to either land in the turn short of the water or draw a longer tee shot round the trees on the right. But there's sand about 50 yards round the corner. Watch approach shot length too. There's a road right behind.

#5 - Par 5.
C: 522 yards
R: 510 yards
F: 457 yards

Tough on tough. Another challenge, sweeping left over the hill. Tee shot has to be hit over trees in front to land centre-right on fairway upslope. Hideous coulee trouble left up to the green where the problem becomes liquid. Your second shot should be aimed towards tall trees visible over the hill towards the right. Water and sand guard the front left of the green.

#6 - Par 4.
C: 392 yards
R: 383 yards
F: 332 yards

Classy dogleg right with OB left, huge trees on the outside of the turn and smaller trees and bushes all the way along the right. Ideal tee shot should land centre right in the area of the turn. There's major sand trouble left and right. Guess what? There's a back-to-front slope.

#7 - Par 4.
C: 388 yards
R: 370 yards
F: 345 yards

Centre tee shot is good. Straightaway hole but right-left fairway lean develops into a sharp downhill approach to the green. It is noticeably tilted towards the fairway to accept downhill approach shots. But that, of course, means a vicious back-front slope. The green might welcome your advances but be below the pin!

#8 - Par 3.
C: 167 yards
R: 155 yards
F: 144 yards

This one, slightly downhill can bite, but there is a knack. The green has significant sand problems front left and on the right side. The trick is to aim tee shot slightly short right to hit downslope starting about 25 yards out from front edge of green and run on.

#9 - Par 4.
C: 404 yards
R: 374 yards
F: 356 yards

Slightly uphill, fading around receding line of trees on the right. Good tee shot target is highest roof on distant townhouses. The green is tucked in the shadow of surrounding trees and has a big trap front left.

#10 - Par 4.
C: 376 yards
R: 366 yards
F: 366 yards

A downhiller twisting right and left. There's water straight out through the trees. The ideal tee shot landing area is in the twist between the two big trees flanking the fairway about 220 yards out. Then it's a mid iron across water in front of the green and avoiding the pond on the right. Back-front slope is Himalayan. So as you negotiate all the hazards, remember to stay below the pin too!

#11 - Par 4.
C: 415 yards
R: 399 yards
F: 350 yards

Full steam ahead. The only real trouble on this one should be the deep high-lipped bunker front-left of the green and, of course, the back to front slope.

#12 - Par 3.
C: 175 yards
R: 152 yards
F: 138 yards

Strong shortie with water all the way along the left up to the green. It is almost flat, but has trees hugging the right approach and sand to catch the overhit behind.

#13 - Par 5.
C: 495 yards
R: 487 yards
F: 402 yards

Good par 5 with intimidating start and finish. Tee shot, aimed towards big green spruce on left side of fairway, has to negotiate pond, the edge of an island left and trees hugging the right. Then it's go for it or lay up. Either way a deep pond-filled gully about 40 yards in front has to be mastered. High banks on both sides of this treed amphitheatre green bring the ball down and on.

#14 - Par 4.
C: 391 yards
R: 374 yards
F: 312 yards

Slightly uphill and straight. Tee shot should be aimed centre right to take water creeping in on left side of green out of play as much as possible for the approach. Trees ring the right side and behind and there's also sand between the water and the green.

#15 - Par 5.
C: 530 yards
R: 514 yards
F: 460 yards

Highest handicap hole and probably deserves it. Aim tee shot along centre left line to open up the best avenue for eventual approach shot. There's sand front-left and front-right, the left one a few yards in front of the right. The problem is an overlap killing any possibility of running on between them. Approach must be lofted. And on this roller, you're in for interesting putting experiences too.

16 - Par 4.
C: 407 yards
R: 398 yards
F: 345 yards

Excellent, testing dogleg left with OB left. Hit tee shot straight out about 220 yards towards the large tree. That sets you up with approach down narrowing avenue of trees. You won't be surprised to hear it's got a severe back-front slope and drastic drop-off behind.

#17 - Par 3.
C: 165 yards
R: 155 yards
F: 145 yards

High-lipped trap front-right and sand left. Guess what! Yup, a back-to-front slope.

#18 - Par 4/5.
C: 436 yards
R: 422 yards
F: 390 yards

A solid, slightly-uphill finishing hole. Tee shot should be hit centre to avoid clusters of trees in landing area both sides, and water left short of the landing area. There's sand left and right of the green.

2802 - 13th Avenue SE
Medicine Hat, Alberta, T1A 3P9
Telephone: (403)526-0737

Cottonwood Coulee Golf Course

"Short but oh so sweet..."

Par 66

If the well-travelled among you can imagine a shorter cross between Calgary's Cottonwood and Lethbridge's Paradise Canyon, Medicine Hat's Cottonwood Coulee is what you'd have. With a par of 66, it's not long by any means, but it's scenically breathtaking and tremendous fun. Accuracy, not length, is what matters here. The course, although it has one shortish but difficult par 5, is mainly made up of short par 4s and tricky par 3s. It winds, ducks and weaves its way along the valley floor with uphill shots, downhill shots and doglegs. There's trouble to be found everywhere. Designer Harold Pasechnik has added to the excitement by making use of water hazards, natural in the form of the Seven Persons Creek, or otherwise in the shape of manmade ponds, on well over half the holes. Tactics can vary depending on weather conditions. It's one that tempts you to go for it with the driver but perhaps it's best to play more cautiously, and more sensibly, with fairway wood, iron and wedge.

#1 - Par 4.
C: 304 yards
R: 289 yards
F: 274 yards

Nice uphill opener with prairie grass trouble on the hill out right. Tee shot centre left works for approach into green with sand front left, heavy mounding left and sharp drop-off right. Unusual feature is back end of green is lower than the front beyond a middle ridge.

#2 - Par 4.
C: 341 yards
R: 325 yards
F: 310 yards

A super-attractive golf hole with elevated tee boxes. Tee shot should be centre left landing right of the lone pine on the left. There's ugly creek and bush trouble right. On this one, because of another ridge, the right side of the green is higher than the left.

#3 - Par 4.
C: 257 yards
R: 239 yards
F: 225 yards

Short and driveable, but the creek is immediately in front of the green and there's sand over there on the left too. So, unless you're super-accurate with the driver or three wood, the better approach is a centre-left lay-up and wedge. You've still got a birdie chance.

#4 - Par 3.
C: 100 yards
R: 85 yards
F: 70 yards

It's short, but uphill with sand lurking in the mounds front left and immediately behind. There's a little basin on the front right of the green that makes for tricky putting in that area.

#5 - Par 4.
C: 256 yards
R: 241 yards
F: 220 yards

Again, driveable, but is it worth it? The coulee cliff threatens all the way left. There's fairway sand 200 yards out right, a pot bunker short left and four more traps behind in the almost overpowering mounding surrounding the green. Green has front-end slope. Placement makes more sense than power (but is it as much fun?)

#6 - Par 4.
C: 285 yards
R: 271 yards
F: 266 yards

Toughest hole in these parts, and it's a beauty. Severely uphill with a 90-degree dogleg right about 200 yards out under the cliffs at the top. There's killer sand in the drop-off inside the turn. The only other threats are the huge maintenance shed and the horrific banking traps just below the green! Common sense dictates tee shot straight out to turn. But that green looks tantalisingly close . . . Naw!

#7 - Par 3.
C: 158 yards
R: 140 yards
F: 136 yards

Scenically stunning. Coulee cliff on the left and creek far below threaten that side in addition to two left side traps. Only real danger right is the mounds. So that side of the green makes sense. Club down! And maybe down again! And . . .

#8 - Par 4.
C: 259 yards
R: 238 yards
F: 217 yards

(Sigh!) Yes, I know it's driveable, but . . . going for it means very accurate drive across a loop in the creek sneaking in from the left and there's also front left sand to catch anything short. Doesn't it make sense to hit nice long iron or fairway wood out towards cart path on right of green for wedge approach? A birdie could be the reward.

#9 - Par 3.
C: 119 yards
R: 107 yards
F: 97 yards

It must be an optical illusion. This hole looks even shorter than advertised. But, believe me, it plays the posted length with gigantic trees hugging tight left and a semi-circle of sand looping round the right from front to back.

#10 - Par 4.
C: 273 yards
R: 255 yards
F: 238 yards

Uphill dogleg left round bluff. After ensuring the way is clear with use of the mirror provided, cut the corner over the shoulder of the bluff onto comfortably-large hidden landing area round the bend, or play iron up centre. Sand in front left banking of elevated green. And if you drop behind railway tie wall on left of green, it's a one-stroke penalty and a drop. Hmm. Lots of divots in the drop area.

#11 - Par 4.
C: 246 yards
R: 223 yards
F: 213 yards

This one is worth the risk. Go for it by hugging bluff rising up on the left. Even if you hook, there's a chance it'll come back in. Green is guarded by pot bunkers front right and behind.

#12 - Par 3.
C: 115 yards
R: 100 yards
F: 63 yards

Picturesque signature hole. Shot from elevated back tees on bluff must avoid the left side with twin-fountained pond and winding cart path far below boding disaster. There's sand on that side of the green too. Right side of the green is almost a must target area. And club down, maybe as many as two clubs.

#13 - Par 3.
C: 122 yards
R: 100 yards
F: 80 yards

Another pretty one with cliff rising on the left. There are two traps front right and the green's flattish on top but sloped in front.

#14 - Par 5.
C: 461 yards
R: 431 yards
F: 369 yards

Yup, it's shortish but what a great par 5. OB all the way left. There's water left, water short right, and more hidden further out right short of the mounds. A centre tee shot is good. But it's decision time. The ravine about 100 yards in front of the green is home to the creek. Go for the elevated green on the hillside in two or lay up to ravine edge for wedge in. The green's left is distinctly higher than the right.

#15 - Par 4.
C: 301 yards
R: 291 yards
F: 223 yards

It's one fun hole after another hereabouts. This one requires a tee shot straight out across ravine bridge. Aim it towards cart path on left of green. But be aware of water in the bush just left and short of the path and more on the right side of the fairway. This narrow green has a major back to front slope so below the pin is best.

#16 - Par 3.
C: 141 yards
R: 127 yards
F: 87 yards

A great par 3. All that's required from the back is a shot across a pond, over a tall tree, across a creek, to a green surrounded by bushes and with hidden sand right and two traps in the mounds left. Wow! Things are a little less severe from the other tee boxes.

#17 - Par 4.
C: 290 yards
R: 270 yards
F: 254 yards

Big trees on the inside turn of this dogleg right really dictate a tee shot down centre or even centre left to open up a (for once) flattish green with sand right and more heavy mounding on the left.

#18 - Par 3.
C: 140 yards
R: 119 yards
F: 92 yards

Nice short finisher across the creek to a green with big sand front right and severe mounding left. This green has a sharp front-end slope.

3245 - 10th Avenue SW
Medicine Hat, Alberta, T1B 4B3
Telephone: (403) 529-1010

Cottonwood Golf and Country Club

"Down in the valley..."

Par 72

The glory of Cottonwood isn't hard to discern. It is there for all visitors to see from a near-aerial perspective as soon as they crest the bluff overlooking the Bow River valley. The course is a lush multi-patterned carpet covering nature's floor far below. And is it by design or mere coincidence? The course's signature hole, the superb island green par 3 12th, and the popular choice for most difficult, the par 4 14th, are very much in the foreground for the player's first impression from the hilltop. At valley level, the semi-private Cottonwood, a personal favorite I confess, lives up to its promise. It's a toughish course with a fair amount of sand and water around, but it's mostly forgiving with the sizeable mounds along most fairways often acting as much ally as enemy. It's only been in existence for six years, but the fairways and greens have the look and feel of a long-established track. With river, trees and bluffs, it's hard to imagine a finer spot to play.

#1 - Par 5.
C: 501 yards
R: 469 yards
F: 383 yards

Testing opener where tee shot should be aimed centre left, followed by second towards right side to open up the green for final approach. It is makeable in two for longer hitters but sand front left and water in the right approaches can cause unnecessary headaches.

#2 - Par 3.
C: 141 yards
R: 116 yards
F: 89 yards

As short a par 3 as you'll get, but it has its moments. It's well trapped and the green could make you seasick if you stick around too long.

#3 - Par 4.
C: 387 yards
R: 344 yards
F: 274 yards

Elevated tee shot should be hit down through trees towards centre right. This opens up green with sand front left and right side. This one's higher left, lower right.

#4 - Par 4.
C: 371 yards
R: 348 yards
F: 301 yards

Solid uphill dogleg left requiring accurate tee shot centre right. Good position there will give best approach into kidney-shaped green up the hill. Sand front left and grass bunkers behind make it a tricky target. And, take my word, there's a heavy back-to-front slope on this one.

#5 - Par 4.
C: 372 yards
R: 351 yards
F: 316 yards

One of the more straightforward holes on the course if you do keep it straight. Good position for tee shot is just beyond fairway sand left. With traps left and right, the green slopes back to front.

#6 - Par 3.
C: 185 yards
R: 151 yards
F: 121 yards

Crosswind from left is usually a factor here. Shot from elevated tee shot has to avoid sand front left, back left and right. The green slopes mainly left to right.

#7 - Par 5.
C: 568 yards
R: 541 yards
F: 432 yards

Officially, the number one toughest hole. It double doglegs left so much it's like going three-quarters the way round a horseshoe. Tee shot should be hit down centre. Second shot corner-cutters, be warned. There's OB left and although you may get lucky the mounds down the left to the green and sand front left of it are deadly. Sensible second is a hit down into second fairway turn, opening things up.

#8 - Par 4.
C: 390 yards
R: 337 yards
F: 292 yards

Pretty dogleg left along the banks of the Bow River left. A drive centre right keeps play away from fairway sand left and opens up the approach to the green nicely. There's sand on the right of the green and nasty mounds on the left.

#9 - Par 4.
C: 385 yards
R: 378 yards
F: 301 yards

It's straight but the river and a creek are not too far away left. Tee shot centre left is heavily favored because lake eventually encroaches on right side affecting approach to green. It's two-tiered, has sand on the left and is covered right by water.

#10 - Par 5.
C: 504 yards
R: 473 yards
F: 390 yards

Demanding opener to the back nine requiring centre-left approach all the way to heavily-trapped green tucked away to the right at the end of the trip. It's two-tiered, back to front.

#11 - Par 4.
C: 416 yards
R: 394 yards
F: 278 yards

Dogleg left where it's a good idea to hit tee shot centre left if possible. There's fairway sand on left and further out on right. There's sand right of the green which slopes from right to left.

#12 - Par 3.
C: 179 yards
R: 143 yards
F: 77 yards

It's a beauty all right and it provided the cover photograph of this book. As if the water on this island hole is not enough, they've put sand immediately over it front left, and more on the right and behind. The green slopes back to front. Magnificent.

#13 - Par 4.
C: 423 yards
R: 383 yards
F: 325 yards

Nice hole doglegging right. Tee shot should be aimed centre left for best approach route into green with sand front right and back left.

#14 - Par 4.
C: 451 yards
R: 423 yards
F: 329 yards

Most regulars say it's the toughest here. I agree. Dogleg left, with fairway sand left, plays long and requires a good start with a tee shot centre right. The water on the right causes nightmares for players hitting through a narrow-looking gap into green which has sand behind and rolls off the right side into the water.

Southern   Alberta

#15 - Par 4.
C: 357 yards
R: 330 yards
F: 298 yards

Dogleg left which eventually becomes a slight uphill approach to green. With severe banked mounding problems left and abundant water trouble obvious right, the sensible approach here is a careful 200-yard placement shot straight out, leaving a short or mid-iron approach. It's well-bunkered right and rolls from left to right.

#16 - Par 5.
C: 491 yards
R: 463 yards
F: 394 yards

Scene of my most bizarre par. The only time my ball touched grass was the one bounce it took before hitting the stick and dropping in after a greenside bunker shot. You work it out! Suffice to say I call this one Sahara, with sand all along both sides. Best start is tee shot just right of fairway sand left. It can be reached in two but it's much more sensible to lay up into the throat of this back-to-front sloped green.

#17 - Par 3.
C: 171 yards
R: 164 yards
F: 121 yards

Tricky shortie. The water right is daunting and there's a pot bunker right and full bunker on the left. If the pin is towards the back of this tiered green club up like crazy.

#18 - Par 4.
C: 455 yards
R: 435 yards
F: 333 yards

One of the more demanding finishing holes in these parts. It doglegs right off elevated tee boxes set in trees. Tee shot should be hit as near centre as possible. Water runs all the way up to the green on the left and along its left side. And there's sand on the right of the green which tilts back to front.

Box 28, Site 2, R.R. #1
DeWinton, Alberta T0L 0X0
Telephone: (403) 938-7200

The island 12th green and 15th tee in foreground

Crowsnest Pass Golf and Country Club

"Don't pass Crowsnest by..."

Par 36

This course on Highway 3 under the gargantuan bulk of Crowsnest Mountain is an excellent one ... and some time in the near future, maybe even the tail end of the 1996 season, it's going to get even better with the opening of a new back nine which pundits say will project this track into being one of Alberta's best. I'm certainly going back to check once the work is done. The existing nine already present challenge enough with tree-lined fairways and smallish sloping greens set amid astounding mountainside scenery. The star is undoubtedly the spectacular downhill par 3 fourth which can require a multi-club decision depending on the wind. Regulars here refer to it, affectionately I think, as the S.O.B. hole. Suffice to say it's been known to shatter the respectability of many a scorecard.

#1 - Par 5.
C: 482 yards
R: 462 yards
F: 428 yards

Best tee shot is centre right to open up the green tucked left round the late dogleg. Somewhere right of the trees left in the fairway is ideal. The green has a heavy front-end slope and is trapped front left, back left and front right. Too far left off the tee and you run into problems with trees in the turn and having to clear the bunker on approach.

#2 - Par 4.
C: 415 yards
R: 365 yards
F: 368 yards

Highest handicap hole. Hit straight out ensuring the ball reaches the turn. The slightly-uphill approach, maybe club up one, is complicated by water spreading halfway across the fairway from the right. No traps here but a severe slope on the front.

#3 - Par 4.
C: 372 yards
R: 351 yards
F: 265 yards

Centre right is best off the tee again avoiding a nasty hollow in the fairway about 140 yards out left. Hit it leftside and it just may run down into the trees. Tough green sloping right to left has traps on the left and back right.

#4 - Par 3.
C: 138 yards
R: 126 yards
F: 114 yards

What can I tell you? A stunning hole to match any anywhere. It's really wedge time but ... look at the flag and try to get a sense of what is normally a head-on wind. The tiny-looking shallow green far below is guarded by a front pond and there are trees slap-bang behind. Good luck!

#5 - Par 4.
C: 366 yards
R: 341 yards
F: 303 yards

Another beauty with one of the most glorious fairway views you could wish for. It has fairway trees about 140 yards out from the regulars. Fly 'em or fade round 'em on the left with an iron. This is the toughest green here with a drastic slope

	running back to front and down from back-right. Traps left, right and back left further complicate life.
#6 - Par 4. C: 382 yards R: 372 yards F: 322 yards	Perfect drive is a 200-yard draw down centre left to the left turn to ready for slightly uphill approach to the green. It has a large trap front right. It has a back-front slope with the ball tending to roll off front right. Best be below the pin.
#7 - Par 3. C: 169 yards R: 144 yards F: 123 yards	Shot is played slightly downhill to one of the flatter ones here. Bunker front left spreads across two-thirds of the approach to the green. Watch the smaller trap right and one back left.
#8 - Par 5. C: 562 yards R: 526 yards F: 449 yards	Hit drive straight down the middle towards the grandeur of Crowsnest Mountain. To see the green for your second you have to be on top of the plateau 210 yards out from the regulars. Long hitters can reach in two but the rest of us should lay up downhill making sure we reach the flat for a wedge on. Four traps protect another flattish green.
#9 - Par 4. C: 372 yards R: 343 yards F: 333 yards	A tough finishing hole. Ideal straight-out hit will land on the flat in front of the water which is about 20-30 yards in front of the green. Big slope on this one demands being below the pin.

Box 332
Blairmore, Alberta T0K 0E0
Telephone: (403) 562-2776

The spectacular 138-yard, par 3, 4th hole

D'Arcy Ranch Golf Club

"When the going gets tough..."

Par 72/73

Taken as a whole, this extremely strong prairie links-style golf course in Okotoks must rate as one of the toughest in southern Alberta. Forgiveness is not the game here even though in the last year or two the primary cut of rough has been extended further back from the fairways than before. But don't despair, the track is far from unfair. It's just that it's one which requires accuracy. And wide-ranging variations on the tee boxes make it enjoyable and playable for all calibres of player. It rolls up and down the coulees west of the town with the Rockies a striking backdrop further towards the sunset. There are many memorable holes on this one, perhaps the most celebrated, and feared, being the tremendous par 5 number seven. Save this track for mid-season form.

#1 - Par 5.
C: 520 yards
R: 500 yards
F: 445 yards

Tough, slightly downhill dogleg right with a gully running down the right and a large trap on that side too. Ideal target line for the tee shot is the distant cart path. For those who can't reach in two, favor the left for a lay-up but watch the traps short left and short right. There's a bunker front left and another set in the downslope right.

#2 - Par 4.
C: 420 yards
R: 395 yards
F: 344 yards

Still going downhill and still veering right. Farm barn on far hill just left of the fairway sand right is a good tee shot line. The green, with two traps left, drops off sharply on that side and there's a large bunker right too.

#3 - Par 3.
C: 148 yards
R: 128 yards
F: 114 yards

Did I say downhill? *This* is downhill. Club down, down, down, for this shot onto a well-trapped tiered green probably 80 feet below with water hugging the right. Wind can be a major factor here so make allowances.

#4 - Par 4.
C: 400 yards
R: 372 yards
F: 321 yards

Back on top. Hit tee shot straight out avoiding largish fairway sand in the left landing area. The approach to a plateau green really must get there. Anything short right in a major dip or worse down in the gully will cause all sorts of problems. There are two traps left and the green tilts back-left to front-right.

#5 - Par 4.
C: 365 yards
R: 345 yards
F: 307 yards

A dogleg right where the tee shot really should be hit centre, even centre left to stay away from rightside fairway trap in the turn. Good drive will set up downhill approach into a green guarded by major sand in the upslope front right and more on the left and behind.

#6 - Par 3.
C: 217 yards
R: 189 yards
F: 129 yards

A tough downhill shot to a green guarded by water left and a trap between it and the green. A prevailing right-to-left wind can usually be used to bring a right side draw down and onto the green.

#7 - Par 5.
C: 550 yards
R: 521 yards
F: 465 yards

A great par 5. Downhill tee shot down centre of coulee has to hit the fairway. Left or right is trouble. Intimidating. Then its decision time on whether to go for the green or lay up into the thin neck between the bluff left and water right. Intimidating. Ridge across the front third of the narrow green can cause putting nightmares. Intimidating.

#8 - Par 4.
C: 392 yards
R: 368 yards
F: 320 yards

Dogleg left where tee shot should be hit towards clubhouse with a draw steering clear of huge traps on the slope inside the turn. Those traps really should discourage cutting corners unless you're really long. Green is set down the hill atop a nasty slope left. Big bunker front left too.

#9 - Par 4.
C: 425 yards
R: 398 yards
F: 343 yards

Straightaway hole with the only serious threat on the way heavy mounding along both sides. The green too is very open to approach with sand front left and middle right. Two straight shots and it could be birdie time.

#10 - Par 5.
C: 538 yards
R: 486 yards
F: 390 yards

A challenging start to the back nine in the shape of a downhill dogleg right. Tee shot should be hit to land inside traps on the left of the fairway turn. The second should begin favoring the right side of the valley to best open up green to wedge approach from close in. There's too much sand trouble left, short and alongside.

#11 - Par 4.
C: 384 yards
R: 367 yards
F: 317 yards

Dogleg left where drive should be hit towards or just left of the traps on the outside of the turn. Take care with club selection, the traps can be reached. Either hit lofted approach onto green or pitch and run onto its right side. There are sand and downslope problems left.

#12 - Par 3.
C: 200 yards
R: 155 yards
F: 118 yards

All the trouble off the green lies left down the slope or in the traps on the four corners. On the dance floor itself, two ridges can cause putting problems.

#13 - Par 5.
C: 545 yards
R: 521 yards
F: 470 yards

It sweeps left, then right. Aim tee shot to land left of fairway sand right and then lay up left, avoiding traps short of the green, for approach. Watch out for a huge grass bunker straddling the fairway immediately in front.

#14 - Par 3.
C: 169 yards
R: 149 yards
F: 119 yards

Shot has to travel across the valley to a green roughly tee box high. Watch the sand front right and pot traps back left. Best advice here is aim for the fat of the green and go for the hole when you get there.

#15 - Par 4.
C: 366 yards
R: 348 yards
F: 301 yards

Squeeze centre tee shot between large traps left and right in the landing area on this uphill challenge. Maybe think of clubbing up for high approach into green guarded front left and back right by traps. This one slopes back to front.

#16 - Par 4/5.
C: 450 yards
R: 417 yards
F: 358 yards

Slight dogleg right with fairway dipping into valley in front of green. Tee shot should ideally be aimed down centre left towards road in the distance and land on the plateau looking down on the green. It's patrolled by bunkers on the right.

#17 - Par 4.
C: 410 yards
R: 383 yards
F: 347 yards

Dogleg left where tee shot should be hit towards the mounds and the 150-yard marker right. There's huge coulee, sand and rough trouble left. And you'd never guess but there's more sand and downslope problems left of the big green.

#18 - Par 4.
C: 420 yards
R: 382 yards
F: 321 yards

Aim for our old friend, the big barn, in the distance again and a good shot could hit the downslope and roll down left towards the green. A good drive, accurate mid or short iron and you could end the day with birdie. But, hmm, there is a lot of sand around the green, isn't there?

Corner of Highway #2A & Milligan Drive
Okotoks, Alberta, T0L 1T0
Telephone: (403) 938-4455

The 420-yard, par 4, 18th hole and clubhouse

Dinosaur Trail Golf and Country Club

"Unique and stunning beauty in the Badlands . . ."

Par 71/73

Carved beautifully among the bluffs, coulees and hoodoos of the world-famous Drumheller Badlands, Dinosaur's new nine, opened in August 1995, is a true marvel, both in terms of desert-style, target golf and in how it was co-operatively achieved by the club, designer and palaeontology buffs. There will no doubt be detractors who say it is unfair in places, with hits across wasteland to far off fairways, with deliberate 'blind' shots in abundance. But Canadian snowbirds know that Arizona is full of holes like these. It's fun, it's exciting, it's unique, an experience. Go into it with that attitude and you'll have a ball – if you start with a plentiful supply. And you'll be ready for the back nine test by the time you complete the original front nine. In total contrast, it's a true and testing parkland track, once played by Clint Eastwood. Yup. The back nine would have made his day.

#1 - Par 4.
C: 367 yards
R: 358 yards
F: 322 yards

Magnificent tree-lined fairway has nice open landing area for drive. Easy mid-iron into green, sand left, will set up good birdie shot.

#2 - Par 5.
C: 552 yards
R: 499 yards
F: 409 yards

More treed elegance. Approach time brings a large, solitary tree, front left, into play, so ideal incoming is from centre right fairway.

#3 - Par 4.
C: 305 yards
R: 300 yards
F: 249 yards

Definitely reachable from tee. But beware inconvenient cluster of trees screening front right of green. If you're going down left, tail of pond intrudes 50 yards out from the green.

#4 - Par 4/5.
C: 450 yards
R: 427 yards
F: 348 yards

A charmer. Highway all along right, with fairway easing right to left. Be centre right off tee to open up larger part of green. Who put that tree 50 yards out on right side?

#5 - Par 3.
C: 139 yards
R: 122 yards
F: 80 yards

Time for a solid wedge. Hidden hollow in front of green with right to left lean will throw short shot into sand left front. Beach back right, too.

#6 - Par 5.
C: 540 yards
R: 487 yards
F: 406 yards

Favor right-side tee shot over mini-gully in front of tee box. Eventually a shot over pond 25 yards in front needs to be negotiated. Character-building hole.

#7 - Par 3.
C: 132 yards
R: 120 yards
F: 91 yards

So-pretty hole. Requires tee shot back across pond into arena-type green ringed by trees.

#8 - Par 4/5.
C: 403 yards
R: 352 yards
F: 305 yards

Hit tee shot towards left, with slight fade and ball will be in fine shape. Position slightly right of centre makes the approach more appealing.

#9 - Par 3.
C: 215 yards
R: 215 yards
F: 158 yards

Unusual closure to the front nine. Straightaway, slightly uphill towards clubhouse. But the hedge a few yards in front of tee box can play mind games.

#10 - Par 5.
C: 515 yards
R: 476 yards
F: 418 yards

The Hyde in Jekyll & Hyde makes his appearance with a vengeance. As in every back nine hole, getting in the air is a must off the tee. Hit straight and trust there is a comfortable landing area across the emptiness. There is.

#11 - Par 4.
C: 320 yards
R: 278 yards
F: 255 yards

From the back it's a 180-yard carry to another fair landing area with scary bluff on left. Have faith!

#12 - Par 3.
C: 149 yards
R: 115 yards
F: 97 yards

Destined for greatness. Tee shot hit down onto island of green in sea of brown and grey. The new signature hole. Simply breathtaking. Think of clubbing down on this one.

#13 - Par 4.
C: 374 yards
R: 350 yards
F: 302 yards

A challenging 167-yard carry to the grassy stuff from the back. But believe! There is a large landing area out there for a straight shot.

#14 - Par 4.
C: 366 yards
R: 307 yards
F: 254 yards

This one will raise eyebrows. Aim tee shot with fade towards round-topped bluff. Depending on length it will land on one of four distinctly down-stepped stages of a fairway that can hardly be detected from the tee box. Then its an *uphill* approach to gorgeous green.

#15 - Par 4.
C: 377 yards
R: 305 yards
F: 232 yards

O.K. Trust me. Two choices for tee shot off back. Lofted club over 50-foot high butte bang in front, or fade another club round left side of it. There's ample parking on the other side. Green, hung out left, has 'island' feel once more.

#16 - Par 3.
C: 197 yards
R: 192 yards
F: 150 yards

A wonderful hole. Tee shot drops 80 feet down across water and sand. Depending on the wind this one could take anything from an 8 iron to a 3 wood. Thinking caps on.

#17 - Par 4.
C: 383 yards
R: 348 yards
F: 287 yards

The back nine's only genuine tree, a lone poplar, is your line of fire. It's about 190-200 yards out in the fairway. Murphy's Law dictates one in every foursome will hit it.

#18 - Par 5.
C: 521 yards
R: 496 yards
F: 438 yards

Simply a great golf hole along the valley floor. Hit straight out and enjoy the scenery. Beware the creek 30 yards in front of green. A good approach between the cliffs left and right will live in your mind's eye forever.

Box 1511
Drumheller, Alberta, T0J 0Y0
Telephone: (403) 823-5622

The 149-yard, par 3, 12th hole

Elbow Springs Golf Club

"Enjoyment by the Elbow..."

Par 72

A treat awaits on Calgary's western doorstep. Elbow Springs is a very pretty course with one or two real stings in its tail. Set atop natural springs in the Elbow River valley, the course is extremely walkable but with enough gentle undulations and twists and turns to provide a real golfing test, especially from the back tees. The two nines vary with the front mainly played without the threat of water. The back nine is a different story with water present at some stage on eight of the holes. The course running east-west has some stunning views of the foothills and mountains to the west. With four tee boxes, players of any calibre can relax and enjoy this one.

#1 - Par 4.
C: 376 yards
R: 366 yards
F: 286 yards

Gentle uphill starter, OB and the road left, with tee shot played across a creek and hopefully hugging the fairway traps left. Good position on a line right of them will set up easy-swing mid or short iron into a large green trapped front left and side right. Comfortable back-front slope here.

#2 - Par 4.
C: 398 yards
R: 375 yards
F: 317 yards

The road is even closer on this one all the way left but it's shielded by mounds. Again favor centre left with tee shot skimming fairway sand left. That's best for approach that has to avoid water short right of the elevated green which also has sand front left. The slope is more pronounced here.

#3 - Par 3.
C: 187 yards
R: 164 yards
F: 128 yards

Tricky par 3 with shot played from chute of trees to a tiered green. Two traps guard the left and one the right. It's important to be on the same level as the pin on this one. A putt from the back down to the hole on the front can run forever, not to mention the possibility of some extreme sidehill putts.

#4 - Par 5.
C: 528 yards
R: 510 yards
F: 446 yards

Hit tee shot straight out through chute of trees to land right of the left fairway bunkers. The second is often *the* shot on this one. Favor centre left with it to reach the late dogleg right round the trees right. A wedge should do the rest. This green is well-trapped short left, left and front right.

#5 - Par 4.
C: 405 yards
R: 373 yards
F: 327 yards

Hit straight down centre away from the trees lining the left. An accurate mid-iron second could set you up for birdie on a front-sloping green with traps left and right. The bushes short right threaten anything resembling a push or slice.

#6 - Par 4.
C: 381 yards
R: 366 yards
F: 302 yards

Really good golf hole requiring a tee shot hit centre to land somewhere left of the fairway traps right. Slightly elevated green is guarded front left by a huge bunker. Putting can be interesting on this undulating green.

#7 - Par 4.
C: 379 yards
R: 347 yards
F: 314 yards

Another good hole. This time tee shot should be hit centre to clear the narrow neck between traps and mounds on both sides in the landing area. Things open up just beyond them. Another elevated green is protected by traps front left and front right.

#8 - Par 3.
C: 213 yards
R: 198 yards
F: 145 yards

Tough short hole requiring hit across water and through funnel between copses of trees guarding the approach. There's sand left and front right of a tiered green. Important on this one to be on same level as pin.

#9 - Par 5.
C: 531 yards
R: 499 yards
F: 438 yards

Longish tee shot centre, centre left gets you into decision time position. Long hitters can make this green tucked right immediately behind pond in two. Others, like you and me perhaps, should lay up left of the water's left edge and wedge in from there. The green, well-trapped left, behind and right, leans back down towards the water. Good, good hole.

#10 - Par 4.
C: 382 yards
R: 355 yards
F: 302 yards

Dogleg right with water threatening first leg left. Either hit tee shot straight out to turn (a three wood isn't such a bad choice) or go for it through narrow gap in trees inside the turn. Either way you'll have a mid or short iron into a green tilting back to front and guarded left and right by traps. It's a shot at birdie.

#11 - Par 4.
C: 395 yards
R: 356 yards
F: 312 yards

Another dogleg right with water straight out and reachable with a driver. Best shot is centre right into the turn setting up a mid or short iron into a green with water left, and trapped left, front right and back right.

#12 - Par 5.
C: 571 yards
R: 526 yards
F: 437 yards

Monster dogleg right needing tee shot centre right to land inside traps on the right. Then the second should be played up the right side to open up the green hanging left round the water. This is a flattish one protected by a trap front right.

#13 - Par 3.
C: 175 yards
R: 161 yards
F: 104 yards

Picturesque signature hole. Tee shot has to flirt with lake all the way left and round behind the green. The green's huge but has heavy mounds and sand on the right. In my own bitter experience, the trap back right is the bunker from hell.

#14 - Par 4.
C: 419 yards
R: 398 yards
F: 334 yards

The perfect target for a fade tee shot across the water is the large grey house on the far hill. That should land you somewhere right of the left fairway trap. Then it's an iron approach into a green guarded heavily by sand front left and front right. This green slopes back to front. Being below pin is best option.

#15 - Par 5.
C: 552 yards
R: 517 yards
F: 444 yards

Another intimidatingly long hole veering slightly left. Tee shot hit across water straight down centre is best, then it's a case of being straight from there until you get to the green protected by traps front left and front right. This rolling green can produce some horrendous putts.

#16 - Par 3.
C: 196 yards
R: 170 yards
F: 125 yards

It's made difficult by railway-tied traps short left and more sand centre-right in front. Another sloping, undulating green where putting can be a lottery, especially at the back. Who rated this the easiest on the course?

#17 - Par 4.
C: 379 yards
R: 357 yards
F: 285 yards

A fine dogleg right round water and trees on the right and with water left further out. Perfect tee shot here is a controlled fade down centre to round the turn and open up the elevated green to mid or short iron approach. Mounded green has a trap left and an awkward bank and trees tight right.

#18 - Par 4.
C: 441 yards
R: 403 yards
F: 346 yards

Challenging finish requiring a good tee shot and an even better approach to the green. There's water over the mounds left, folks, and it sneaks in unseen quite a ways into the fairway left. Best drive is a draw hit centre right to carry on round the slight dogleg left. The slightly-downhill approach is daunting, through narrow neck between water on both sides, into a slightly-tiered green with bunkers left and behind.

Box 16, Site 8, R.R. #1
Calgary, Alberta, T2P 2G4
Telephone: (403) 246-2800

The 175-yard, par 3, 13th hole and clubhouse

Fort Macleod Golf Club

"Historic as a golfing outpost too..."

Par 35/36

The Northwest Mounted Police were the first here in the late 1880s. It was inevitable that the men who made up the detachment soon introduced golf as one of their main forms of recreation. A fine stretch of land was prepared down by the banks of the Old Man River, and so it was that the Fort Macleod golf course became probably the first to be built west of Winnipeg. It claims to be anyway. The fine track is still there, a three-wood from the old NWMP fort, claiming its own place in Canadian golfing lore. With such an excellent nine-hole course available, why not take in a round as well as visiting the fort and museum? It makes for a splendid day out.

#1 - Par 4.
R: 344 yards
F: 335 yards

Nice opener, usually into headwind, with OB and high bank left, trees all along the right. Centre-right is best drive to open up good line into a long green flanked on the left, back and front, by traps. There's a sharp drop-off right and it slopes back to front and left to right. Watch club selection for approach.

#2 - Par 5.
R: 467 yards
F: 398 yards

Into the wind again but reachable in two if it isn't blowing too hard. First half of the fairway slopes left towards OB so best line for tee shot is centre right for a flat lie for the approach. The fairway pond is 30 yards out from the green so if you're not going for it in two lay up short of it. Traps left and right and more water right and behind.

#3 - Par 4.
R: 313 yards
F: 247 yards

A tricky dogleg left with water on the inside of the turn, a trap adjacent to it and another on the right in the landing area. An iron into the turn is best for approach into a green trapped front right. Green is about 25 yards long front to back.

#4 - Par 3.
R: 173 yards
F: 180 yards

Crosswind from the left is a regular player here. The diagonal left-right sloping green is trapped left and front right. Fade in with the wind if you can.

#5 - Par 4.
R: 425 yards
F: 372 yards

Basically straightaway with OB left and trees right. Play centre left off the tee to avoid intruding trees right front of green on approach. This two-level green runs off at the back. Bunker front right and another on the left side.

#6 - Par 3.
R: 160 yards
F: 154 yards

The high road with its cross-bunker about 10 yards in front of the circular green cannot be avoided. Be careful with club selection as prevalent tailwind can have a major say here. Pot bunkers left and right.

#7 - Par 5.
R: 505 yards
F: 425 yards

With a following wind, this hard dogleg left plays shorter than advertised. Centre tee shot is good. Two-level green with the top tier three feet higher than the front has traps front left and front right. Hit and stick on the right level. OB left, behind, create more problems.

#8 - Par 3/4.
R: 205 yards
F: 200 yards

This long par 3 for the men plays even longer if the usual headwind is blowing. Ball really has to be brought in from the right because of a big poplar tree 40 yards short left. The circular green is probably 25 yards deep.

#9 - Par 4.
R: 333 yards
F: 324 yards

Trees left and right and usually with the wind. Centre tee shot sets up well for approach into an elevated green with a horseshoe-gully surrounding it. This green narrows considerably at the back.

270 Lyndon Road
Fort Macleod, Alberta, T0L 0Z0
Telephone: (403) 553-4664

The 333-yard, par 4, 9th hole

Hanna Golf and Country Club

"A treasure on the prairies..."

Par 36/37

Tucked away almost secretly several blocks north of Highway 9 is this fine nine hole circuit, rightly treasured by the locals. Like many small town courses, it's not just a golf club but more a part of the town's life. But the secret is getting out with more and more travellers stopping off to enjoy the facility, including the striking, expanded clubhouse. It's fine prairie golf here, with startlingly good fairways and greens, and ponds and treed landscaping proving an oasis in this vast, normally sunburned land.

#1 - Par 4.
C: 349 yards
R: 335 yards
F: 309 yards

Nice opener doglegging left. Canny shot off tee is hit into centre right of bend. That leaves a medium, short iron into green with pond front left and sand right 20 yards from green's edge.

#2 - Par 3.
C: 166 yards
R: 149 yards
F: 117 yards

Shoot iron of choice down funnel of trees. Sand left and small bunker back right. Be careful here. It's harder than it looks.

#3 - Par 5.
C: 515 yards
R: 482 yards
F: 462 yards

A lovely open hole. Let 'er rip. The second or third shot is slightly uphill. Only headache is sand front left.

#4 - Par 4.
C; 343 yards
R: 313 yards
F: 285 yards

A narrow charmer. If you can conjure the shot up there's space round large tree on right. Good tee shot there opens up green ridged across centre.

#5 - Par 4.
C: 399 yards
R: 399 yards
F: 325 yards

Aim downhill drive right of left fairway sand. Left dogleg turn is a handy 150 yards from green. Sandy left, right and behind.

#6 - Par 4/5.
C: 470 yards
R: 446 yards
F: 401 yards

Drive straight down the middle, avoiding water in left turn of dogleg. Too far left and you're dicing with pond on approach shot too.

#7 - Par 5.
C: 515 yards
R: 482 yards
F: 447 yards

Be straight until you reach approach range. Then be aware of rushes-edged pond sneaking in front of green right. Sand left and back left. Nice hole.

#8 - Par 3.
C: 150 yards
R: 127 yards
F: 110 yards

Don't be left. Steep bank will throw ball down for nasty chip back onto narrow green. Scenic, elevated hole.

#9 - Par 4.
C: 391 yards
R: 368 yards
F: 298 yards

Tee shot straight. Hold on to your approach or that water front right will come into play. Sand front left and right back.

Golf Course Crescent, Box 955
Hanna, Alberta, T0J 1P0
Telephone: (403) 854-3722

The 166-yard, par 3, 2nd hole

Heatherglen Golf Club

"Maturing with the years..."

Par 72/73

It's really not so long ago that this course on Glenmore Trail east of Calgary was, on good days at least, a relatively straightforward affair. But times have changed. The trees have grown. They've matured into telling obstacles along fairways that were always good underfoot but trouble-free and they're sprouting inside dogleg turns drastically reducing the chances of successfully taking shortcuts. More water has been introduced in subtle places, and there have been a number of other cosmetic changes that have raised the calibre of the lay-out. This is no longer a place where players can spray it around with some abandon and survive. There's trouble out there now and it's getting easier to find all the time.

#1 - Par 4.
C: 384 yards
R: 380 yards
F: 360 yards

Dogleg left. Tee shot across creek should ideally land centre right between fairway sand left and right. That side opens up green for mid-iron approach. This one, like most greens around here, is flattish, but well guarded by sand.

#2 - Par 4/5.
C: 448 yards
R: 434 yards
F: 389 yards

Use mirror to ensure fairway is clear. Dogleg left starting slightly uphill with water close along left side and major marsh trouble over mounds on outside of turn. Aim tee shot inside mounds for straight approach shot to green which has traps front left and front right.

#3 - Par 4.
C: 362 yards
R: 348 yards
F: 324 yards

OB left, water right, off the tee box and later along the right side the of green. Good drive down centre sets up safer approach into green trapped left and right.

#4 - Par 3.
C: 202 yards
R: 197 yards
F: 162 yards

A testing shortie with OB all the way close along the left and a dry creek running most of the way along the right approach to green. It's guarded well by sand right front and behind.

#5 - Par 5.
C: 510 yards
R: 490 yards
F: 405 yards

A fine roadside par 5 requiring a tee shot hit over pond in front of tee boxes. A good landing area is centre right alongside fairway sand right. Next shot should be hit to the right of large tree centre left in the fairway. There's sand left of green with a ridge making the back higher than the front.

#6 - Par 5.
C: 530 yards
R: 522 yards
F: 510 yards

Dogleg left with water straight out about 230 yards. This is one hole where it's still possible to take a shortcut across the corner with a good hit of 240 yards or so. Next shot should favor left side to open up green, water front right. Good birdie hole.

#7 - Par 4.
C: 358 yards
R: 351 yards
F: 329 yards

Good hole, a dogleg right. Ideal tee shot is aimed just left of major sand on the fairway's right. Success will set up nice mid-iron approach into green guarded by sand left. Another birdie chance.

#8 - Par 3.
C: 189 yards
R: 182 yards
F: 166 yards

Toughish par 3. Really needs a slight draw shot to fly into green on hole which seems to slip left. There's sand left and right too.

#9 - Par 4.
C: 398 yards
R: 388 yards
F: 370 yards

Good dogleg right finisher for front nine. Ideal tee shot is centre inside fairway sand left. That sets up mid iron down left side into green where water is squeezing in on front right edge.

#10 - Par 4.
C: 314 yards
R: 304 yards
F: 273 yards

A little teaser. Fly your tee shot over the twin trees in the middle of the fairway or choose which side to go. My advice is left of them. Fairway sand is dangerously close right.

#11 - Par 3.
C: 155 yards
R: 149 yards
F: 130 yards

A tricky shortie. There's water threatening immediately in front on the left and there's more on the right up beside the narrow green. There's sand front right, right and left and there's a severe back to front slope.

#12 - Par 5.
C: 504 yards
R: 473 yards
F: 400 yards

Dogleg left. There's hidden water left starting about 75 yards off the tee and more on the right side straight out starting at about 250 yards. Ideal tee shot target line is the distant house beyond the turn.

#13 - Par 4.
C: 376 yards
R: 370 yards
F: 353 yards

Always tricky. There's water right and a deep (for now-) grassed ditch across the fairway. Aim tee shot just to the right of the wooden bridge. Good one carrying the ditch will set up mid iron into green guarded by trees left and right, water back left, and sand front left, front right.

#14 - Par 3.
C: 154 yards
R: 134 yards
F: 116 yards

Never easy. If precision is ever part of your game, now's the time. Short, but there's water left and water right of narrow green sloping back-to front. Wind often a factor. There's sand too, left, right and back.

#15 - Par 4.
C: 288 yards
R: 282 yards
F: 268 yards

Fine, short par 4 dogleg left. Tee shot across pond immediately in front. Long hitters could probably reach the green but be warned, there's water perfectly placed short left of the green to catch any inadequate shortcut attempt. Safe way is tee shot left of fairway sand straight out followed by a chip on.

#16 - Par 5.
C: 516 yards
R: 489 yards
F: 419 yards

Major intimidation factor from OB field all along the right. It can be like a magnet despite a vast landing area. The safe shot is centre left but beware water starting on left about 250 yards out. The most difficult shot should be the final approach into green between OB fence right and trees encroaching from left. As you leave, this one might have you shaking your head at how difficult you made it.

#17 - Par 4.
C: 306 yards
R: 299 yards
F: 234 yards

Long hitters can get close, but watch out. Too far left and there's major unseen water problems in the landing area and there's a road and OB tight right to make you pay for any unwanted push or slice.

#18 - Par 4.
C: 405 yards
R: 392 yards
F: 313 yards

Quality finishing hole. There's trees left and road and OB right to watch out for. Tee shot should be hit straight out to land somewhere around 150 yard markers. Then it's a matter of flying the water, starting about 100 yards in front of the green which has a severe back to front gradient.

Glenmore Trail & 100 Street SE
Calgary, Alberta
Telephone: (403) 236-4653

The 154-yard, par 3, 14th hole

Henderson Lake Golf Club

"A little piece of country in the city . . ."

Par 70/75

It's as if they built the golf course first and then designed Lethbridge around it. It's not true of course but this fine parkland track, nearly eighty years old now, lies in the heart of the city. With only two par 5s for the men, both on the front nine, par sits a mite deceptively at 70, but don't be fooled. Note the ladies' par is 75. If this course has trademarks it's its higher-than-usual share of long par 4s and mostly small greens and they do take their toll on the scorecard. With Henderson Lake itself nearby, the famous Japanese Gardens lurking delightfully on the fringes, and the magnificent mature trees lining the fairways, this one's a delightful walk in a country setting despite its proximity to the downtown bustle of a thriving southern Alberta city.

#1 - Par 4.
C: 405 yards
R: 381 yards
F: 357 yards

Nice opener with trees along both sides. Aim tee shot centre left to avoid several nasty traps on the outside of a very faint dogleg left and water tucked in tight behind the trees right in the landing area. Approach has to negotiate little pot bunker centre front, and traps right and left.

#2 - Par 4.
C: 337 yards
R: 320 yards
F: 309 yards

Short but be careful with trees and OB right. The long green sits diagonally left-right with a large trap left centre and another back right. Tee shot down centre is good.

#3 - Par 5.
C: 529 yards
R: 509 yards
F: 495 yards

Needs to be played like a double dogleg, left then right. Good tee shot landing in the right side short of the fairway traps on the outside of the turn is essential. Second should be aimed to the left side of the fairway well away from a trap short right. The green has sand middle left, a pot middle right and a trap behind. Depending on placement, approach could vary two clubs.

#4 - Par 3.
C: 161 yards
R: 134 yards
F: 112 yards

Nice short hole with water the danger all along the right. There are traps left, right and behind. Watch out for a curious basin in the front right of the green that can cause some tricky putting predicaments down there.

#5 - Par 5.
C: 565 yards
R: 539 yards
F: 487 yards

Long dogleg right that usually plays downwind in this usually windy city. Favor the right side for tee shot if you can but watch out for trees all the way and OB on that side too. The green is protected by two substantial traps on the left side.

#6 - Par 4/5.
C: 447 yards
R: 430 yards
F: 418 yards

This one's special. Best, and they say, toughest here. Dogleg right with threatening group of cottonwoods clustered on the outside of the turn. Fade down centre is the best bet but watch for a prevalent left-right crosswind that can turn it into a slice into OB right. The kidney-shaped green has a distinct back-right to front-left tilt and has sand right.

#7 - Par 4.
C: 373 yards
R: 366 yards
F: 359 yards

Others say this is the hardest. I'd agree. Dogleg right with a green which is virtually an island with an inlet creeping behind and down the left from Henderson Lake on the right. Add the fun provided by a headwind and OB right and you get the picture. Good position for tee shot is left side beyond the 150-yard markers. Sand right too.

#8 - Par 3.
C: 126 yards
R: 120 yards
F: 117 yards

A good one. Tee shot has to cross water about 90 or 100 yards out to a green marked by a severe back-front slope. The back is three feet higher than the front end. Beware too of the fact it's downhill and usually downwind. There's sand left and right.

#9 - Par 4/5.
C: 432 yards
R: 417 yards
F: 403 yards

This tree-lined beauty is a long one with OB right. Take heart. The landing area is wider than it looks. Successful centre tee shot is happiness here. The green, lower at the front than back, has sand left and trees back and right.

#10 - Par 4.
C: 311 yards
R: 307 yards
F: 242 yards

Tricky. It's a 160-yard carry over the water right. But there's water straight out too on the outside of the turn about 190 yards away. Good spot is between the two but safety is only about thirty yards wide. Also, trees on the inside should make you think twice about going for the flat green. Sand front left and front right. Iron time.

#11 - Par 3.
C: 172 yards
R: 163 yards
F: 109 yards

Pretty hole. The problem is it's more or less dead into prevalent west wind. Shot to huge green has to avoid small pond short right thirty-or-so yards in front. There's sand left and right too and the green has some subtle breaks in the front right corner.

#12 - Par 4.
C: 389 yards
R: 385 yards
F: 381 yards

Long and straight and straight downwind. Hit centre tee shot cleanly and you'll be left with a short iron-wedge into a green which is flattish on top but has a tilted front end. OB at the back and sand left, right and behind.

#13 - Par 4/5.
C: 426 yards
R: 419 yards
F: 412 yards

Hit tee shot centre left on this gentle dogleg right with grove of trees tucked inside the turn. This is one of the bigger greens around here and has sand hugging the left side.

#14 - Par 4/5.
C: 421 yards
R: 415 yards
F: 407 yards

Tough drive with trees hugging right side but it's downwind and you could be left with mid-iron approach that requires care. There's sand left and putts from the back on this highly-elevated green tend to be noticeably slow because you're hitting into the (usual) wind.

#15 - Par 3.
C: 224 yards
R: 217 yards
F: 210 yards

A tough test. Low tee box, low green and long and narrow. Watch the tailwind again and don't expect to repair any ball marks on this one. Nasty sand front left and back left.

#16 - Par 4.
C: 363 yards
R: 353 yards
F: 348 yards

Big trees on the inside of this dogleg left pose a problem and there are smaller trees right too. Good tee shot with fairway wood or long iron is a draw down centre. Favor right with approach as anything too far left can kick off this green. Its right side is higher than the sloped left. Two traps front right and back right. Fun!

#17 - Par 4.
C: 405 yards
R: 396 yards
F: 396 yards

Tee shot, usually dead into the wind, should be hit centre right for best approach into a green set diagonally to the fairway. There's one trap on the left but watch out for possible problems with a severe right-left slope at the back. Some nasty putts in that territory.

#18 - Par 4/5.
C: 426 yards
R: 417 yards
F: 414 yards

A tough finishing hole. Tee shot centre right is likely to be into that west wind again. One thing to watch for on this green which has a trap left. The lower front end is usually much softer than the top. So it's trickier to hold back there and there's OB right behind.

Box 1094
Lethbridge, Alberta, T1J 4A2
Telephone: (403) 329-6767

Heritage Pointe Golf and Country Club

"Simply one of Canada's best . . . "

Its reputation has spread far and wide and deservedly so. Among the many accolades bestowed on Heritage Pointe was being named Canada's best new golf course by Score magazine in 1994. Architect Ron Garl says the exciting and spectacular course off Dunbow Road just south of Calgary is without doubt his finest work to date. The course is in fact three in one, three nines of divergent character, enjoyment and challenge. They are the Heritage and Pointe nines down in the valley and the intimidating treeless Desert Nine. Whatever combination you play, you'll know you've been in a golf game by the time you finish. Outstanding.

Par 36

Pointe

#1 - Par 5.
C: 520 yards
R: 511 yards
F: 374 yards

Daunting tee shot down into the valley. It really makes sense to use an iron or fairway wood to hit on a line to the cluster of target rocks on the fairway left in the distance. From that region a longish lay-up short right of the green is best to open things up.

#2 - Par 4.
C: 402 yards
R: 364 yards
F: 268 yards

Use an iron to aim tee shot towards the pine tree just left of the greenside trap. Some say the shot to the elevated green is the toughest second on the course. Aim high approach over the trap for the fat of the green which has a severe front-end slope.

#3 - Par 4.
C: 418 yards
R: 383 yards
F: 315 yards

Aim tee shot straight down centre avoiding water along the left. This is a pretty flat green accepting an approach with anything from a three iron to a wedge. Beware the major trap left.

#4 - Par 4.
C: 403 yards
R: 350 yards
F: 277 yards

Best line off this tee with a long iron or fairway wood is centre right as all the sand and water trouble is along the left. The green is tiered right to left.

#5 - Par 5.
C: 518 yards
R: 454 yards
F: 405 yards

Toughest tee shot on the golf course. Accuracy is the thing here so hit a fairway wood, even a long iron, out towards the rock pile on the outside of the turn. From there the percentage shot is short left of the elevated narrow green. This one slopes severely back to front. Important to be on the same level as the pin.

#6 - Par 3.
C: 183 yards
R: 165 yards
F: 96 yards

Downhill so club down at least one. It slopes back to front so be below the pin if possible.

#7 - Par 4.
C: 406 yards
R: 382 yards
F: 304 yards

This is what you call an elevated tee. Often best to play long iron or fairway wood here to stay short of the creek. The 150-yard markers are a good target. Maybe club down for approach which has to avoid a mini-desert short left to hit a green which slopes mainly back to front. However, a slight crown in the middle does cause some tilt off the back

#8 - Par 4.
C: 361 yards
R: 301 yards
F: 234 yards

Off the elevated tee, aim iron tee shot down a line right of the pine on the left of the fairway ignoring the invisible cross creek below the tee boxes. Watch the smallish grass bunker short right in the approach to a fairly level green. It has a tier on the back left corner.

#9 - Par 3.
C: 187 yards
R: 165 yards
F: 102 yards

They call this one the Augusta Knock-off hereabouts. It is similar to the renowned 12th there. Try and hit the correct tier on the three-level green. Although there's water and sand in front it really is better to be short than long. Chipping back down from behind can be a nightmare.

Par 36   Desert

#1 - Par 4.
C: 411 yards
R: 389 yards
F: 308 yards

Grip it and rip it! Aim left of the rightside sand avoiding the heavy mounding on the left. Then take one club less for your approach into an elevated flat green.

#2 - Par 4.
C: 385 yards
R: 373 yards
F: 253 yards

The green is invisible and perspective is difficult so hit tee shot towards target rocks through the fairway. You'll need reasonable length here to see the green for your second. Club down for the approach into this long, flattish one.

#3 - Par 3.
C: 214 yards
R: 189 yards
F: 127 yards

Daunting long iron shot into a slightly-elevated green with major sand trouble in the shape of a large bunker and three pot bunkers front left. The slope on this one is mixed between left-right, back-front.

#4 - Par 5.
C: 546 yards
R: 510 yards
F: 425 yards

Ideal tee shot should come to earth right of the array of fairway traps left. It can be reached in two but the rest of us should spot the old metal barn and that's our lay-up shot. There's water and sand on the right of this two-tiered green.

#5 - Par 3.
C: 178 yards
R: 160 yards
F: 122 yards

Take an extra club here to be there if you know what I mean. There's a huge waste bunker right so if you're going to bail out, bail out left.

#6 - Par 4.
C: 463 yards
R: 440 yards
F: 309 yards

Basically a straightaway hole. Let 'er rip but you don't want to be in the deep sand on the right of the fairway. The final approach is uphill so even a good drive will leave you a longish iron onto a flattish green, You may well feel you have to club up no matter what.

#7 - Par 5.
C: 517 yards
R: 503 yards
F: 422 yards

A golfer could die of thirst in what they say is Canada's longest bunker all along the left. Long drive down centre is a good start on this monster. Then lay up short left of the green with your second. From there, chip up and on to the three-level, clover leaf green. Wow!

#8 - Par 4.
C: 424 yards
R: 379 yards
F: 306 yards

Those target rocks sure come in handy. Aim for them from the back, maybe for the roofs of the houses beyond the green from the whites. Then at least think of clubbing down for approach into this green which has a back to front slope. Oh, by the way, he said, stating the obvious, avoid the myriad of pot bunkers right.

#9 - Par 4.
C: 400 yards
R: 373 yards
F: 297 yards

If the wind is behind you, watch your club selection here. The water can be reached down a gentle downslope. This huge green slopes back to front and has water dangers short left and left.

Par 36/37

Heritage

#1 - Par 5.
C: 566 yards
R: 518 yards
F: 414 yards

Back down in the pined valley, at least after the tee shot from the severely elevated tee box. With an iron or fairway wood, make your line the horseshoe trap in the desert of bunkers. Then lay up right short of the elevated green. Try and stay below pin on one which slopes sharply back to front.

#2 - Par 4.
C: 374 yards
R: 363 yards
F: 320 yards

A great hole. Even long hitters should rethink flying the fairway traps on the left. Right of them is the line to take off the tee and the ideal spot to set up the second. Club up for the approach into an elevated green with OB behind.

#3 - Par 3.
C: 187 yards
R: 177 yards
F: 87 yards

Club down for this downhill shot with the wind usually at your back. There's major sand headaches short and water problems not too far behind this elevated green. Choose your weapon carefully.

#4 - Par 4/5.
C: 479 yards
R: 422 yards
F: 355 yards

Hit tee shot centre right out over the creek. A longish drive should leave a medium iron into a severely back-front sloping green which will accept the shot. But it's tiered so go for the bonus and try and be on the same level as the pin.

#5 - Par 3.
C: 221 yards
R: 170 yards
F: 108 yards

Tricky to say the least. This one usually needs one more club as it's straight into the prevailing wind. Green is tiered left to right.

#6 - Par 4.
C: 406 yards
R: 383 yards
F: 246 yards

Iron is best here along a line towards the clump of trees through the fairway. That sets up short iron, even a wedge, across the water to a green multi-trapped in the short left approaches. They are deep and plentiful.

#7 - Par 4.
C: 413 yards
R: 366 yards
F: 293 yards

Hit straight out towards the outside of the turn. A landing just beyond the 150s is ideal for a short iron approach into the slightly elevated flattish green. Be long rather than short on this shot.

#8 - Par 4.
C: 353 yards
R: 312 yards
F: 187 yards

Your tee shot target has to be the leftmost bunker through the fairway as all the trouble here lies in the gorge right. Important: check flag position from the tee as you won't be able to judge as you set up for approach. Its position on the three-level green can mean a several-club difference for that shot. Green has left to right slope too.

#9 - Par 5.
C: 497 yards
R: 463 yards
F: 383 yards

Long hitters can let 'er fly here for a chance of getting on in two. Drive should be aimed towards the two towers up towards the driving range. Go for it or lay up short of the water in front of this island green. It slopes predominantly back to front but an overhit will roll off into the water behind.

#1 Heritage Pointe Drive, R.R. 1
DeWinton, Alberta, T0L 0X0
Telephone: (403) 256-2002

Highwood Golf and Country Club

"High quality by the Highwood . . ."

This challenging traditional riverside course in High River was transformed a few years back now with the unveiling of a new links-style nine to complement the existing 18-hole parkland circuit. The facility by the Highwood River now comprises three nines, Heritage, Spitzee and Montainview, any combination of two providing a testing and enjoyable 18-hole round for players of varying calibre. Heritage and Spitzee are the original wonderfully-treed eighteen, Mountainview, wending its way round water hazards and flanked in places by new housing, providing the more open links aspect of the track. It's simply a very good course and a very nice place to play.

Par 35

Heritage

#1 - Par 4.
C: 403 yards
R: 392 yards
F: 381 yards

Ever-so-gentle dogleg left with trees lining the left and more open on the right. A draw tee shot down centre sets up best mid-iron approach into a small green, shaded by trees, and which falls away slightly back left. It can be a bit damp underfoot in here.

#2 - Par 4.
C: 437 yards
R: 393 yards
F: 349 yards

Ideal tee shot is a long controlled draw centre left tightish to the trees and river left. But turn the ball too much and you'll have approach problems with a large tree guarding the green short left. There is more landing area space for your drive straight out but watch the three traps perhaps 220 yards out from the regulars. Green is narrow and single-tiered.

#3 - Par 4.
C: 360 yards
R: 318 yards
F: 283 yards

Interesting decision time. Positive drive of 230 yards or so can be hit across the water through gap in trees on the inside of the right turn. Or a solid iron hit about 170 yards straight out will land nicely in the turn. Take your pick. There's sand left and right of a big green which slopes back to front.

#4 - Par 3.
C: 201 yards
R: 179 yards
F: 144 yards

Toughish par 3 with trees all the way left and water right and short right of the green. There's an ugly pot bunker front left and more sand right and behind. Best shot is a slight draw hit along the water. But be warned the pond seems to suck the ball down. Get the right club!

#5 - Par 4.
C: 364 yards
R: 348 yards
F: 315 yards

Tee shot from within chute of trees should be hit centre, centre right onto open side of fairway. But watch the big tree short right of the tee box. Good drive that side will set up nice approach into a long, diagonal green which has sand left and trees and bushes right.

#6 - Par 3.
C: 129 yards
R: 119 yards
F: 109 yards

Wedge time. But beware the grassy bump in front of a green which slopes back-front, left-right. There's sand right behind and the trees beyond it aren't too far away either.

#7 - Par 4.
C: 353 yards
R: 353 yards
F: 316 yards

Be centre left off the tee staying well away from steep bank right that will take ball down into trees and trouble. The approach is ever-so-slightly uphill to a green trapped behind and with trees providing some danger short left. Flattish on top, the green has a front-end slope and big drop-off right.

#8 - Par 4.
C: 357 yards
R: 320 yards
F: 271 yards

Centre left off the tee is good on an almost straightaway hole with trees coming into play right in the landing area. Go in high on approach because a huge trap guards most of the green's front end. There's more sand left too.

#9 - Par 5.
C: 588 yards
R: 524 yards
F: 483 yards

A monster not only in length but in challenge. Hit tee shot across fringe of waste bunker right down a line inside fairway traps left. Stay left with your second too on a fairway that dips down then back up with moguls left and trees right. Water left, major trap short right and one behind on a green lower left than right.

Par 35/36 **Spitzee**

#1 - Par 5.
C: 488 yards
R: 475 yards
F: 428 yards

Long elegant par 5 sweeping right down an avenue of trees. Centre left for the tee shot and stay on the left all the way to a long, narrow tiered green sloping back to front with sand left and right.

#2 - Par 3.
C: 175 yards
R: 160 yards
F: 129 yards

A new green since the devastating floods of '95. But there's still sand front right and the elevated green still undulates and the water's still close back right.

#3 - Par 4.
C: 376 yards
R: 344 yards
F: 313 yards

A straightaway hole on which all the trouble lies right in the shape of bushes, trees and water beyond. A tee shot down the middle is perfect to set up mid-iron approach into a back-front sloping, crested green. Be careful with approach shot length. The trees are not too far behind.

#4 - Par 4.
C: 330 yards
R: 316 yards
F: 301 yards

Attractive hole with main source of trouble again all along the right. Another centre tee shot is best but watch your length. Creek crosses about 70 yards in front of the green. Centre tee shot will also take two huge trees left out of play for lofted approach into a narrowish tiered green with traps left, right and behind.

#5 - Par 4.
C: 348 yards
R: 322 yards
F: 311 yards

Hit drive straight down the middle left of the fairway trap on the right and avoiding the big tree on the left. This is a very long green which can vary approach by up to two clubs depending on flag placement. It also dips slightly at the back end.

#6 - Par 4.
C: 350 yards
R: 342 yards
F: 326 yards

Straightaway hole with a fairway that dips. Trees creep into play in the landing area right so a centre left tee shot best sets up the hit into a flat green, trees right and bushes behind.

#7 - Par 4.
C: 360 yards
R: 341 yards
F: 287 yards

A fine hole wriggling first left then slightly right. A good drive will travel centre left between the trees avoiding contact with water that starts about 230 yards straight out and carries on up towards the green. A new feature is an approach further complicated by a creek that now crosses in front of the green from the big tree on the right.

#8 - Par 3.
C: 173 yards
R: 164 yards
F: 130 yards

Trees down both sides but closer on the right. And they're all around the narrow, flattish green. Watch the wind here.

#9 - Par 4/5.
C: 442 yards
R: 422 yards
F: 407 yards

A lovely hole. Dogleg left needs a tee shot right up the centre avoiding any chance of water problems on the outside of the turn. Centre drive also sets up best approach between sentry trees guarding a crazily-undulating green with water quite close behind.

Par 35

Mountainview

#1 - Par 4.
C: 405 yards
R: 389 yards
F: 347 yards

Toughish dogleg left with water threatening both sides. Accurate tee shot centre to land in line with large tree on the left is best. That sets up best approach into a large diagonal green with sand front right and back left. Predominant slope here is back to front.

#2 - Par 4.
C: 366 yards
R: 345 yards
F: 320 yards

Ideal tee shot is one centre left away from the fairway trap right to be in best position for approach into a long green with traps left and right.

#3 - Par 3.
C: 182 yards
R: 161 yards
F: 127 yards

The large green is trapped left, right and behind. It also has a dipping tier back left and two other levels centre and right. Calling card putts available on request.

#4 - Par 5.
C: 474 yards
R: 448 yards
F: 426 yards

A fine downhill hole with traps both sides in the landing area. Be straight down the middle to set up approach to a green with water left and right and a creek crossing immediately in front. Go for it with your second or lay up. And it's best to be below

#5 - Par 3.
C: 197 yards
R: 142 yards
F: 112 yards

the pin on a very sharply sloped green with sand back left and back right.

The joys of owning a house on a golf course . . .This tricky par 3 is all about accuracy both for the scorecard and for peace of mind. Water hugs the left of the green and houses the right.

#6 - Par 4.
C: 421 yards
R: 386 yards
F: 350 yards

This is one fine golf hole requiring a brave tee shot from elevated tees to thread the needle between water left and fairway traps right. A good one will run through the fairway dip and end up on the top of the plateau. Aim approach to the left side of the tiered green which runs down right. But watch for huge trap left and another back right.

#7 - Par 4.
C: 353 yards
R: 331 yards
F: 281 yards

Best option on a shortish uphill dogleg left is an accuracy iron or fairway wood off the tee to land between traps left and water right. Lose the approach right and it's wet. The large flattish green has traps back left and back right.

#8 - Par 4.
C: 306 yards
R: 287 yards
F: 269 yards

A driveable dogleg right around water, but really do you need the angst? Common sense play is a mid iron played short of the creek in the turn and go from there with a nice easy wedge.

#9 - Par 4.
C: 427 yards
R: 410 yards
F: 393 yards

Best drive from elevated tee box is straight down the middle keeping clear of the water running along the left. The next problem is an approach over the creek about 75 yards in front of the elevated green. It has water close on both sides, a basin on its front end, and traps left and back right. Good finisher.

Golf Course Road, Box 5503
High River, Alberta, T1V 1M6
Telephone: (403) 652-2402

Inglewood Golf and Curling Club

"A natural beauty in the shadow of the city . . ."

Par 71/73

Inglewood golf course is unique. At certain points on this challenging track along the banks of the Bow River, it seems almost possible to lob a fairway wood shot into the heart of downtown Calgary, its glass, steel and concrete towers seem so close. But here we are, on a country-style course a mere ten-minutes drive from the hub of the city's business world. It's really a minor miracle. The setting with huge old trees and holes bending around with the river provides spectacular views and at times really tough golf. The 'natural' country feel here is often augmented by the sights and sounds of the Inglewood Bird Sanctuary just across the river.

#1 - Par 4/5.
C: 426 yards
R: 418 yards
F: 403 yards

It's the highest handicap hole on the course. Why? It's narrow and tree-lined all the way, not an unusual occurrence around these parts. Middle is the way all the way to a slightly elevated green which has sand front left and back right. Deceptively tricky opener.

#2 - Par 3.
C: 161 yards
R: 150 yards
F: 131 yards

Picturesque shortie. Tee shot needs to be hit over or along the edge of a river inlet creeping in from the right. There's major sand right of the green and again behind it. This one has a marked back-to-front slope so below the pin makes sense.

#3 - Par 4.
C: 388 yards
R: 378 yards
F: 361 yards

Sharp dogleg right with river and huge trees on the inside of the turn. Be centre left off the tee to open up the green surrounded by mounds, hidden sand front left and a nasty grass bunker front right. Ridge across the front of the green causes a major slope on the front edge.

#4 - Par 4.
C: 417 yards
R: 401 yards
F: 376 yards

Wobbles left, then right through avenue of trees. A tee shot centre left is good. Again this rolling green is surrounded by troublesome mounds. If the early holes are anything to go by, your short game better be up to scratch today.

#5 - Par 4.
C: 391 yards
R: 375 yards
F: 347 yards

A tester. It's straight but there's trouble on downslopes behind trees and bushes on both sides. And the neck into the green is exceedingly narrow between trees left and semi-hidden water creeping around the back from front right. There's sand off the back too.

#6 - Par 5.
C: 568 yards
R: 548 yards
F: 448 yards

A solid par 5. Tee shot should be aimed centre left. From then on be aware of the trees and sand on the right side that come into play on approach to the green. There's big bunker trouble

#7 - Par 3.
C: 183 yards
R: 161 yards
F: 140 yards

#8 - Par 4.
C: 376 yards
R: 356 yards
F: 339 yards

#9 - Par 5.
C: 452 yards
R: 440 yards
F: 420 yards

#10 - Par 3.
C: 145 yards
R: 143 yards
F: 105 yards

#11 - Par 5.
C: 530 yards
R: 512 yards
F: 509 yards

#12 - Par 4.
C: 338 yards
R: 330 yards
F: 317 yards

#13 - Par 4.
C: 397 yards
R: 395 yards
F: 338 yards

#14 - Par 4.
C: 333 yards
R: 317 yards
F: 307 yards

left on this elevated, back-to-front sloping green. It also has severe drop-offs on both sides and behind.

A quality short hole. Water creeps in from the left about halfway out and the cart path and trees hug the right side tight. There's a trap front right and a major ridge halfway across the green causes a front-end tilt.

Another good one. It's straight but there are two huge trees in the middle of the fairway. They look to be side by side, but in fact the left one, about 250 yards out from the back, is nearer by fifty yards. Either side of it is a good tee shot landing area. The green here has a severe front right slope and sand front left.

Just a superb dogleg left sweeping along with the Bow River left, that's all. It's almost mandatory to hit tee shot centre right. Long hitters can reach in two, but a safer alternative is to keep advancing down the right until you have a nice wedge shot onto a green guarded front right by water and sand left.

Classy little opener to the back nine. Shot must travel along edge of water right to hit green heavily-sloped back-to-front and surrounded by trees and bushes. Be below the pin.

Another fine hole. Either side of the large tree in the middle of the fairway is okay for the tee shot. Then it's a case of being patient until you have to negotiate the narrow neck into a green guarded front left and front right by sand.

Tee shot on this dogleg left has to be hit out of chute of trees, avoiding river and OB left, to land centre right. Happy landings there provide a nice short iron, wedge into a green covered heavily by sand and grass traps front right and behind.

The oft-present Bow is with us again on this one and there's fairway sand on the right. Good tee shot target is just left of that sand. Good one sets up mid-iron approach into narrow green protected on both front edges by traps. It slopes mainly back to front.

Slightly downhill (a surprise on this course). Aim tee shot towards sand visible on left. A hit of around 220 will land you just short of it and in fine position to short iron or wedge your way onto sloping green guarded front right by a scary railway-tie-backed trap. There are trees all around and another trap behind.

#15 - Par 3.
C: 176 yards
R: 172 yards
F: 146 yards

Nice shortie. There's an extremely narrow access neck between traps front left and front right and there are major potential sand problems back left. My way is the high way.

#16 - Par 4/5.
C: 446 yards
R: 443 yards
F: 419 yards

Perfect tee shot on this super dogleg left is a 240-yard hit landing centre right in the turn. Too far left and you have to negotiate huge trees on left for approach. A good tee shot away from them opens up a long-iron fairway-wood approach into a green which has sand left and drop-off mounding right. The green slopes back to front.

#17 - Par 3.
C: 198 yards
R: 190 yards
F: 176 yards

This is the one you can see from Deerfoot Trail. Straightaway hit with a four or five iron should do the trick. But there's hungry sand left and right on a fairly narrow green.

#18 - Par 5.
C: 506 yards
R: 489 yards
F: 484 yards

Chance to go out with a bang . . . or a whimper. It's straight and slightly downhill. Aim tee shot just right of tree in centre of fairway about 260 yards out. There's another tree bang in the middle affecting the approach too. Long hitters can make this in two. Others will likely be hitting a lay up to chip left of, or over the water covering right half of green. Birdies happen here.

26th St. & 34th Ave., S.E. Overpass
Calgary, Alberta
Telephone: (403) 299-9666

The 145-yard, par 3, 10th hole

Innisfail Golf Club

"Undoubtedly one of Alberta's best . . ."

Par 72

Let me put it on record now. There are precisely eighteen level lies on this wonderful course just over an hour's drive north of Calgary on Highway 2. They're all on the tee boxes. After that, this exciting track will give you every uphill, downhill and sidehill lie you can imagine, will test your ability with every club in your bag, any others you can borrow from your partners, and demand the best of your course management. And I'll make a recommendation. The course is not overly long from the tips at 6 459 yards, but fascinatingly severe elevation changes and one or two minor, albeit scenic, treks between green and tee boxes really require you play from the comfort of a power cart. The original nine is about 70 years old and it wasn't until 1986 that the course became what it is today. Innisfail, with narrowish tree-lined fairways swooping through the spruce and poplars, is a great one.

#1 - Par 4.*
C: 358 yards
R: 348 yards
F: 326 yards

An opener that hints of the great things to come. And it's been changed for the 1996 season. The green is tucked further right round the bend. Downhill with thick bush on both sides. Good tee shot from elevated tee box hit down left side will hit downslope and kick along nicely to open up the new green round the bend. It is trapped on both sides.

#2 - Par 3.*
C: 214 yards
R: 190 yards
F: 158 yards

OB left. This one has become a water hole. There's sand too between the water and front right of the green. But there's a 15-yard landing area beyond the sand to provide some relief.

#3 - Par 5.
C: 498 yards
R: 455 yards
F: 408 yards

This dogleg left doesn't take any prisoners. Tee shot should be hit centre onto uphill fairway which has a deadly gully off to the left. Make sure group in front has moved on before manoeuvring down through a narrow funnel of trees towards a green which is higher on the left side.

#4 - Par 4.
C: 361 yards
R: 335 yards
F: 325 yards

A class act. A tee shot favoring left side will do the trick on this uphill hole on which the fairway starts out with a distinct left to right lean. Up near the green, however, it develops a right to left tilt, so your approach should be hit in on that side.

#5 - Par 5.
C: 545 yards
R: 515 yards
F: 472 yards

Downhill tee shot should hit centre in a flattish landing area where the hole begins sweeping majestically right. Then it's sharply uphill on a fairway that develops a serious right-left tilt topped by a large trap on the right. Club up drastically for the hit into the smallish green.

#6 - Par 4.
C: 351 yards
R: 339 yards
F: 321 yards

Another downhill sweeper to the right. Tee shot should be leftish towards group of small blue spruces on the edge of the left-right leaning fairway. That side is best for mid-iron approach into green perched on the hillside.

#7 - Par 3.
C: 161 yards
R: 144 yards
F: 130 yards

Don't be long! There are three traps directly behind this green. Even if you do manage to miss them, it'll still take a perfect chip from back there to hold this green that slopes mainly back left-front right. Oh, there's a centre pot bunker in front. Short but deadly.

#8 - Par 4.
C: 399 yards
R: 384 yards
F: 362 yards

For the men, the highest handicap hole and it's a beauty. Aim elevated tee shot centre left but longer hitters beware trap 275 yards out left, and slicers watch those trees about 230 yards out right. Then, guess what. It's uphill to a narrow green with a sharp front end slope, sand left and back right. Savor any par on this one.

#9 - Par 4.
C: 373 yards
R: 340 yards
F: 325 yards

Ideal tee shot on this dogleg right is centre left to land somewhere short of the fairway sand 250 yards out on the outside of the turn. That sets up a comfortable mid-iron into a trap-surrounded, three-tier staircase green. But watch out. There's also a 'secret' left-right slope on this one to complicate matters.

#10 - Par 4.
C: 381 yards
R: 371 yards
F: 335 yards

This late dogleg right seems to dogleg forever. Unless you're a precise fader, tee shot should be hit centre left to clear the trees on the inside of the turn. Anything too far right would have to negotiate more trees protruding short right of heavily-bunkered green with severe back-front tilt. Warning: Make the turn on this one or it's nothing but trouble.

#11 - Par 3.
C: 182 yards
R: 172 yards
F: 167 yards

Interesting. Traps front left and front right and vicious little grass bunker immediately behind. Two curiosities here. There's a little basin in the front edge of the green and a mound in the green can throw the ball left or right at the back.

#12 - Par 4.
C: 372 yards
F: 362 yards
F: 352 yards

Elevated downhill tee shot should be hit centre right to ready for uphill approach into a two-tier, back and front, green with a trap front right.

#13 - Par 4.
C: 316 yards
R: 306 yards
F: 255 yards

Be sensible. Iron or fairway wood tee shot should land about 200 yards out just short of the sand on the outside of the turn. Make the turn or die! Trees creep in from the right for the approach and there's huge sand problems left. Green tilts right to left.

#14 - Par 5.
C: 521 yards
R: 508 yards
F: 493 yards

Wow! Just a glorious view from a spectacular elevated tee box looking down on a fairway receding right as it approaches the lake. Ideal drive is a fade shot starting towards the tall birch on the left and landing centre away from tree and mound trouble right. Then patience is a virtue up a green trapped front left, front right and behind.

#15 - Par 4.
C: 362 yards
R: 352 yards
F: 303 yards

Signature hole on a course of wonders. The unseen water of Hazelwood Lake starts just beyond trees on the left. So hit tee shot down towards lone pine on the outside of this dogleg left. Then it's decision time. Lay up into the neck of the peninsular green hung out left or go for it. Tricky to stick though, and there's a beach between water and green and more sand back left and back right.

#16 - Par 4.
C: 413 yards
R: 365 yards
F: 345 yards

Another fine hole. Good drive centre just beyond trap left is best here to open up approach into pear-shaped green with traps front left and front right and sharp drop-off at the back.

#17 - Par 3.
C: 182 yards
R: 165 yards
F: 112 yards

Best chance here is a slight draw through funnel of trees to come into the green from the right side avoiding major sand problem front left and more on the right side.

#18 - Par 5.
C: 510 yards
R: 459 yards
F: 444 yards

A marvellous finisher. It's your choice what side you go to get past the spruce trees short in the middle of the fairway on this left-to-right leaning fairway. Left is maybe best. Then keep going up to extremely elevated green with major sand headaches front right and a smaller trap back left.

*Exact new yardages not available for #s 1 and 2 at publication time. Check scorecard or tee box marker.

Box 6068
Innisfail, Alberta, T4G 1S7
Telephone: (403) 227-3444

Kananaskis Country Golf Course

"A world-class Rockies showpiece..."

You have to be there... to fully appreciate the glory with which Albertans have been blessed. This 36-hole beauty set in some of the world's most stunning surroundings draws golfers from across the globe. It's a fair bet their day here is in the Top Five memories of Canada they take away. But the news is good for Albertans too. There is a misconception that with bookings taken a couple of months in advance, it is difficult to book tee times. Wrong! A phone call a few days in advance usually pays off and remember that Alberta citizens get a handy green fees discount which brings them well within the realm of most pocketbooks. The courses, designed by famed architect Robert Trent Jones, are scenic wonders and full of challenge and fun for the most varied handicaps. They say the Mt. Kidd course has less water than the Lorette track. Personally I don't see much difference between water on eleven of Mt. Kidd's holes compared with fourteen on Mt. Lorette. Kananaskis Country, rated by Golf Digest as the top 36-hole public golf facility in North America, is golfing at its most spectacular.

Par 72

Mt. Kidd

#1 - Par 4.
C: 455 yards
R: 439 yards
F: 348 yards

A challenging opener requiring a tee shot hit over creek about 180 yards out from back tees. Hit it down centre, centre right with a good landing area as tight to right fairway sand as you dare. A long iron can take you into green protected by sand both front edges.

#2 - Par 5.
C: 615 yards
R: 578 yards
F: 514 yards

A monster with water left off tee box and eventually again left of green. Tee shot should be aimed to hit ground somewhere left of the rightside fairway sand. The next should favor the right of the fairway too to open up most open approach into green heavily guarded by sand. Be careful with approach club selection as wind and green size are factors.

#3 - Par 4.
C: 437 yards
R: 391 yards
F: 316 yards

They're all 'nice' hereabouts but this is a *nice* one. Tee shot should be aimed at right side of banked fairway starting about 200 yards out from the back. One on that side will leave best approach angle into a green which leans distinctly right to left. Lovely hole.

#4 - Par 3.
C: 197 yards
R: 182 yards
F: 129 yards

Virtually an island green. Downhill club selection, it can vary by three or four clubs, is vital here. Wind can be another player. But if you're going to stick on this one, it's best to take the high road.

#5 - Par 4.
C: 339 yards
R: 324 yards
F: 262 yards

Shortish but tricky with water crowding both sides. Accuracy is the name of the game here so an iron or fairway wood off the tee landing right of the fairway sand left is the idea. Position in that area will leave a high short iron or wedge into a green with beach at every corner.

#6 - Par 5.
C: 553 yards
R: 515 yards
F: 469 yards

Challenging. Ideal tee shot centre right will keep you away from water threat left and set up best route into green ringed by water. With sand in front, it's best to lay up until you're in comfortable approach range of the tiered green sloping back to front.

#7 - Par 4.
C: 415 yards
R: 384 yards
F: 305 yards

If you're allergic to water, you're in a tough spot with water surrounding the tee boxes and travelling all along the left up to the green. Common sense dictates a tee shot centre right. And do beware that water round the green and the traps in front.

#8 - Par 3.
C: 183 yards
R: 142 yards
F: 89 yards

Take the wind into account here. It can be significant. And your work is not all done when the water has been negotiated. This is a small rolling green which sets up some tricky putting scenarios.

#9 - Par 4.
C: 408 yard
R: 378 yards
F: 337 yards

Fine inward finisher. Good tee shot target is left of the fairway sand about 250 yards out from the back tees. Warning. When you hit approach across the creek, try and stay below the pin on this severely-sloped green. It goes without saying there are one or two traps around too.

#10 - Par 4.
C: 405 yards
R: 392 yards
F: 334 yards

Aim tee shot down centre right of fairway to line up best approach. And this is definitely another one where it's almost compulsory to be below the pin. The back-front slope is that sharp. Putting back down can be disastrous.

#11 - Par 4.
C: 355 yards
R: 342 yards
F: 285 yards

Fine hole with the river crowding the right. But you've really got to take a risk and land tee shot somewhere in the vicinity right of the fairway trap in the middle. And with sand bang in front, you've really got to attack this elevated tiered green from the air.

#12 - Par 3.
C: 183 yards
R: 167 yards
F: 112 yards

Tricky with water all along the right, a large trap front right and another back left. For best results, hit a high fade favoring the left side of this green no matter where the pin is.

#13 - Par 4.
C: 392 yards
R: 385 yards
F: 326 yards

Bordering on claustrophobic. Accuracy a must here so maybe a fairway wood or long iron off the tee might help. Good landing area is somewhere left of the fairway sand right. And now for something completely different. This green runs off towards the back.

#14 - Par 5.
C: 525 yards
R: 491 yards
F: 404 yards

A tough one. Aim tee shot to come to earth right of slope coming down from the left. Try and stay right for the next one to set up a short iron or wedge onto a two-tiered green set high above the fairway. There's a traditional back-front lean on this one.

#15 - Par 4.
C: 402 yards
R: 379 yards
F: 318 yards

A personal favorite. Three wood or long iron is best here to set up lofted approach through narrow neck between slopes into the green. By the way, bid farewell to anything too far back left on this one. A sharp slope back there will run the ball off.

#16 - Par 3.
C: 207 yards
R: 164 yards
F: 121 yards

Tee-box differential at its finest. The wind can be a major factor here so be careful with club selection on this downhill shortie. Again try and land below the pin. Putts from the back here can be brutal.

#17 - Par 4.
C: 370 yards
R: 361 yards
F: 324 yards

Boldness be your friend. Hug those bunkers right with your tee shot for best approach into a small, severely-trapped green. Particularly watch the little pot bunker in front. Putting on this one can be an experience.

#18 - Par 5.
C: 642 yards
R: 576 yards
F: 546 yards

Ever wish some rounds could go on forever? Here's a finishing hole that does. Favor the right side off the tee and in approach to the green well-trapped short and left.

Par 72

Mt. Lorette

#1 - Par 4.
C: 412 yards
R: 397 yards
C: 358 yards

Well, well, maybe there is more water on Lorette after all. Ponds down the left and a creek running all the way right. Fairway wood or longish iron off tee to centre of fairway is safest option. That still leaves you a longish hit into a green protected by front right sand and water close behind.

#2 - Par 4.
C: 416 yards
R: 381 yards
F: 325 yards

Stream all the way left and it's a mini-desert out there with all those traps. Hole feels its way right. Ideal drive lands somewhere just left of all the sand on the right about 250 yards out from the back. Then, it's a mid or short iron onto a green which slopes from back to front.

#3 - Par 4. C: 395 yards R: 376 yards F: 317 yards	Good tee shot comes to earth just right of fairway sand. That should leave a short iron, wedge from rolling fairway onto elevated green covered front and both sides by traps. This green has a distinct left-right lean. Oh, surprise, surprise. There's water all along the left.
#4 - Par 3. C: 254 yards R: 219 yards F: 148 yards	From the back, the longest par 3 I encountered during the summer of '95. This is a real challenge. Don't be surprised if you feel the driver should come out. Go with your instinct.
#5 - Par 5. C: 541 yards R: 502 yards F: 412 yards	Talking of challenges . . . a good drive will drop somewhere right of the fairway sand left. It's the next shot that's important. Long hitters could probably make it in two but there's hidden water lurking near the sand front right and it carries on tight all along the right of an extremely narrow green. A lay up and wedge are the much safer option.
#6 - Par 3. C: 195 yards R: 174 yards F: 93 yards	Difficult. Water runs along right side of tee box and shot is required to cross it in front. Long iron should be aimed to left side of green even though there's potential sand trouble on that side. The main threat though is the green's left-to right tilt down towards the water right.
#7 - Par 4. C: 482 yards R: 439 yards F: 368 yards	Plays long. Tee shot again across water has to miss the leftside fairway bunkers on the right. Even then you've still got a hike to a rolling green which is guarded front, left and right by traps.
#8 - Par 4. C: 408 yards R: 374 yards F: 340 yards	No water but this fairway is as tight as it gets. However, to get your par or better you really need to be fairly long too to get in a position to hit a mid or short iron approach into green. Big sand problems front left.
#9 - Par 5. C: 560 yards R: 522 yards F: 451 yards	Epic! The best start is a tee shot right of the fairway traps starting around 250 yards out. Then if you can squeeze a second shot into the gap between the lake left and traps right you're in wonderful shape! And the contours of the green looping round the water make for some interesting putting propositions.
#10 - Par 4. C: 402 yards R: 392 yards F: 333 yards	Centre left is a good idea for the tee shot on this sharpish dogleg right. A successful one will leave you a short, mid iron into a thin green, sand left, with a marked lean back to front.
#11 - Par 5. C: 497 yards R: 475 yards F: 392 yards	A shorter par 5. Longer hitters can easily reach in two if they're careful about placement. Ideal tee shot lands alongside fairway sand left but it's fairly tight in there. Solid shotmaking can pay off here with a birdie.

#12 - Par 4.
C: 394 yards
R: 371 yards
F: 302 yards

A fade shot off the tee landing in the centre just beyond the turn can pay dividends here too. A nice one will leave a high mid or short iron into a tricky elevated and shallow green guarded well be sand.

#13 - Par 4.
C: 407 yards
R: 396 yards
F: 313 yards

A tester. But if you hit a draw into the right side of the fairway, it'll set up best approach into a big, well-trapped green which has a back to front slope.

#14 - Par 5.
C: 523 yards
R: 506 yards
F: 410 yards

The water right follows this dogleg left all the way round to the green. Good tee shot will hit ground right of the fairway sand and then caution really dictates a lay up somewhere in the area of the next sand on the left. The well-trapped green is not noted for excessive width.

#15 - Par 3.
C: 188 yards
R: 165 yards
F: 115 yards

Daunting shortie requiring hit across the river to a green so large it can vary club selection two or three options. Two large traps left and one behind add to the intimidation factor.

#16 - Par 4.
C: 380 yards
R: 367 yards
F: 265 yards

More water torture. Best tee shot is one across the river to hit centre left of fairway. That would leave a mid or short iron into a green noted for the large trap left.

#17 - Par 3.
C: 185 yards
R: 158 yards
F: 126 yards

Watch your club selection here too. Again it can vary a club or two depending on the wind factor. Tee shot has to flirt with the river and hit a pretty shallow green bordered heavily by traps. Good hole.

#18 - Par 4.
C: 463 yards
R: 427 yards
F: 361 yards

Long, difficult finisher. Tee shot should be aimed centre right, right of fairway sand on the left. Next shot is decision time. Lay up to the creek starting about 75 yards out from the green on the left and about 55 yards out on the right or fly it is the choice. The green is cruelly trapped on all corners. Wow!

Hwy. #40, South of Hwy. #1
PO Box 1710
Kananaskis Village, Alberta T0L 2H0
Telephone: (403) 591-7272

Keho Park Golf Club

"Pure links golf by the lake . . ."

Par 36

For those whose passion is natural links golf with a "seaside" feel, a trip of just under two hours southeast of Calgary will take them to a touch of paradise on the edge of Keho Lake, near the village of Nobleford. For the Scots among you, imagine playing the Solway Firth area. The gravel road approaches from all points of the compass tend to make visitors wonder whether they've got the directions right, but arrival and first sighting of this nine-holer strung along the lake shore immediately dispel any misgivings. For 20 or so years until 1987, sand greens were the order of the day, but now fine, challenging elevated grass greens mark the march of progress. There's challenge here with narrowish fairways, and a marvellous day out surrounded by remarkable prairie lake views.

#1 - Par 4.
R: 372 yards
F: 306 yards

Testing dogleg left opener. The superintendent reckoned cutting the corner was too easy. That was soon rectified with strategically-placed boulders on the inside of the turn. Hit them and watch it fly. There's sand there too. Sensible play is straight hit out 220 yards into turn. Elevated green, sand left and right, slopes forward, and slightly right.

#2 - Par 5.
R: 461 yards
F: 395 yards

Great hole curling left with Keho Lake on the right and a smaller lake on the inside. An ideal start usually into the wind is a tee shot some 230-250 yards down the left. Big hitters might find themselves ready to go for the green behind the little lake in two. Others hit down into neck of green. It has sand right and is mounded.

#3 - Par 4.
R: 341 yards
F: 287 yards

Three wood or long iron might be the way to go on this one which narrows and widens as you go and is normally into the prevailing wind. Solid shot left will land you in largish landing area for shortish approach into a green with a slight left-right lean and sand on the right.

#4 - Par 4.
R: 358 yards
F: 308 yards

What you see is what you get. Again maybe think three wood or iron to land inside fairway traps on the right. The green with a slope welcoming approaches has sand front left . . . and water right behind down a steep bank. Don't be long!

#5 - Par 3.
R: 122 yards
F: 95 yards

Virtually an island green with water problems front, left and behind and sand left. The right side of the green sloping towards the tee box is always best and if you're going to err there's a bit of a landing area short right. Short but tricky.

#6 - Par 4.
R: 332 yards
F: 262 yards

Feeling adventurous? The corner can be cut with a clean hit of just over 200 yards. Otherwise hit straight out and slightly uphill into turn short of fairway sand 240 yards out. There's sand front left and the green tilts slightly left-to-right.

#7 - Par 4.
R: 368 yards
F: 310 yards

The downhill fairway has a left to right lean and a fairway bunker left. Ideal tee shot is a slight fade hit down left side to land centre in the turn. There's more sand left and right in the approaches to the green which has a marked back to front slope which screams "Be below the pin." Anyway there are trees and all sorts of nasty stuff right behind.

#8 - Par 5.
R: 500 yards
F: 434 yards

In a perfect world your tee shot would land some 250 yards out somewhere left of the fairway trap. Your second would come to earth somewhere left of the bunker short right of the flattish green. Chip on for par or better and walk away . . . Hmm.

#9 - Par 3.
R: 157 yards
F: 113 yards

Downhill shot, usually with a left to right wind, with traps left of the elevated green with some dramatic drop-offs. Just hit the green. What could be simpler? Hmm again.

Box 278, Nobleford
Alberta, T0L 1S0
Telephone: (403) 824-3666

The 157-yard, par 3, 9th hole

Lakeside Greens Golf and Country Club

"Water aplenty in rolling terrain..."

Par 71

There will be some excitement around this solid links course a few kilometres east of Calgary this 1996 season with the opening of its brand new clubhouse. Since it began operating a few years back, this testing track at Chestermere Lake has been working out of makeshift facilities but it's finally coming of age. And another change, equally important. Since I began playing here I've mind-wrestled with the legitimacy of the number five hole. Now that they've altered it, maybe it's time to come out and state officially that its old configuration was to me, and others I know, a genuinely unfair hole. By substantially extending the landing area on this dogleg left round an elevated pond rendering the green invisible and introducing a couple of new traps straight out, it has finally become honest. This course can be a pleasant breeze or in the wind, a full-blown nightmare.

#1 - Par 4.
C: 413 yards
R: 400 yards
F: 329 yards

Opener drifts right and slightly uphill towards green. Ideal tee shot is hit centre, centre left to avoid possibility of nasty landings on mounded embankment right. Good one sets up mid, short iron approach into a narrow three-tiered green with dramatic back to front slopes.

#2 - Par 3.
C: 201 yards
R: 151 yards
F: 101 yards

This large flat green is perched on a peninsular jutting into the lake with water front, left and behind. Wind varies club selection drastically. There's front sand wedged between water and green and a large trap behind. A grassy mound in front can also serve up some disappointments when you arrive at the green. Too left, too bad.

#3 - Par 5.
C: 522 yards
R: 510 yards
F: 396 yards

One of the more challenging long holes in the Calgary area. Tee shot should be hit centre, centre left across water avoiding nasty banking right with more hidden water just beyond. Long hitters can reach the hillside green in two but it's well-trapped in the left approaches. Lay up right and chip maybe? Serious tiers run down left to right.

#4 - Par 4.
C: 374 yards
R: 350 yards
F: 291 yards

Cut the corner on this dogleg left if you like. But nasty mounding and traps in there can be a problem. The percentage shot is straight out 200-plus yards towards traps on the outside of the turn. Then it's an uphill wedge or short iron to the green guarded by traps front left and front right. Nasty putts to be had here too.

#5 - Par 4.
C: 390 yards
R: 351 yards
R: 291 yards

That's better! Now it's a proper golf hole. There's an elevated pond on the inside of this fierce dogleg left beyond which is the invisible green. Now that they've extended the fairway further out left, that's the place to be to actually have a line of vision into the green sloping heavily left to right down to more water.

#6 - Par 3.
C: 169 yards
C: 161 yards
R: 119 yards

A fine hole across water demanding a two or three-club selection difference depending on pin placement and wind. There are two traps right and one in front just across the water. Huge, heavily sloped green, mainly back-left to front-right, produces putting nightmares.

#7 - Par 4.
C: 369 yards
R: 348 yards
F: 297 yards

Dogleg right round rock-banked ponds right. Sensible tee shot is a fade down centre left to land inside fairway traps left. Anything too right tends to run down tilted fairway to the water. The slightly-elevated green is well trapped front left, back left and back right.

#8 - Par 4.
C: 438 yards
R: 406 yards
F: 345 yards

I do like this one even though it's nothing fancy. Maybe that's why. Slightly uphill straightaway links hole with serious banking and mounding on both sides. Straight-out tee shot will set up long or mid iron approach into back-front leaning green with sand front left. Some interesting putts here too.

#9 - Par 4.
C: 404 yards
R: 380 yards
F: 307 yards

OK. Along with its "twin" finisher #18 running parallel on the left this one requires strategy. Water is straight out about 200 yards from the front fringes of the tee boxes. Lay up with an iron or seven wood down right to ready for approach across water. (There is a bit of bail-out room right of green on this one).

#10 - Par 4.
C: 380 yards
R: 350 yards
F: 250 yards

Birdie time. Hit tee shot up centre to land somewhere right of fairway traps on the left and you have a nice short iron, wedge into a back-front sloping green with traps left and right and one pot back right. Best be below the pin.

#11 - Par 3.
C: 168 yards
R: 149 yards
F: 130 yards

Tougher than it looks for some reason. Sand front left and on both sides further back. Long green, maybe requiring two-club adjustment depending where the pin is, has marked back-to-front slope.

#12 - Par 5.
C: 611 yards
R: 561 yards
F: 421 yards

Tee shot is everything on this dogleg left. There's hidden water on the left that can be carried by long hitters. But the sensible ploy is to hit iron or fairway wood straight down the hill right of tree on left water's edge and land short of visible water straight out. Then its straight to back-front tiered green with traps left and right.

#13 - Par 3.
C: 188 yards
R: 180 yards
F: 114 yards

Daunting hole with water along the right to a hillside green with three railway tie-backed traps on the left and huge sand on the right. By the way, you may notice it has a vicious back-front slope on the front end.

#14 - Par 4.
C: 435 yards
R: 401 yards
F: 304 yards

Another solid, nothing-fancy hole with the highway and mounds on the left. Tee shot down centre does the trick for mid iron into tiered green running away from front right to back left. There's sand short right and another trap front left. The lower front-right section is a bit of a basin.

#15 - Par 4.
C: 384 yards
R: 360 yards
F: 298 yards

Getting into some potentially expensive damage territory now as houses crowd in on the right of this dogleg right. Kindest on the nerves and on the wallet is a tee shot straight out to land left of rightside fairway sand. That leaves a comfortable approach into a flatter green with traps front right and behind.

#16 - Par 4.
C: 395 yards
R: 365 yards
F: 301 yards

Hit an iron or fairway wood straight out both for position and pocketbook protection. Landing in the turn just beyond the huge fairway traps right sets up a short iron or wedge into green tucked round ninety-degree corner. Be warned, make the turn. There's major unseen sand front right if you have to cut corner with your approach.

#17 - Par 5.
C: 542 yards
R: 520 yards
F: 425 yards

Three solid shots on this gradual uphiller with the road and OB left can set you up with a good chance of a birdie. There's sand front right and back left of another rolling, back-to-front sloping green.

#18 - Par 4.
C: 409 yards
R: 395 yards
F: 344 yards

A tough finisher with care being needed on the tee shot to leave ball short of lake crossing in front of green about 240 yards out from the back tees. There's little bail-out room left here between the water and OB left. Iron or fairway wood tee shot will leave you either a mid iron or long iron second (or third) over water no matter what.

555 Lakeside Greens Drive
Chestermere, Alberta T1X 1C5
Telephone: (403) 569-9111

Land O Lakes Golf and Country Club

"Where water rules the day . . ."

Par 71/72

I declare here and now that I do not particularly like golf courses where water has been introduced for water's sake. So it was with some trepidation that we arrived at this course with a name inferring watery hell on the flatlands around the southern Alberta township of Coaldale, east of Lethbridge. Four hours later, there was no doubt in my mind that we'd just played one of the finest water-links courses we'd come across all summer. Yes, there's water on fifteen of the eighteen holes. Heck, there are seven lakes scattered through the lay-out. But no, it's not a case of design gone nuts. Water is indeed ever-present, but its placement is subtle not overpowering. It can be avoided, it can be carried, but err and it'll punish. It just means that accuracy and shotmaking are the order of the day.

#1 - Par 4.
C: 364 yards
R: 346 yards
F: 308 yards

Get used to it, there's water left off the tee box. Good tee shot is centre right into the turn on this slightly uphill dogleg left with nasty sand on the inside just beyond the water left. That should set up a high short iron, wedge into a large well-trapped green.

#2 - Par 4.
C: 420 yards
R: 409 yards
F: 351 yards

Hit tee shot centre right into area right of left fairway sand traps. Beware grabby rough and mounds on that side too. This heavily-trapped two-tier green has a major ridge running diagonally across it giving the front end a distinct slope. Up top, back left, it's flattish.

#3 - Par 3.
C: 160 yards
R: 140 yards
F: 92 yards

Here we go! Tee shot, usually with a crosswind from the left, has to cross the lake from the back tees. Fly it down the length of the water right from the others. This huge green slopes back to front and has a pot bunker in front, and traps left and right.

#4 - Par 5.
C: 520 yards
R: 493 yards
F: 432 yards

Highest handicap for women. Water short right off the tee on this slight dogleg left and then again short right of the green. Aim tee shot out towards the bridge and a good one will leave a long or mid iron approach either for the green or in the landing area short left of it. There are traps back left and front right between the green and the water.

#5 - Par 4.
C: 378 yards
R: 360 yards
F: 307 yards

Quite a hole, this one. Slightly uphill dogleg right with water short right off tee box. Drive should be hit centre left to land somewhere between fairway traps on both sides. Then it's a careful mid-iron approach into a green with water left, right and behind. There are traps both front edges. It has a sharp back-right, front-left slope.

#6 - Par 3.
C: 217 yards
R: 196 yards
F: 156 yards

Uphill long iron or fairway wood to seriously-tiered green. Top tier of three tilts left-right, and drifts down two levels to serious front-end slope. Club selection on a hole which usually has a tailwind is everything. Traps left and right too.

#7 - Par 4/5.
C: 445 yards
R: 428 yards
F: 382 yards

The men's highest handicap hole needs centre right tee shot out across the creek. Why centre right? To stay away from the invisible water starting left not too far over the hill. But be careful with strategically-placed traps in the landing area right. The water then continues all the way up to the green guarded by sand left and right.

#8 - Par 5.
C: 510 yards
R: 485 yards
F: 445 yards

Toughish dogleg right around expensive houses and nasty bunkers on the inside of the turn. OK, maybe you can cut the corner with a hopefully-accurate long fade. Chancy with sand, mounds, and houses. Call me chicken, but my way is iron or fairway wood out into 90-degree turn and proceed to the well-trapped green from there.

#9 - Par 4.
C: 340 yards
R: 311 yards
F: 261 yards

A great hole. Hit tee shot across the creek centre right out into the landing area right to land inside fairway traps. Then it's a mid iron back across the creek to the left, that's left, pin on the double green. (The right flag is the 18th). The green is heavily-trapped and has a serious back-front slope.

#10 - Par 4.
C: 401 yards
R: 384 yards
F: 315 yards

The signature hole and the most difficult here. It's a beauty. Dogleg right with a lake on the inside and one on the left. Trick is to hit (iron?) between them and land dry in the turn. (Warning: It's longer across the water than it looks if you like cutting corners, maybe 250 yards). Then everything drifts left to right down to the water for the long, mid iron approach. Trapped green leans that way too. Wow!

#11 - Par 3.
C: 196 yards
R: 176 yards
F: 130 yards

A good par 3, usually into the wind, with water all the way along the right side. This side-trapped green has a major ridge diagonally across the middle causing downslopes left at the back and down at the front.

#12 - Par 5.
C: 525 yards
R: 499 yards
F: 429 yards

Every hole's getting to be fun around here. This uphill monster needs centre tee shot then go for it if you like. But sensible play is lay-up short and left of the green away from the water starting short right of it and going up towards the front-right edge. This green drifts left-right.

#13 - Par 4.
C: 435 yards
R: 418 yards
F: 365 yards

Houses and OB left. Tee shot centre right is ideal but watch for fairway sand over there especially as the fairway tends to lean left to right. This is, shall we say, a rolling green. Putts are the luck of the draw here.

#14 - Par 3.
C: 165 yards
R: 145 yards
F: 90 yards

Another solid par 3, with lake running all the way along the right and creeping across the right front of the green, and the creek all the way along the left. Nice, eh? There's sand left and right and a marked downslope on the front end.

#15 - Par 5.
C: 497 yards
R: 472 yards
F: 435 yards

The water right of the tee box extends out about 130 yards on that side. Good tee shot lands between fairway traps left and right. On the approach(es) watch out for more water that really creeps in from the left across the front edge of the green. Maybe lay up right into the area of the fairway trap short right? Green tilts back left-front right.

#16 - Par 3.
C: 170 yards
R: 154 yards
F: 125 yards

#14's evil twin. Water, water everywhere on the right at least and OB left. This green, trapped back left and back right and with water guarding front right, is a putting lottery.

#17 - Par 4.
C: 296 yards
R: 275 yards
F: 245 yards

Slightly uphill and definitely driveable. Go for it if you like but there are vast expanses of sand short on both sides, around it and dead in front. And the road's OB right. Percentage chance of birdie really is tee shot straight and short of the green, chip and a putt.

#18 - Par 4.
C: 420 yards
R: 403 yards
F: 353 yards

Ideal tee shot on this challenging finishing hole is a centre left fade avoiding nasty fairway bunkers both sides in the landing area. Then it's case of negotiating the creek just in front of the elevated green on the right (Remember, it's doubled with #9). Back-front slope here is severe too.

102 Fairway Drive
Coaldale, Alberta, T0K 0L0
Telephone: (403) 345-CLUB (2582)

Lee Creek Valley Golf And Country Club

"Heading for the 49th Parallel . . ."

Par 36/37

When you reach Cardston, originally a large Mormon settlement complete with Temple, you're really getting within a long tee shot of the border with the United States. Maybe it was the border's proximity that lured the township's most famous daughter south to fame and fortune. Fay Wray who will be forever remembered clasped in the loving paws of the mighty King Kong was born and raised here. The town's tough nine-hole golf course can play havoc with golfers in its clutches too.

#1 - Par 4.
C: 370 yards
R: 361 yards
F: 330 yards

Out of bounds left. All boundary fences are OB here. The fairway downslope should carry your ball far enough to allow a short iron into the green. One hop it onto the green which is backed by Indiana Jones country. A nice confidence builder.

#2 - Par 5.
C: 500 yards
R: 480 yards
F: 430 yards

A long dogleg right with OB left and right. Your tee shot should ideally land centre right in the fairway allowing a likely long or mid-iron lay-up for a chip or pitch onto the green. It slopes back to front.

#3 - Par 3.
C: 232 yards
R: 208 yards
F: 191 yards

A tough, tough par 3. It's usually downwind, so a lofted club could fly the ball onto the green. But there's a horseshoe-shaped, moat-like ditch in front of the green.

#4 - Par 4.
C: 330 yards
R: 315 yards
F: 265 yards

A solid hole. A good drive centre left will land you somewhere in the region of 100 yards out from the green, leaving you a wedge on. But the last 50 yards and the green are maybe 20 feet higher than the rest of the trip. Putts from the back of this difficult green are extremely fast.

#5 - Par 3.
C: 140 yards
R: 135 yards
F: 125 yards

Testing hole. You're hitting from low tee box to green wedged on shelf on a hillside perhaps 40 feet above the fairway. You don't want to miss right. The clever trick is to hit just beyond the green left and roll back on.

#6 - Par 4.
C: 392 yards
R: 360 yards
F: 298 yards

Signature hole and the best here. Dogleg left with OB left and thick trees, especially near the green, on right. Good tee shot sticking as close to left as you can get it, will leave you a medium iron into the green from a good angle.

#7 - Par 4/5.
C: 390 yards
R: 378 yards
F: 344 yards

An extremely difficult driving hole with the river and 60 feet high cottonwoods on the left inside the slight dogleg. Centre right off the tee is a good idea. Putts from the back of this green are fast too.

#8 - Par 5.
C: 530 yards
R: 517 yards
F: 442 yards

Keep your eyes peeled here. Interesting set-up with two, that's two, greens. If the pin is on the left green, the older one, okay. But if it's on the right, the elevated green, club up to take care of altitude difference. And on this one watch for fast putts left to right and back to front.

#9 - Par 4.
C: 335 yards
R: 305 yards
F: 272 yards

Straightaway drive from elevated tee box. Favor right side as there are some high trees on left fairway up towards the green, a mere shelf, hard to hold, about 25 feet above the fairway. And then enjoy the tow rope from the green up to the clubhouse. Fast putts to be had from back to front and they break right to left.

P.O. Box 1886
Cardston, Alberta, T0K 0K0
Telephone: (403) 653-4198

The fairway on the 335-yard, par 4, 9th hole

Magrath Golf Club

"Water and wind provide the challenge..."

Par 72

Y ou know what can happen when you hit a pothole. The wheels can come off. Here it's Pothole Creek and it winds and weaves its way through this entire prairie layout. It's an old golfing adage, but "trust the locals" to know what they're doing. This course may be somewhat remote but they come from all over the southern part of the province to play it. 'Nuff said. It's a test all right even though length is not its strength. With the wind and water so prevalent play canny and really think each shot out especially in terms of what you have available in the bag. If you consider shotmaking to be one of your strong points this one will tell you where you stand in that department.

#1 - Par 4.
C: 335 yards
R: 320 yards
F: 282 yards

Elevated tee shot should be hit down centre to land in fairly open fairway on this dogleg right with the creek winding along the inside of the turn. There's sand to be negotiated front left on what should be a reasonably straightforward short-iron approach.

#2 - Par 4.
C: 415 yards
R: 402 yards
F: 300 yards

A real toughie. It's a dogleg left with OB on that side. The drive is usually bang into the wind and really should be hit centre right for best approach into a mound-encircled green with small firs also in attendance. It has major sand front right.

#3 - Par 3.
C: 163 yards
R: 145 yards
F: 145 yards

A strong left-right wind is usually a player here, so take it into account. Shot must go across creek in front of tee boxes and hit a green heavily-trapped left, right and behind.

#4 - Par 5.
C: 527 yards
R: 494 yards
F: 485 yards

Straightish but has water right early and left later. And there's a wettish area on the left of the fairway about 100 yards out from the green which has sand front left, right and behind.

#5 - Par 3.
C: 159 yards
R: 150 yards
F: 158 yards

To say this one's well-trapped is an understatement. The rolling green, elevated maybe five feet, is surrounded by sand. And there's a severe back-right to front-left slope. Some tricky putts to be had here.

#6 - Par 4.
C: 358 yards
R: 333 yards
F: 328 yards

A fierce dogleg right with a veritable jungle OB right and the creek as well. Time for an iron off the tee? Certainly. Aim to land centre-leftish in the turn about 200 yards out. Good one sets up comfortable approach into a for-once trapless, but small green.

#7 - Par 5.
C: 513 yards
R: 504 yards
F: 450 yards

Can be a nasty customer. It's a dogleg right with a strong wind usually blowing from the right. There's a vast waste bunker just inside the water on the inside of the turn. The right-left sloping fairway tends to run everything down in that direction. Tee shot centre left is the name of the game.

#8 - Par 4.
C: 408 yards
R: 375 yards
F: 330 yards

A sweeping dogleg right with a hidden green at the end. Usually only the flagtop is visible. Tee shot should be hit centre for best approach into a green which has huge sand front left and troublesome mounds surrounding it. Oh, and Pothole Creek is just behind.

#9 - Par 4.
C: 437 yards
R: 428 yards
F: 357 yards

Straight tee shot down centre should avoid tree trouble left and creek-OB headaches right. Unusual feature is six-foot step-up in fairway about 300 yards out.

#10 - Par 4.
C: 320 yards
R: 310 yards
F: 307 yards

Nice hole from elevated tee box across valley to elevated green which has right-to-left slope. Yes, with the wind blowing, it's driveable, but bear in mind the green is 35 feet above the fairway. The sand here is front right and left side. Very fast putts if you're coming from the back.

#11 - Par 4.
C: 423 yards
R: 410 yards
F: 369 yards

Toughest par on the course. Extremely difficult hole with a giant cottonwood dominating the rightside landing area. If you can, squeeze the tee shot left of the tree into the 35-yard wide gap between it and the leftside shrubbery and creek. A good one will leave a longish mid iron into a green trapped left. Luck be a lady . . .

#12 - Par 5.
C: 548 yards
R: 522 yards
F: 476 yards

Late dogleg right, longest hole on the course. Good tee shot will be aimed just inside the big tree crowding in on the right side. Watch the creek crossing the fairway 240 yards out on the left and further on the right. Second should land left of the traps guarding the inside of the turn. Traps left and right of green.

#13 - Par 4.
C: 350 yards
R: 337 yards
F: 312 yards

Sweeps gently right with creek and OB right. What you get is really what you see but the big, newish two-tiered green is higher at the back than the front. Two nasty traps guard the front edges.

#14 - Par 3.
C: 182 yards
R: 169 yards
F: 163 yards

The problem on this pleasant shortie is that it's usually into a strong west headwind and it's a semi-blind green with only the top half of the flag visible. Don't be long.

#15 - Par 4.
C: 441 yards
R: 425 yards
F: 337 yards

Tee shot should be hit down centre left. But be careful with this one if you are a long hitter. With a strong wind directly behind, the creek crossing the fairway 290-300 yards out is very reachable. After the creek, the hole wriggles right to a green trapped front left and on right side and with trees tight behind.

#16 - Par 5.
C: 527 yards
R: 508 yards
F: 415 yards

Sweeping dogleg left. Good landing spot for drive is just right of trees on the inside of the gentle turn. Slicers beware major fairway trap right with your second.

#17 - Par 3.
C: 180 yards
R: 152 yards
F: 140 yards

Tricky par 3 along Pothole Creek on the left and with sand front right of the rolling green. And watch out for a nasty swamp area short left on this one.

#18 - Par 4.
C: 380 yards
R: 370 yards
F: 286 yards

Favor a hit down the left to cross the creek again and land on top of a plateau probably 12 feet higher than the tee box area. The shot is usually into a headwind too. Traps and mounds surround this finishing green.

Box 208
Magrath, Alberta, T0K 1J0
Telephone: (403) 758-3054

McKenzie Meadows Golf Club

"Newcomer is a 'natural'..."

Par 72

Jim Thompson, co-owner of this new links course just north of Highway 22x on Calgary's present southern fringe is not ashamed in using the word "barren" to describe what he, his partners and Calgary landscaper and architect Gary Browning are trying to achieve in terms of look and feel on this brand new addition to the Calgary-area circuit. It's no mistake that there are few young trees in view or in the plans for the track lying in the meadows between the community of McKenzie on top of the bluff and the Bow River. The aim is to have as true a links course as it is possible to design nowadays and, to a very large extent, it has been achieved on a course more undulating than it would appear from the bordering highway. Natural maturing on a course which opened for a two-week dry run in 1995 will surely do the rest. A nine-hole executive course will follow in the future.

#1 - Par 5.
C: 525 yards
R: 491 yards
F: 431 yards

Architect Browning didn't fool around with this starter, a tester right off the bat. The slightly downhill dogleg left has three large traps on the outside of the turn, heavy mounding on the inside. Good tee shot will draw down centre left. Watch out for more sand short right of the green in mounds. Two-tier green ringed by trees has slope at front.

#2 - Par 4.
C: 351 yards
R: 344 yards
F: 314 yards

Hole sweeps left along the bank of the Bow with water short right of the green. Your call. Hit tee shot centre right or fly rightmost mound on the left but watch trap on left about 280 yards out. This green also has a ridge producing a front-end tilt.

#3 - Par 4.
C: 375 yards
R: 368 yards
F: 296 yards

Fine hole, a dogleg left with the Bow keeping you company along the left. Centre right is good for the tee shot. There's water starting on the right just round the turn and running up alongside the green. On this left-right leaning green, everything runs down towards the water and also a greenside trap right.

#4 - Par 3.
C: 190 yards
R: 181 yards
F: 127 yards

First of four stand-out par 3s here. There's a major trap front left among the mounds and the bushes hug disconcertingly tight to the right side. The green runs back-left to front-right with a diagonal ridge making it a two-level affair.

#5 - Par 4.
C: 344 yards
R: 338 yards
F: 287 yards

Ideal tee shot here is hit down centre left where there's more room away from the bushes and trees tight right. The two-level green is the left side of a huge double green. There's ugly bushes trouble left and major sand front right.

#6 - Par 4
C: 419 yards
R: 411 yards
F: 349 yards

Fine, fine golf hole. There's threatening mounding and sand on the inside of this dogleg right. Tough to fly it all. There's water about 300 yards straight out. All in all, good spot for tee shot is in turn around the 150-yard markers. There's sand left and right of the green.

#7 - Par 3.
C: 165 yards
R: 160 yards
F: 76 yards

Super short hole with tee shot needing to be hit along or over water left. Green creeps left with a beach between it and the water. Oh and just to make things interesting there's more water short right and a pot bunker immediately in front.

#8 - Par 4.
C: 345 yards
R: 339 yards
F: 248 yards

Water, water, water . . . left, right and straight out. Aim tee shot centre right to land around the 150-yard marker. With your mid-iron approach watch the water left and a vast crescent-shaped trap on the right.

#9 - Par 5.
C: 481 yards
R: 473 yards
F: 395 yards

Not overly-long but a challenge nonetheless. Thread the needle with your drive to negotiate narrow strip between water left and right. Then it's quite sharply uphill to a narrow green that continues invisibly quite a way left behind the traps and bank front left.

#10 - Par 4.
C: 391 yards
R: 374 yards
F: 325 yards

First of three holes running below the bluff. Anything too right on these is gone forever in the frighteningly-thick bush on the slope. The view of the fairway (or lack of it) from the highly-elevated tee box is scary. My advice is a safety iron with a fade to land centre beyond the left 150-yard marker. Green has sand front left.

#11 - Par 5.
C: 505 yards
R: 481 yards
F: 432 yards

Great one vying for signature hole honors with #7 and #15. Beware the bush again by aiming tee shot down centre. Mere mortals should lay up to ready for severe uphill approach into a green elevated with a vengeance. Watch out for hidden sand in the slope front left and two front right.

#12 - Par 4.
C: 448 yards
R: 439 yards
F: 362 yards

Yup! The bluff's still with you. Make the region around that left 150-yard marker your landing area again and you'll be all right. The hillside bushes creep right in beside the green right side and there's a large amount of sand on the left.

#13 - Par 5.
C: 530 yards
R: 506 yards
F: 458 yards

Phew! Away from the bluff but don't be lulled to sleep here with all this space. A solid straightaway tee shot is a good start on this dogleg right towards the river. Keep going but watch the sand left of the green, the other half of the double with #5.

#14 - Par 4.
C: 324 yards
R: 318 yards
F: 242 yards

This dogleg right is driveable with a tail gale, but is having to cross the water and the sand worth the chance? Especially when a nice mid iron into the turn will set up a safe approach to give you a good birdie shot anyway.

#15 - Par 3.
C: 196 yards
R: 188 yards
F: 96 yards

Longish shortie requiring hit across water from the back tees. Depending on wind and pin placement on this large tiered green, I could see a variance of up to four clubs. No kidding! Watch sand front right too.

#16 - Par 4.
C: 355 yards
R: 350 yards
F: 281 yards

Nice hole, water all the way right. It's really a straightaway trip but the green hangs out right round the water. There's a trap front right between green and water, and heavy mounding on the other side and behind. Tee shot centre left is best for safety and approach.

#17 - Par 3.
C: 152 yards
R: 136 yards
F: 106 yards

Not too long but there's danger with water left and a large trap directly behind. And ridges on this one make for some interesting putts.

#18 - Par 4.
C: 412 yards
R: 372 yards
F: 307 yards

Uphill dogleg right round water where it's best to aim drive towards leftside 150-yard marker but watch the trap just outside it. The narrow green has a strategically-placed trap on the left.

Lake McKenzie
Calgary, Alberta
Telephone: (403) 253-7473

The green on the fine 505-yard, par 5, 11th hole

Medicine Hat Golf and Country Club

"A sense of grandeur and tradition..."

Par 72

In the short walk between the second green and the third tee box, golfers pass a simple ten-foot high stone cairn. It marks the original 1893 site of the Northwest Mounted Police barracks overlooking the spectacular South Saskatchewan River several hundred feet below the bluffs. It somehow focuses visitors on the fact that here, they are surrounded by tradition. The long-established course, with its velvety fairways, strategic water hazards and dozens of varieties of mature trees lining every fairway positively reeks of grandeur. In a sense, a step onto the first tee box here is a step back into a more elegant past. Many of the holes are nothing short of magnificent both in terms of scenery and golfing challenge.

#1 - Par 5.
C: 556 yards
R: 543 yards
F: 508 yards

Highest handicap hole is an impressive dogleg right starting out along an avenue of trees and then dropping down to the green. Tee shot should be hit centre followed by a second favoring left to open up the green properly for short iron or wedge approach. Green, sloping from back right to front left has two traps right and one left.

#2 - Par 4.
C: 406 yards
R: 396 yards
F: 384 yards

Dogleg right with water short left off tee box. Aim tee shot to land just right of leftside 150-yard marker in the turn. That leaves best approach into green with a big trap front right and one on the left. Take a minute to read the cairn and look at the stunning river view.

#3 - Par 5.
C: 536 yards
R: 501 yards
F: 491 yards

Lovely straightaway hole played down narrowing avenue of trees. Just keep going as near centre as possible until the green, trapped twice front left and once front right, is reached.

#4 - Par 3.
C: 194 yards
R: 155 yards
F: 102 yards

Well-spread elevated tee boxes require hits over varying amounts of gully trouble on way over valley to elevated green. There's nothing but OB and major trouble on the right. Green has a major trap in the bank front right, another on the left and a pot bunker back right. Left side of the green is a safe bet.

#5 - Par 4.
C: 345 yards
R: 331 yards
F: 289 yards

Seemingly non-threatening hole along a lovely line of trees left, but squeeze approach to green is affected by two sentry spruces, one left, one right. The one left has sand immediately behind it and, whoops, there's hidden water short right of green. Mmm.

#6 - Par 4.
C: 341 yards
R: 330 yards
F: 296 yards

Testing little dogleg left. Just right of the tree on the left of the turn is good for the tee shot. Beware the water lurking on the left too discouraging a straight drive towards the green. There's sand left and right.

#7 - Par 3.
C: 144 yards
R: 129 yards
F: 106 yards

Short, requiring accuracy. There's two traps front right, one left and one pot bunker back right. A sharp ridge crossing the green makes for some, shall I say, interesting putts. You're on your own.

#8 - Par 4.
C: 400 yards
R: 379 yards
F: 320 yards

Elegance personified. Late dogleg left with line of superb trees along the left side. Play tee shot centre right to stay away from them and open up tight approach to green between two more sentry spruces. This green also has a ridge causing a front-end slope.

#9 - Par 4.
C: 386 yards
R: 359 yards
F: 314 yards

True quality. Straight and slightly uphill through the trees. But there's invisible water starting about 150 yards out on the left and more later to the left of the green. So favor centre right off the tee. Two deep fairway basins can give awkward lies on the way to another approach between two trees onto a narrow, flattish green.

#10 - Par 4.
C: 393 yards
R: 383 yards
F: 270 yards

The handicappers say it's the easiest around here. But what a fun hole with a drive straight across water from the back tees to a landing area dipping down and right. Catch the slope and you'll have a wedge onto a ridged green for a birdie chance.

#11 - Par 5.
C: 520 yards
R: 503 yards
F: 483 yards

Gorgeous signature hole, a winding downhill par 5. There's water about 230 yards straight out behind the trees. A good tee shot down centre right will set up either a dangerous second onto green with water left, or a more sensible mid iron towards the chubby little spruce on the right side for an approach third. Two traps right.

#12 - Par 4.
C: 397 yards
R: 373 yards
F: 355 yards

Yet another striking hole requiring straight tee shot towards the cliffs in the distance. Two trees, not spruces for a change, narrow the neck into this green which has a serious bump running across it.

#13 - Par 4.
C: 404 yards
R: 375 yards
F: 332 yards

There's OB all along the right and behind the green. There's water behind the tree left starting about 150 yards out. Good tee shot target is area just inside lone spruce out on the right. This green has a very severe front-end tilt.

#14 - Par 3.
C: 205 yards
R: 185 yards
F: 154 yards

A tester. There's water on the left with sand just inside it and two major traps front right. Ideal shot is draw into the right side of a green which has two ridges running halfway in on both sides tending to funnel ball down towards centre.

#15 - Par 4.
C: 400 yards
R: 379 yards
F: 362 yards

Slightly uphill dogleg left requiring tee shot centre right to open up a green with sand front left and back right. It also has an intriguing basin front right.

#16 - Par 3.
C: 140 yards
R: 122 yards
F: 106 yards

Another short one, but it has a narrow approach alley between trees and two traps left and one right. The tiered green has a basin in the middle.

#17 - Par 5.
C: 482 yards
R: 473 yards
F: 438 yards

Straight hole starting slightly downhill and then up again towards the green with traps on each corner. Tee shot centre right is best approach.

#18 - Par 4.
C: 363 yards
R: 343 yards
F: 296 yards

Gentle uphill dogleg left with fairway leaning right to left. Tee shot centre right is a good idea to set up long, mid-iron approach through yet another narrow neck of trees into elevated green with traps front left, back right and back.

Box 232
Medicine Hat, Alberta, T1A 7E9
Telephone: (403) 527-8086

The 406-yard, par 4, 2nd hole
with the South Saskatchwan River in the background

Milk River Country Club

(North of the Border Golf and Bowl)

"Prairie golf at its most natural..."

Par 34/36

Don't expect anything fancy round these parts, but what a fun place to play golf at its most natural. The fairways are unmanicured and undulating and the greens aren't the biggest. But if you like playing the game with a feel for its origins, this small town course just north of the United States border is just what you're looking for. It's a family-run concern and that spills over into what the nine-hole course is, an ideal two-hour stopover for the vacationing golfing family . . . heading north or south. But watch out for those breezes.

#1 - Par 3.
R: 164 yards

The big trees out on the left pose the problem with the left side of the green tucked behind them. The landing area short is heavily mounded and the small green itself is elevated with a sharp drop-off behind. A high draw centre right is best if you can.

#2 - Par 4.
R: 350 yards

Trees left and the Milk River all the way right along this roller coaster fairway which can throw your ball any which way. It's another tiny green with big drop-offs both sides and behind.

#3 - Par 4/5.
R: 400 yards

Trees left and right on another mogul-riddled fairway. Hit tee shot straight out through chute of trees towards the large grain elevator in the far distance. Don't lose it right or a reed-filled pond in the landing area will come into play. Guess what? Another elevated, mounded green.

#4 - Par 3.
R: 150 yards

An educated guess says there's usually a tailwind on this one heading due east. Club selection then is important to a small elevated green with trees and a pond immediately behind it. Careful!

#5 - Par 4.
R: 256 yards

A little gem. It's uphill through chute of trees and bullrushes. The extremely shallow green (memories of the 13th at Waterton) is carved into the facing hillside probably 40 feet above the fairway atop a fierce bank. Go for it if you like but maybe a lay up to the foot of the slope for a close-in wedge is the answer.

#6 - Par 3/4.
R: 204 yards

OB all the way right on a dipping fairway to a green with nasty sand short front left. Watch for a left-right crosswind.

#7 - Par 4.
R: 356 yards

It's straightaway but the road is threatening all the way on the right. Good tee shot down centre will set up slightly downhill approach aimed towards the telegraph poles in the distance. Just be straight.

#8 - Par 4.
R: 325 yards

Straightaway and uphill where tee shot should be aimed towards the thickest part of the copse of trees at the top. What's this? A square green with a huge drop-off behind which makes for almost impossible chip back onto a back-front sloping green. Best be short with your second and pitch on.

#9 - Par 5.
R: 470 yards

Downhill where centre tee shot works best. But beware, anything that drifts even slightly right is bringing reed-filled, marshy pond short right into play for your approach. There's also a substantial trap short right. A good golf hole.

Milk River, Alberta T0K 1M0
Telephone: (403) 647-2502

The 470-yard, par 5, 9th hole

Nanton Golf Club

"A Tale of Two Nines . . ."

Par 71

Seventy years ago, some locals decided it would be fun to have two golf holes built to while away their evenings and weekends. Gradually seven holes were added along with traditional prairie sand greens and clubhouse. Now this fine track, with grass greens of course, consists of a full 18 holes. The big attraction, it lures golfers from far afield, is the best of both worlds provided by the contrasting old and the new nines. The pretty front nine is cosy, treed and not overly long, but be warned, with small greens and tree cover, it has its moments. The homeward nine? This is prairie links golf at its finest, with immaculate, bunkered fairways, large, undulating greens and water aplenty. A super test, particularly on breezy days.

#1 - Par 5.
C: 525 yards
R: 503 yards
F: 485 yards

Elevated tee shot with fairway fading right. Avoid flirting with trees right and drive middle. Long hitters can hit the green in two but for most it is the third, likely a wedge, that decides the outcome.

#2 - Par 4.
C: 425 yards
R: 404 yards
F: 354 yards

Always plays long. Drive middle left. The second or third is a difficult hit into a two-tiered, back and front, green often "invisible" in tree shadows. Hit to green's left side.

#3 - Par 3.
C: 175 yards
R: 150 yards
F: 107 yards

Club up for deceptive uphill shot. Ideally, hit the high side of green sloping severely right to left and trickle down towards hole. Difficult to stick left side.

#4 - Par 4.
C: 330 yards
R: 330 yards
F: 324 yards

Birdie hole. Be centre left off elevated tee. There's only trouble in the trees right, including a hidden pond. Good drive means a short iron or wedge into green.

#5 - Par 4.
C: 385 yards
R: 365 yards
F: 355 yards

Happiness here is par. Good drive vital. It's a tricky second (or third) up a hill onto "hidden" green fifty yards back on top. Club up for that blind hill shot.

#6 - Par 4.
C: 327 yards
R: 321 yards
F: 311 yards

If you save the driver for special occasions, get it out now. Only hint of trouble is right with roughed slope dropping towards third fairway.

#7 - Par 4.
C: 376 yards
R: 366 yards
F: 356 yards

Dogleg left. Favoring left side, shoot between 150-yard markers. Good placement allows a straight 5-to-8 iron into shaded green. Birdie time?

#8 - Par 3.
C: 136 yards
R: 118 yards
F: 1107 yards

Intriguing newcomer to the original front nine. Sand all the way on both sides. Pin placement can vary shot by a couple of clubs. Be straight.

#9 - Par 4.
C: 315 yards
R: 310 yards
F: 305 yards

Sure, the long hitter can reach. But there's out of bounds all along the left and the green is tiny and totally treed. Oh, yeah, the hidden pond on the green's right . . .

#10 - Par 5.
C: 492 yards
R: 456 yards
F: 402 yards

Drive left of right fairway bunker. Decision time. Go for green over the second fairway bunker or lay up left for wedge approach on third shot.

#11 - Par 4.
C: 405 yards
R: 356 yards
F: 320 yards

So that's Mosquito Creek! It's close all along the left of the left-sloping fairway. Hit drive centre right. For some reason my buddies and I find this green, bunkered on both sides, hard to hit.

#12 - Par 4.
C: 397 yards
R: 374 yards
F: 320 yards

It looks simple, but plays long and the green is raised and slopes back to front. Your drive should be a straightaway hit.

#13 - Par 3.
C: 164 yards
R: 150 yards
F: 100 yards

Great water hole with green perched on far edge of pond. There is an invisible brick wall or wind shear just in front that often spells "W-E-T." Club up!

#14 - Par 4.
C: 323 yards
R: 303 yards
F: 249 yards

Feeling the heat yet? Good hole doglegging left round lake. Sensible shot is three wood straight at orange (Please don't repaint it!) grain elevator. Chip and a putt from there? Could be.

#15 - Par 5.
C: 523 yards
R: 491 yards
F: 428 yards

Solid, solid hole. Longer hitters can shoot over bunker, others left of it. Some are tempted to go for green in two. Lay up safer. Yes, there's a wildlife-filled pond to right of green.

#16 - Par 4.
C: 385 yards
R: 340 yards
F: 275 yards

Warning! More hidden water about 260 yards out. Ease up. Shoot for position maybe 220 yards out just beyond 150-yard markers. A medium to short iron second to the sloping green should do the trick after that.

#17 - Par 3.
C: 221 yards
R: 199 yards
F: 148 yards

Second superb par 3 on back nine. Water along the left. Ideal is something like a seven-wood or four-iron draw starting at mounds to right of green. But beware a head-on wind.

#18 - Par 4.
C: 374 yards
R: 347 yards
F: 279 yards

Tricky! My way is to avoid driving beyond 150-yard markers or a murderous downhill lie or even the creek await. Time for a fairway wood or long mid iron. It's far better to stay up top for level shot across the creek to the hillside green.

Box 972, Nanton
Alberta T0L 1R0
Telephone: (403) 265-4235

The dangerous 164-yard, par 3, 13th hole

Oyen & District Golf Club

"A one-dollar clubhouse and much more"

Par 35/36

It's an eye-catching log structure, imposing on the flatness of the surrounding prairie. But it only cost the folk of Oyen a single dollar. An oil company with interests in the area had the disused building shipped across the province from a plant closing in the shadows of the Rockies. And the sealing of that deal basically gave the final green light for a new golf course to be built in the 1 100 population community. Only a few years old, the course has challenges galore and will get even better with maturity.

#1 - Par 4/5.
C: 469 yards
R: 434 yards
F: 394 yards

This is a long hole. A creek crosses the fairway 280 yards out and there's sand left just short of it. Go for it if you dare, or if you're Daly. Sand on right side, fifty yards in front of green.

#2 - Par 3.
C: 180 yards
R: 147 yards
F: 118 yards

Longish hit up slight slope. Sand front left and right. And a pond sits ten yards behind green.

#3 - Par 4.
C: 364 yards
R: 319 yards
F: 297 yards

Nice dogleg round water right. Smart play from tee box is three wood fade landing 90-100 yards from green. Watch the creek with your approach second. And there's another pond right behind green.

 # 4 - Par 4.
C: 410 yards
R: 386 yards
F: 322 yards

Out of bounds left. But you can fly your tee shot 150-190 yards across the dogleg and still avoid the cluster of sand in the left angle. Triangular green welcomes approach from right.

#5 - Par 5.
C: 560 yards
R: 535 yards
F: 493 yards

Plenty of wide open spaces in Eastern Alberta and this one proves the point. Highway 41 is uncomfortably close left, but try and keep tee shot as far left as you dare. Stay left for your second. Another big green will gobble up approach from that side.

#6 - Par 3.
C: 126 yards
R: 105 yards
F: 95 yards

Cute, cute hole. Big trap left of smallest green on course.

#7 - Par 4.
C: 409 yards
R: 393 yards
F: 374 yards

Disconcerting pond 50 yards in front of tee box and big-time traps 230 yards right. But that's the side you want. Skinny green sloping right to left.

#8 - Par 3.
C: 151 yards
R: 130 yards
F: 102 yards

Tricky. Mid-iron over pond and between two copses of trees. If the pin is on front side, be below!

#9 - Par 5.
C: 577 yards
R: 536 yards
F: 471 yards

You're kidding! 'Fraid not. Swamp left and bunker right, both about 220-240 yards out. But favor left with tee shot and just keep going and that includes approach over creek.

P.O. Box 114
Oyen, Alberta, T0J 2J0
Telephone: (403) 664-2555
Toll Free Tee Times: 1-800-884-8771

The 364-yard, par 4, 3rd hole

Paradise Canyon Golf and Country Club

"Desert-style delights by the Old Man . . ."

Par 71

This outstanding desert links course is located inside a loop in the Oldman River in the canyon west of the city of Lethbridge. Its lush, green fairways, signature mounds, and greens contrast sharply with the harsh grey-brown grandeur of the surrounding cliffs and bluffs and provide a lay-out distinctly reminiscent of courses down Arizona and Utah way. The floods of 1995 did, however, exact some toll with several riverbank holes being severely swamped by the raging waters of the Old Man, but work continued through the late summer, fall and winter to restore them to their former glory. I'm told they'll be more or less as they were before the storms, even though the river might encroach even more than it did before. Wind might be a factor in a city famed for it although the day I played, the breezes were shooting across the canyon tops without dropping in for a visit. A day here gives the itinerant player a different challenge. It's tough and it's fun.

#1 - Par 4.
C: 418 yards
R: 386 yards
F: 321 yards

A nice straightaway opener with a heavy downslope onto the fairway from the left, so hooking is not a good idea if you want a good start. Ideal tee shot is centre, centre right to land somewhere inside the right fairway traps. That would leave a comfortable iron into a multi-layered green with sand left and right.

#2 - Par 3.
C: 190 yards
R: 175 yards
F: 131 yards

Club selection here is important to hit a two-level green guarded by sand short front left, side right and back left. Have a look at the flag for wind strength before you hit on this one.

#3 - Par 4.
C: 433 yards
R: 413 yards
F: 357 yards

It's the highest handicap hole and it's special. It's a case of taking the high road or the low road on a twin fairway. Best to take the upper route right well away from lake trouble alongside the low way left. Just short of the sandtrap is good for a long, mid iron approach into a green threatened by water short left, sand left, back left and right.

#4 - Par 5.
C: 544 yards
R: 528 yards
F: 473 yards

A fine par 5 with water stringing along for company all the way on the left. Best tee shot on this one is centre right into the region of the trap on that side and continue down that side until you're ready for a wedge or pitch onto a tiered green tucked away left. There isn't much landing area back to front on this one guarded by sand in front.

#5 - Par 4.
C: 416 yards
R: 391 yards
F: 327 yards

A good drive down the centre beyond the fairway bunker left and short of the last of two traps right will set up a comfortable hit into a long green that may require a club or two difference depending on pin placement. There are severe traps on both sides.

#6 - Par 3.
C: 211 yards
R: 197 yards
F: 153 yards

Long and difficult. The green is guarded by a large trap front left and three pot bunkers behind. Accuracy with a long iron or even fairway wood is a must on this one.

#7 - Par 4.
C: 446 yards
R: 416 yards
F: 352 yards

Now the Oldman is with us on the left. On river holes double check tee-box maps for any alterations on holes since I passed through. But assuming the lay-out is the same, a tee shot straight out is best on this fine hole bending right late into the green. A narrow land bridge between traps on the front allows a pitch and run approach if you like.

#8 - Par 5.
C: 547 yards
R: 519 yards
F: 448 yards

Check the tee box map. The Oldman is keeping us company again. Best tee shot will travel down centre left to set up another lay up shot into an area around the fairway trap left further up. That leaves a nice wedge onto a two-tiered green guarded front right by a veritable beach and left by a trap. Fine, fine hole.

#9 - Par 4.
C: 382 yards
R: 355 yards
F: 308 yards

The first leg of this dogleg right was washed out by the floods so towards the end of 1995 it was being played as a par 3 from temporary tee boxes in the turn. But assuming all is well now, you have a choice. Play safe into the turn with an iron leaving a comfortable short iron or wedge on, or go for it over the trap on the inside of the turn with a solid fade. Traps left and right of elevated green.

#10 - Par 4.
C: 381 yards
R: 347 yards
F: 257 yards

From the back, it makes no sense whatsoever to try and cut the corner on this uphill dogleg right. That ball will just get hung up in horrendous hillside rough. Better to play the course and hit out into turn. Then club up anywhere from one to three clubs depending where the flag is on a tricky three-tiered staircase green. It's guarded short left and short right by sand. Wow!

#11 - Par 4.
C: 306 yards
R: 289 yards
F: 249 yards

Iron time with a vengeance. Longish mid iron will set up a short approach into a green hidden below the bluff at the end of the fairway. Any tee shot too long on this one is bound for oblivion in wasteland below the bluff. I'm told, though, that some long-hitting members regularly go for it. Good luck!

#12 - Par 3.
C : 148 yards
R : 131 yards
F : 109 yards

The Canyon's signature hole where club selection on a series of bluff-top tee boxes is everything, especially in the wind. The rolling green with traps left, right and back left is a carpet spread out in the valley far below with the Oldman River behind. Look at the flag!

#13 - Par 5.
C: 518 yards
R: 499 yards
F: 408 yards

A downhill hole with the fairway leaning left to right into tree trouble. Tee shot down centre left is best here to land somewhere in the vicinity of the fairway sand left. Lay up next shot into open part of the fairway short of the green. This allows a high approach over traps front left and front right. Gaining a shot is a definite possibility.

#14 - Par 3.
C: 184 yards
R: 167 yards
F: 114 yards

The Sahara beckons short of the green right and all along that side. So try and hit high fade in from the left side but beware trap over there too. Left-to-right crosswind could complicate matters even further.

#15 - Par 4.
C: 436 yards
R: 403 yards
F: 366 yards

On a hole which drifts right a good tee shot will split the fairway traps left and right. If you have to land in one opt for the left. That leaves a longish mid iron into a green covered front right by water and sand back left. Trickier than it looks, this one.

#16 - Par 4.
C: 475 yards
R: 437 yards
F: 346 yards

Go for it, but avoid the traps left and right in a huge landing area. A long mid iron should get you to the green trapped short left, back left and side right. There are some tricky putts to be had on a multi-tiered green.

#17 - Par 3.
C: 217 yards
R: 185 yards
F: 135 yards

Check tee box map for flood alterations. But all being well, it's a case of avoiding the Oldman all the way right and flying the major trap short right. Watch traps left too. A tough one.

#18 - Par 5.
C: 558 yards
R: 534 yards
F: 428 yards

Check that map again. Stay left, well away from the river with the tee shot. Then hit an iron into the fairway right to set up high wedge into green tucked away left. It's trapped left and right.

185 Canyon Boulevard
Lethbridge, Alberta, T1K 6V1
Telephone: (403) 381-7500

Picture Butte Golf Club

"The potential to be a great one..."

Par 72/73

This is a good, solid golf course right now. But there's something about it, the many maturing trees, the thickening rough, that hints of potential greatness in years to come. The lay-out on the mainly flat terrain is sound. But take care out there. Even now, it's one of those sneaky courses that doesn't look as if it'll provide too much difficulty, but somewhere on your travels, you'll realize that you're having to think a lot, having to pick your spots. And of course it boasts a unique hole. Lying in wait is the so-ugly-its-beautiful par 3 16th, its green nestling around a mountain of ash discarded from the now-disused Shaughnessy coal mine. Miss this putting surface and a hitherto good round can become a disaster.

#1 - Par 5.
C: 537 yards
R: 531 yards
F: 394 yards

The hole goes straight into the prevailing west wind and consequently can become an endurance test right off the bat. Pretty straightforward, but favor the right route. There's water encroaching from the left about 130 yards out from the green.

#2 - Par 4.
C: 392 yards
R: 357 yards
F: 320 yards

Hit tee shot, likely into a headwind, through trees left and right, aiming to find a spot somewhere on the left side. This green is heavily guarded by three bunkers, one left and two right.

#3 - Par 4.
C: 339 yards
R: 281 yards
F: 233 yards

The OB here speaks for itself, a sheer drop into the coulee right and also behind the green which is ever-so-slightly elevated with sand front left and back right. Good birdie hole.

#4 - Par 4.
C: 280 yards
R: 273 yards
F: 280 yards

You'll love it or hate it. Me? Well... it's a 90-degree dogleg right around the pond. Go for the green in one if you dare. The sensible approach is a lay up about 200 yards out followed by short iron-wedge into green falling left to right towards water. Sand left side, right front and centre back.

#5 - Par 3.
C: 198 yards
R: 161 yards
F: 123 yards

Good short hole with water down right. Sand front centre and back left. One small curiosity. A little pocket in the middle front of the green is lower than the rest of the surface.

#6 - Par 5.
C: 476 yards
R: 433 yards
F: 397 yards

Straightaway par 5, shortish in fact, the only obvious problem being a likely headwind. This really should be birdie territory.

#7 - Par 3.
C: 112 yards
R: 102 yards
F: 87 yards

And while we're on the subject of birdies . . . not much real estate used here. Only threats are sand front, left and back and the ever-present wind.

#8 - Par 4.
C: 445 yards
R: 420 yards
F: 365 yards

Out of bounds all the way left. The following wind will help you merrily along the way to a green which tends to break left.

#9 - Par 5.
C: 533 yards
R: 527 yards
F: 400 yards

Long, straightaway hole with slight upslope towards the green. There's OB left, young trees right, and sand in the right landing area. This one's about perseverance – it was designed that way.

#10 - Par 4.
C: 338 yards
R: 332 yards
F: 333 yards

Another solid birdie chance here with OB left, and straightaway fairway up to green shadowed by maintenance building and trees. But beware the two traps left and one right.

#11 - Par 4.
C: 351 yards
R: 328 yards
F: 274 yards

A challenge, this one. It wiggles left and right. It's a 230-yard carry over the sand in the middle of the fairway which signposts the hidden green. A good tee shot into the vicinity of the bunker will give you a good view of the green which slopes back to front and has sand left and right.

#12 - Par 5.
C: 497 yards
R: 472 yards
F: 425 yards

Trees left most of the way, especially for your tee shot. But that's the side you want to favor because there's landing area water behind the fairway mounds right and then just in front of the green right. Big sand possibilities front left and front right with trees not too far behind the green. A good par 5.

#13 - Par 3.
C: 201 yards
R: 162 yards
F: 144 yards

A tough shot with the headwind veering in slightly from the left. Sand back right of the green. Nasty little hole.

#14 - Par 4.
C: 308 yards
R: 303 yards
F: 257 yards

Decision time, folks! It's a 280-yard carry across the water to the front of the green from the back tees. So, common sense should prevail on this dogleg right. The clever way here is a mid iron tee shot straight out, followed by something like an 8-iron over less water. Sand behind, and two in front of, the two-level green. Excellent hole.

#15 - Par 4.
C: 311 yards
R: 305 yards
F: 228 yards

Another thinking hole. Sensible approach might be a long iron off the tee, water right, followed by a short one into the green over more water partially intruding on the left. The front right of the green is decidedly lower than the rest of it.

#16 - Par 3.
C: 154 yards
R: 141 yards
F: 103 yards

The Ash Hole! (At least I think that's what they said.) It's different, isn't it? Three-level boomerang-shaped green snakes round behind the ash heap probably fifty feet below. OB is right and short of the green. The ash mountain will likely bring your ball down onto the putting surface. But anything left is disaster. The rough on that left slope will gobble the ball up. If you've saved a Mulligan, now might be the time.

#17 - Par 4/5.
C: 455 yards
R: 441 yards
F: 389 yards

Testing hole that can suddenly get a lot longer if you get bad tee shot lie among mounds right. So favor the left but watch the trees. Approach is a gradual climb to a green guarded heavily by sand back left and side right.

#18 - Par 4.
C: 423 yards
R: 416 yards
F: 375 yards

Sound finisher. Straightaway, usually with a tailwind, but watch the water left just short of the tee shot landing area. The green's left side is lower than its right.

Box 359
Picture Butte, Alberta, T0K 1V0
Telephone (403) 732-4157

Pincher Creek Golf Club

"Extreme challenge in the wind..."

Par 36

Dotted around southern Alberta are a series of small town nine-hole golf courses too often ignored by the "golf is eighteen holes" brigade. It is they who are missing out. Pincher Creek is a classic case. A short drive from Waterton, Pincher Creek, along with the championship 18 at Waterton Lakes, another nine at Cardston's Lee Valley Creek, and the Crowsnest Pass course in Blairmore, completes a perfect mini-tour for golfers vacationing in the deep south of Alberta. Make no mistake. Pincher provides a severe enough test in its own right, especially when those breezes begin to blow.

#1 - Par 4.
R: 375 yards

Nice opener requiring fairly straight tee shot probably affected by a quartering wind. Three bunkers visible around the green which has a step in the middle. It's fair to say that on all greens here the grain goes from west to east with the wind.

#2 - Par 4.
R: 435 yards

Elevated tee shot has to negotiate a 90 foot drop into a valley with a fairly generous landing area. Then it's a maybe-80 feet climb back up to the green. Club way up for this one especially against the wind. Tricky green too with different levels, front, left and right back.

#3 - Par 4.
R: 410 yards

Accurate tee shot, best a draw, required here with water hazard 150 yards out right, OB down left side. A three-level green from side to side, is guarded dead centre front by pot bunker.

#4 - Par 3.
R: 160 yards

Another three-level green, higher at the back and lower left side. Be careful not to overhit because the wind is usually coming from behind right.

#5 - Par 4.
R: 430 yards

Undoubtedly the toughest hole on the course, a double dogleg, first left, then right. The first turn is just over 200 yards out. Be as left as you dare because your second will have to deal with a water hazard on the right about 100 yards from the green. This green, a bi-level, runs from back right to front left. Sand front right.

#6 - Par 5.
R: 535 yards

Tee shot usually backed by wind will take you up towards an eventual hard dogleg right. Long hitters can reach the green in two on a breezy day. Divided green has a west side higher than the east. There's big sand trouble back left, and a small pot bunker dead in front.

#7 - Par 5.
R: 510 yards

The tee shot at this, another double dogleg left and right, is usually into the wind. A group of trees, right 150 yards from the green, can cause problems. Two-tiered green, guarded front right and back left by traps, rises from front to back.

#8 - Par 3.
R: 210 yards

Try not to be long or short with a tough tee shot dropping about 50 feet down to the green guarded immediately in front by a creek. The one consolation is that it's a biggish green and there's usually a following wind. Club selection important.

#9 - Par 4.
R: 375 yards

Tee shot and approach usually have to take crosswind from left into account. A series of fairway mounds and trees to the right of the green can also interfere with progress. The mound-surrounded green's one of those awkward tiered affairs with the front lower than back and back right

942 Hyde Street
Pincher Creek, Alberta T0K 1W0
Telephone: (403) 627-2126

The 375-yard, par 4, 9th hole

Redwood Meadows Golf and Country Club

"Magnificence among the foothills mcadows..."

Par 72/73

It is hard to imagine a more sumptuous setting for golf than Redwood Meadows, a spectacular course near the hamlet of Bragg Creek, a 30-minute drive west of Calgary. The pine and spruce-lined circuit strung along the banks of the Elbow River on the Sarcee Nation is one of the more satisfying experiences to be had on the Calgary-area tour. At its best, Redwood must rank among western Canada's superior courses. Narrow tree-lined fairways, sand and water hazards and huge greens are the keynotes of this tester. There are, of course, no redwood trees. The Sarcee people named the area following a forest fire which stripped the trees of their bark leaving them an eerie shade of red. This is a course where for many, it's best to leave the driver in the bag, and go with iron or fairway wood. You'll find the high road into most of the greens is the best route but be careful with swirling breezes around the greens unfelt on tee boxes and fairways. This is a special one.

#1 - Par 4.
C: 410 yards
R: 392 yards
F: 374 yards

A gentle dogleg left where you want to be centre right off the tee to land left of the rightside trap in the turn. A good one will leave a mid iron to a huge green with a back to front slope.

#2 - Par 5.
C: 539 yards
R: 523 yards
F: 507 yards

Another dogleg left where you want to be centre right to land maybe 10 to 15 yards right of the leftside fairway trap. Too far left and the approach to the green is blocked by a stand of trees. The first of several par 5s here where most should think of reaching in three rather than two. For most too, a fairway bunker in the left approaches to the green is often invisible until it's too late. Be below pin.

#3 - Par 4.
C: 426 yards
R: 396 yards
F: 384 yards

Pretty straightforward where down-the-middle pays dividends. Be careful with club selection for approach to a very deep, but pretty flat green. If the pin is at the back club up at least one.

#4 - Par 3.
C: 189 yards
R: 173 yards
F: 156 yards

The trees are tight and it's trapped left and right. There's a valley running across the green. Take an extra club if the pin is back but those trees are pretty close behind too.

#5 - Par 4.
C: 416 yards
R: 387 yards
F: 371 yards

Ideal target line is centre right about 15 yards left of the tree encroaching on the right side of the fairway. Don't be left as trouble awaits over there. This green rolls rather than slopes.

#6 - Par 5.
C: 528 yards
R: 462 yards
F: 450 yards

Birdies are chirping especially from the white tee box. Be straight down centre. If you're long enough you can make it in two, but be warned a hidden pond comes into play about 20 yards behind the large tree in the left approaches to the green. The water parallels the green. More complications are traps and OB right.

#7 - Par 4/5.
C: 413 yards
R: 404 yards
F: 404 yards

Highest handicap hole and plays like it. It takes a good drive for the leftside fairway trap to come into play. Best play here is a line centre right of the trap. For the second beware of the large pine short right of the green. If the pin is positioned right at all, go for the heart of the dance floor which runs down back to front.

#8 - Par 3.
C: 155 yards
R: 127 yards
F: 127 yards

Gorgeous water hole. Try and be below the pin on a back-front sloping green with major trouble behind for the over-enthusiastic shot.

#9 - Par 4.
C: 382 yards
R: 355 yards
F: 301 yards

Drive along a line about 15 yards inside the fairway trap left on this sharp dogleg right. Too far right and the chances are you're blocked out by trees in the turn or you'll lose your ball. A good one along the suggested line should leave you a mid or short iron approach into a heavily-trapped green which slopes only slightly back to front.

#10 - Par 4.
C: 417 yards
R: 404 yards
F: 391 yards

Don't venture too far right or the trees will block out your approach again. Rather aim to be centre maybe 15 yards left of the traps right. Another very deep green where the extra club is necessary to reach a back pin. Another slight back to front slope on this well-trapped green.

#11 - Par 4.
C: 415 yards
R: 396 yards
F: 368 yards

Aim to be alongside the first fairway bunker off the tee. A solid one will leave you a mid or short iron into another well-bunkered green.

#12 - Par 3
C: 170 yards
R: 143 yards
F: 119 yards

Another picturesque short hole. The water is wider right than left. Best safety play then is maybe left, centre left, for the fat of another large green.

#13 - Par 4.
C: 367 yards
R: 342 yards
F: 318 yards

Shortish so hit anything you're comfortable with to ensure you go centre or centre right. The last thing you want on this one is to be too far left because your second will be stymied by trees down that side. Traps guard the left.

#14 - Par 5.
C: 524 yards
R: 501 yards
F: 469 yards

A thinking player's hole with water all along the left and crossing in front of the green inside the 100-yard mark. Best approach is to think 200 yards, 200 yards and 100 yards or an approximation of that. There's just too much trouble around to take any chances. Be patient up to a rolling green.

#15 - Par 3.
C: 189 yards
R: 152 yards
F: 119 yards

Voted the best par 3 in the Calgary area in a 1994 *Calgary Herald* poll and with very good reason. Picturesque but there's trouble left, right and behind. On this one the further left you are the more chance there is of your ball taking an unwelcome dip.

#16 - Par 4.
C: 382 yards
R: 366 yards
F: 350 yards

This is maybe one where you can feel totally comfortable with your driver, hitting out centre left. If you are on the right you won't see much of the green for your approach. Best be below the pin on a green with a marked back to front slope.

#17 - Par 5.
C: 606 yards
R: 551 yards
F: 522 yards

Be centre off the tee. Your second or third has to negotiate a tight gap in the trees to the hardest green on the course, narrow and sliding back to front.

#18 - Par 4.
C: 437 yards
R: 427 yards
F: 378 yards

Both a tough finisher and one of the toughest on the course. Aim to be long off the tee landing to the right of the fairway traps on the inside of the turn. A good one will set up a sub-200 yard approach into the green. On this one it is possible to land short and run up and onto the rolling green between the two front-edge traps.

4 km East of Bragg Creek on Hwy. #22
Calgary, Alberta, T2P 2G4
Telephone: (403) 949-3663

River Bend Golf Course

"Where the Red Deer bends..."

Par 72

This fine 18-hole championship course is set inside a loop in the Red Deer River with the river bounding its western, eastern and northern sides. Add two huge lakes to the scenario and a couple of ponds here and there, and you soon realize water is a major player in these parts. But the liquid hazards are not overpowering. They come into play in sensible places and very much add to the attractiveness of a course ranging from challenging from the back tees to comfortable for front tee players. A couple of members I played with insisted this site, known as Waskasoo Park, used to be a series of gravel pits. If that's the case, then here's proof positive golf courses can improve the environment. Golf here is part of a larger recreational picture with camping and picnic sites, hiking trails, and canoeing also on site. A very good golf course in a very pleasant place.

#1 - Par 4.
C: 397 yards
R: 388 yards
F: 347 yards

A gentle dogleg left from elevated tee box requiring hit centre to avoid mounds on the left. That line sets up best approach into a green guarded by a huge trap starting front right and looping round that side, and another back left.

#2 Par - 4.
C: 413 yards
R: 389 yards
F: 374 yards

Tough, sharp dogleg left. Hit tee shot towards hill on the left and make sure you're short of water about 270 yards straight out. The water then continues up the right of the second leg to the side of the green. It's guarded by a back trap and slopes back-left to front-right. Good hole.

#3 - Par 3.
C: 167 yards
R: 115 yards
F: 86 yards

Short but tricky with shot over water and a bridge. The tiered green, lower right than left, has three bunkers, two back right and one back left.

#4 - Par 4.
C: 358 yards
R: 338 yards
F: 325 yards

Attractive hole looping left round the water. Ideal drive is hit centre right for best line into a green trapped left and right. This green too drifts down from back left.

#5 - Par 4.
C: 341 yards
R: 317 yards
F: 302 yards

An extremely late dogleg leg right with the green tucked right beyond water. Perfect line for tee shot here is out towards the tallest poplar beyond the last of the three fairway traps on the left. Good placement will set up comfortable wedge onto a huge green.

#6 - Par 5.
C: 523 yards
R: 487 yards
F: 465 yards

Superb long hole. The blue tees are set on an island. Tee shot should be hit centre across or along the water depending on your tee. There are fairway traps left and the water goes most of the way right. Nearer the green, it's replaced by three large traps and water can come into play short left. Two traps left and one back right of a green which has heavy back-front slope. Wow!

#7 - Par 4.
C: 384 yards
R: 362 yards
F: 316 yards

Straightaway hole with water starting right maybe 170 yards out. Aim tee shot right of the large fairway trap left for best position. On approach watch out for a huge trap short right, about fifteen yards out, and more sand back right and behind. Green tilts back to front.

#8 - Par 3.
C: 172 yards
R: 155 yards
F: 145 yards

The trick here is flying the semi-hidden bunker immediately in front of the green. I learned from bitter experience that this one is St. Andrews deep! You've been warned. More bunkers left and right. Good hole.

#9 - Par 5.
C: 525 yards
R: 500 yards
F: 439 yards

Long hole sweeping gently right. Water starts right about 50 yards beyond the rightside transformer box on the hill. Tee shot centre left then is best here but beware fairway trap left in the landing area. There's a severe hollow in front of the green which is bunkered left and front right. This one too has a back-front slope.

#10 - Par 5.
C: 499 yards
R: 485 yards
F: 455 yards

Good spot for the drive is halfway between the fairway sand left and centre on this gentle dogleg left. Long hitters can make it in two. But others should lay up right of the trap short left for a chip on. Green is trapped front right, left and behind. It slopes from 10 o'clock to 4 o'clock.

#11 - Par 4.
C: 382 yards
R: 351 yards
F: 340 yards

Tee shot should be hit to land between the fir tree left and the middle to set up best approach to a green trickily tucked on away left on a peninsula. Water front left, left, and behind so don't overcook it! There's also huge sand front left.

#12 - Par 4.
C: 398 yards
R: 314 yards
F: 300 yards

Gorgeous and the toughest here. It horseshoes round the water left. Play the course! Tee shot should be hit across or round the water to whatever distance you're comfortable with providing you're dry. Then make sure you don't lose anything right or you'll make the nasty discovery there's more water here than meets the eye!

#13 - Par 4.
C: 334 yards
R: 323 yards
F: 278 yards

Trees thickening up now. They line the right side all the way but there's a bit of space left. Best tee shot is hit centre left and that opens up a tricky green to get to. There are two traps in front, another right and one back left. It slopes back-right to front-left.

#14 - Par 3.
C: 132 yards
R: 123 yards
F: 106 yards

Picturesque. Accuracy has to be the byword with a shot over a dipping fairway to an 'L'-shaped green wide in front, but narrowing away back left. Huge trap guards the right and there are smaller ones front left and back left.

#15 - Par 4.
C: 317 yards
R: 291 yards
F: 282 yards

Dead tree dead centre off the tee. Best to aim iron or fairway wood shot on this right dogleg right of it with a fade. Too much length and too much fade however will carry the ball round the treed corner into unseen water beyond the rightside 150-yard marker, so be careful. Green has back-front ridge causing left-right slopes.

#16 - Par 3.
C: 150 yards
R: 139 yards
F: 95 yards

Another pretty hole with a long green that could cause some careful club selection consideration. There's water right and depending on the time of day you might not notice a trap hidden front right in tree shadows. There are more bunkers left and right of a green which tends to drift right from centre.

#17 - Par 5.
C: 533 yards
R: 510 yards
F: 461 yards

A fine par 5 with trees lining the left and a bunker right narrowing the fairway landing area. This fairway is the first here with a noticeable lean, right to left. Be as straight down the middle off the tee as you can. The green, doubled with #10 is bunkered front right, front left and behind. And if your approach is sliced, one of #10's can come into play wider right.

#18 - Par 4.
C: 426 yards
R: 406 yards
F: 375 yards

A high quality finisher doglegging gently right. There are vast areas of beach lining both sides of the landing area and they go further than is visible. Tee shot should be aimed down the middle at the high point of the fairway. The green has large trap starting front left and continuing that side, and one back right in the bank.

P.O. Box 157
Red Deer, Alberta, T4N 5E8
Telephone: (403) 343-8311

River's Edge Golf Club

"A little gem by the Sheep River..."

Par 35

As a competitive golfer, former Canadian tour player Ed Englehardt was known to favor finesse and shotmaking over pure power. So it was natural that when he designed and opened his own golf course at River's Edge a couple of years back now, it would reflect those qualities. At the moment there are only nine holes, but each and every one of them is a challenge. It is, my friends and I agree, a course which requires much thought for every shot. Placement here is of the essence. And the three-tier course has variety with links type holes up top and three tree-lined beauties down in the valley by the river. It welcomes any grade of player because of substantial differences in tee box positioning. This is a great nine-holer which, played regularly, can do nothing but improve any player's scrambling and shotmaking abilities.

#1 - Par 4.
C: 404 yards
R: 343 yards
F: 335 yards

Up on top and the wind can be a factor. A dogleg left, major downslope and rough trouble left, with the hole visible at the end of the bluff. Ideal tee shot is aimed centre right into the turn to allow the ball to drift left down fairway slope. That allows a nice mid iron into green for par or birdie.

#2 - Par 3.
C: 164 yards
R: 137 yards
F: 125 yards

Excellent par 3 with hilltop tee box. Straight solid shot will bring happy landings on large green. But there's big hillside rough problems left, and a severe downslope into lake right. Breezes might be a concern here too.

#3 - Par 4.
C: 343 yards
R: 336 yards
F: 301 yards

Strong dogleg right with tee shot, from the back tees at least, requiring a near-200 yard carry across the lake. The other major concern is avoiding drift towards cruelly-roughed hillside on inside of turn. Safe fairway touchdown after tee shot just right of fountain will ensure a nice short or mid iron to green. Miss left and you'll have nightmares.

#4 - Par 4.
C: 369 yards
R: 326 yards
F: 317 yards

Dogleg left and one of the toughest driving holes you'll encounter anywhere. Tall trees inside the turn with nasty hidden pond beneath are the problem. It's either a feathered draw shot round them or, my choice, a lofted club over the top. Too far straight out and you're into the adjoining fairway, if you're lucky.

#5 - Par 4.
C: 359 yards
R: 302 yards
F: 290 yards

Tight avenue of trees sweeping right. Another precise driving hole. Ideal is fade shot centre. Good one will set up short or mid iron into green which slopes sharply from back left to front and front right.

#6 - Par 5.
C: 432 yards
R: 408 yards
F: 396 yards

Englehardt let Mother Nature have her way here. It was a questionable riverside par 5, but the floods of '95 introduced a creek immediately in front of the green. Englehardt left it. Now, it's a genuine par 5 with a decision needed. Go for it or lay up for your final approach onto a green which has a cruel back to front slope.

#7 - Par 4.
C: 440 yards
R: 395 yards
F: 335 yards

Funny game isn't it? From the back, this measures longer than the par 5 before it. It needs a good drive centre left to land just right of the mounds left. Watch driving range OB left. Good one opens up comfortable approach to narrow green sloping back to front. Hideous gully trouble right.

#8 - Par 3.
C: 150 yards
R: 150 yards
F: 105 yards

Back tees demand uphill shot across ravine to large green sloping mostly back to front with a right to left lean. For me at least everything off the tee tends to slide left especially in a headwind.

#9 - Par 4
C: 348 yards
R: 323 yards
F: 290 yards

Good finishing dogleg right with substantial hillside problems right. Good tee shot lands straight out in turn. Short iron or wedge will take you onto large undulating green with big putting headaches.

P.O. Box 160
Okotoks, Alberta, T0L 1T0
Telephone: (403) 938-4200

Riverview Golf Club

"Special spot by the South Saskatchewan..."

Par 71

There's a spot on the 16th tee where you can look down several hundred feet and see a flag at the bottom of the coulee. The locals bill it "The most difficult Par 3 in the World." It's a joke, but the real hole is problem enough. This lay-out, much of it running along the towering bluffs above the South Saskatchewan River, causes gasps of awe from the first time visitor, as much for the quality of the golf holes as for the mind-blowing vistas down into the Badlands and across the prairie to distant Medicine Hat. Redcliff? A nice small town. Its golf course is major league. Almost a masterpiece.

#1 - Par 4.
C: 409 yards
R: 388 yards
F: 340 yards

A kind start, straightaway up slight slope. An accurate drive will leave a comfortable mid iron between fairway-flanking trees onto green, front-bunkered left and right.

#2 - Par 5.
C: 524 yards
R: 510 yards
F: 405 yards

Ideal drive is centre left. Second lay-up shot should be to left side. Surprise! Dangerous approach shot, because pond is tucked immediately behind trees right front of green and sand covers the other side.

#3 - Par 3.
C: 160 yards
R: 145 yards
F: 135 yards

Hope you're warming to the task. Solid hole, with water right and encroaching right side of green. Trees left. Be straight.

#4 - Par 4.
C: 410 yards
R: 385 yards
F: 295 yards

The water on the right extends 250 yards so safe tee shot has to be centre left. The green's all yours with a straight long or mid iron approach. Birdie chance.

#5 - Par 5.
C: 482 yards
R: 462 yards
F: 418 yards

When the going gets tough... basic drive but water left comes into play for second or third shot. Safety first. Make sure approach to green is from right side.

#6 - Par 4.
C: 302 yards
R: 287 yards
F: 264 yards

Dogleg left round water. Sand left starting 170 yards out. If you hit 220 or so and dice with the beach, you've got a real birdie opportunity.

#7 - Par 4.
C: 410 yards
R: 395 yards
F: 384 yards

Spectacular. The river valley is with you all along the right but don't get too close to admire the view. There's some cliff erosion. Left side is the name of the game. Small green, sand back and left.

#8 - Par 3.
C: 218 yards
R: 185 yards
F: 157 yards

Prevailing southwest wind is your friend into heavily-protected, small green, with beach left side and behind. Save the view until afterwards.

#9 - Par 4.
C: 416 yards
R: 396 yards
F: 300 yards

Straight, slightly down-sloped hole. What you get is what you see. Sand right front and right rear.

#10 - Par 4.
C: 343 yards
R: 308 yards
F: 267 yards

Water right is with you almost from the tee box. Stay centre left. Sand left and right of green. But good second short iron will pay birdie dividends.

#11 - Par 4.
C: 450 yards
R: 430 yards
F: 360 yards

Magnificent coulee-top dogleg right. The only trip you want to the left is for sight-seeing, but there are fairway bunkers 200 yards out on the right.

#12 - Par 4.
C: 421 yards
R: 380 yards
F: 324 yards

Go centre right off the tee. Water left, and it's a 230-yard carry. Demanding approach into long narrow green.

#13 - Par 5.
C: 522 yards
R: 480 yards
F: 411 yards

Unlucky 13? What a hole. Water right off tee box. Go that route and you'll need to hit around 300 yards to cut the dogleg right. Drive straight out and take the shorter trip across water with your second. Sand 10 yards in front left of green.

#14 - Par 3.
C: 165 yards
R: 142 yards
F: 120 yards

Have a breather. But watch hollow covering right front of green, big bunker right and two traps left. This one is very narrow at the back.

#15 - Par 4.
C: 390 yards
R: 382 yards
F: 279 yards

Camera ready. Coulee in front of tee box and along left of fairway. A daunting tee shot, but there's a large landing area right. Sand front right of green.

#16 - Par 3.
C: 169 yards
R: 135 yards
F: 119 yards

Two holes for the price of one! See if you can spot joke flag in the valley. But keep your concentration for club-up tee shot into prevailing wind to slightly elevated green. A little beauty and major grandeur.

#17 - Par 4.
C: 389 yards
R: 360 yards
F: 327 yards

No rest for the wicked. Wicked is the word for frightening tee shot across coulee cliffs, a 225-yard carry from blue, 200 from white. And then they have the gall to put water front right of green.

#18 - Par 4.
C: 432 yards
R: 398 yards
F: 344 yards

The clubhouse is in sight down the sloped, straight fairway. But watch strings of trees both sides of tee shot landing area. Sand right-front and right-back of green.

700 - 10th Avenue
Redcliff, Alberta, T0J 2P0
Telephone: (403) 548-7118

The 169-yard, par 3, 16th hole, overlooking the South Saskatchewan River

Rolling Hills Golf & Country Club

"Part of local life . . ."

Par 33/34

There are hamlets like this one in inland Scotland and Ireland. The golf course is not just a place to play golf, not just a recreational facility on the community's fringe, but more a part of local people's life, a gathering place, part of their fabric. Whoever named Rolling Hills had a sense of humor, or a deep yearning for some geological feature to interrupt the horizon. But flat isn't necessarily bad. The nine hole set-up is short at 2 116 yards, but has its charms and its surprises, two in particular. The par 5 second and par 4 ninth are superb holes by any standards. Whether by design or accident, these two wouldn't be out of place on any course anywhere.

#1 - Par 4.
R: 307 yards
F: 307 yards

First glimpse of an unusual feature. Two Russian elms slap in the middle of the fairway. Hit tee shot over them centre left. The second is either a low pitch and run through more on the right, or more likely a wedge over them.

#2 - Par 5.
R: 535 yards
F: 471 yards

Surprise! A long straight hole but hang on! There's trees in the middle, and further on a "secret" pond between two larger trees on the left about 280 yards out. The likely second is fired over a creek 240 yards from green. The green's a postage stamp!

#3 - Par 3.
C: 88 yards
F: 88 yards

Have a rest after #2! A bit "pitch and putty" this one, but watch the rough-laden trap right in front.

#4 - Par 3.
R: 159 yards
F: 159 yards

Straightforward mid iron tee shot, but this raised green is a tiny target. And there's enough rough short left to cause problems.

#5 - Par 3/4.
R: 227 yards
F: 227 yards

Another par 3? But wait. If you stick this postage stamp, you deserve a medal. A real tester.

#6 - Par 4.
R: 238 yards
F: 215 yards

Not as easy as it sounds. Tee shot is threatened by pond in front of tee box, and trees immediately beyond catch the player's peripheral vision. And there's one of those sandless "traps" front left of green.

#7 - Par 3.
R: 96 yards
F: 96 yards

An easy wedge. Only problem, a "trap" front right.

#8 - Par 4.
R: 231 yards
F: 231 yards

Hit tee shot across creek 75 yards out towards left dogleg turn. Plenty of prairie spaces. Unless you hit small green, a good chance of a chip and a putt with second.

#9 - Par 4.
R: 321 yards
F: 321 yards

A thing of beauty. Dogleg right, but there's a large pond inside the bend. And you have to carry the creek twice, once on the drive and then in your approach to the green.

Box 37
Rolling Hills, Alberta, T0J 2S0
Telephone: (403) 964-2380

The 88-yard, par 3, 3rd hole

Shaw-Nee Slopes Golf Course

"Parkland course is a challenge..."

Par 72

This testing 18-hole course on the southern fringes of Fish Creek Provincial Park is one of Calgary's more testing parkland tracks. Its hallmarks are lovely treed fairways and mounded, sloping greens which are both difficult to stick, and to putt on. Another feature is the powerful one-two punch carried by the opening two holes. In combination, the par 4 and par 5 represent a start as tough as any hereabouts. If your score is all that counts and you're not careful, your round can be as good as over by the time you walk to the third tee. And if they don't get you, you've also got to negotiate long back to back par 5s on 16 and 17 as you approach the clubhouse. It's possible to shoot really good scores at Shaw-Nee, but chances are somewhere along the line, this one will rear up and bite you.

#1 - Par 4.
C: 404 yards
R: 381 yards
F: 356 yards

Dogleg left round high fence guarding property on the inside of the turn. Get in there and from most lies, the only alternative is a chip back on to the fairway. Best bet is a fairway wood or long iron down centre to land in the turn setting up a long, mid iron uphill approach to the two-tiered green guarded by sand left. Below the pin is best.

#2 - Par 5.
C: 511 yards
R: 488 yards
F: 462 yards

A long-playing dogleg left with fairway on the first half leaning distinctly left to right. Best shot is a draw down centre to get clear of magnificent line of trees along the left. The uphill approach has to avoid sand short right and short left to get to a mounded green on which putting can be a nightmare. It leans back to front and left to right.

#3 - Par 4.
C: 373 yards
R: 351 yards
F: 329 yards

A chance to recover. Downhill, then uphill slight dogleg left. Ideal tee shot is hit down centre right to land in the valley. Uphill mid or short iron approach avoiding sand front right could give you a birdie chance on this one. But watch that back to front slope again.

#4 - Par 4.
C: 398 yards
R: 371 yards
F: 346 yards

Make sure fairway's clear before hitting. Excellent downhill dogleg right. Tee shot should be hit with fade down centre through chute of trees. Anything too right might be OK but there are some nasty tree lies to be had in there. Approach to elevated mounded green, guarded on the flanks by traps, is all important. Extremely difficult to stick.

#5 - Par 3.
C: 153 yards
R: 131 yards
F: 112 yards

Pretty short hole that some days requires only a wedge. But it's approaches are guarded by mounds both front edges and guess what. It has a fierce back-front slope with fall-offs both sides and trees tight on all sides. Be below the pin.

#6 - Par 5.
C: 477 yards
R: 459 yards
F: 404 yards

Superb uphill, downhill, uphill dogleg right. Good drive centre and over the crest will give longer hitters a good shot at making it in two. Mr Average should try and lay up solid second towards the left side of the slope up to the green thereby avoiding line of trees on the right. But there's sand over there too. And yes, the green slopes back to front.

#7 - Par 3.
C: 194 yards
R: 169 yards
F: 146 yards

Pretty, tree-surrounded hole, slightly downhill. The main problem is the creek protecting the green 15 yards in front. But there's water too behind the trees left and not too far behind the green itself. The green itself leans back to front and drops off slightly front right.

#8 - Par 4.
C: 438 yards
R: 414 yards
F: 388 yards

A tough one. Tee shot has to be hit centre avoiding string of trees beginning short right off the tee box. A slight right-left tilt on the fairway will carry the ball towards the left, a good place to be. Tricky approach has to avoid nasty trap front left in the bank of the elevated green. Best route in is to the right side of the long green remembering there's a hidden trap middle right.

#9 - Par 4.
C: 374 yards
R: 351 yards
F: 331 yards

Another tee shot that has to avoid a receding line of trees starting short right. Again hit out down the middle preferably with a fade to set up mid iron approach into another elevated green with major sand left and right.

#10 - Par 4.
C: 387 yards
R: 369 yards
F: 349 yards

Straightaway tree-avenued hole that plays longer than it looks. Centre-left tee shot is best to compensate for ever-so-slight left-right fairway lean. That should leave a comfortable mid iron approach into a green guarded front right and left by traps.

#11 - Par 4.
C: 318 yards
R: 295 yards
F: 273 yards

I'm told this dogleg left round the tall trees is driveable by cutting the corner. I've never done it and I've never seen it done. Best shot is fairway wood or iron draw round the corner or into the turn. That leaves a cosy short iron or wedge into a green and a real shot at birdie. Don't be long with your approach as the water and trees are close behind.

#12 - Par 3.
C: 159 yards
R: 145 yards
F: 137 yards

Picturesque hole with pond along the left and a green guarded tight right by intimidating trees. The wind, usually coming from 10 o'clock is a problem too, so club selection for a large back-front sloping green is vital. Be below flag if you can.

#13 - Par 4.
C: 342 yards
R: 325 yards
F: 312 yards

Perfect tee shot on this downhill, uphill hole is a centre right draw. But beware there is a usually-dry pond out of sight down the slope straddling the fairway probably 80 yards out from the green. Try and ensure your uphill approach stays below the pin on this back-front sloping green too.

#14 - Par 4.
C: 360 yards
R: 345 yards
F: 318 yards

A fine hole with elevated tee box and lake running along the first leg of slight dogleg left. Best tee shot is one of about 230 yards to land on a plateau before a major valley dropping down and then back up to the green. That gives a level lie for preferably-lofted iron approach into a mounded hilltop green. Putts from the back can run forever.

#15 - Par 3.
C: 162 yards
R: 155 yards
F: 145 yards

Daunting hole with Fish Creek Park immediately behind, a ball-devouring ravine immediately in front and a distant elevated green. The wind usually right to left is often a factor here so allow for it. One consolation. It's a big green with the sole trap slotted behind it.

#16 - Par 5.
C: 492 yards
R: 477 yards
F: 440 yards

Necessary tee shot down centre left is made more difficult by introduction of large house-protecting screens. But anything not long enough and too far right will fall down into trees and bushes right. Ideal spot is on the far upslope or on the plateau over a gully 230 yards out from regular tees. Then proceed straight up to a green I call Vesuvius because of its mounding. Good luck on this one!

#17 - Par 5.
C: 516 yards
R: 500 yards
F: 481 yards

Fine long hole doglegging left. Perfect tee shot is draw down centre left but there is a big landing area to the right too. Then it's a case of manoeuvring through a valleyed chute of trees up to a green tucked tight against trees left. There's sand behind a slightly back-to-front sloping green.

#18 - Par 4.
C: 401 yards
R: 375 yards
F: 362 yards

A tough finishing hole. Tee shot should favor centre right to be in best position to deal with two tall sentry spruces guarding the front left of the green on approach. The pin is usually tucked in behind them. I wonder why? Sand short left too and on the right.

820 - 146th Avenue SW
Calgary, Alberta, T2X 3C0
Telephone: (403) 256-1444

Strathmore Golf Club

"There's trouble out there..."

Par 72/74

Canadian Pacific workers built and played the original course as they labored west towards the Rockies. Someone must have spotted the potential in the marshland northwest of the townsite. Rebuilding and extension have made the best possible use of a large lake and numerous other smaller ones. Huge sandstone blocks uncovered in railway excavations serve to landscape this rolling course where trouble stands up to be counted in unexpected places.

#1 - Par 4.
C: 425 yards
R: 389 yards
F: 308 yards

Hit tee shot left of centre. Trouble right in shape of a pond and a creek. A second pond stands guard in the right centre fairway about 75 yards in front of green.

#2 - Par 3.
C: 247 yards
R: 215 yards
F: 198 yards

Long hit usually into prevailing west wind. Cart path, gravel road, canal run full-length right. Enough said.

#3 - Par 4.
C: 414 yards
R: 401 yards
F: 325 yards

Hit tee shot centre left over pond in front of gold/blue tee boxes, but watch fairway sand left. Heavily treed rightside fairway. Big trap back right off green.

#4 - Par 4.
C: 350 yards
R: 325 yards
F: 295 yards

Semi-hidden green is behind copse of trees left. A pond guards front right. So beware prevailing tailwind on this one. Hit tee shot centre right.

#5 - Par 5.
C: 475 yards
R: 470 yards
F: 373 yards

Not overly long, but toughest hole on course. A whale of an approach shot is required onto green which is virtually an island with lake intruding left and left front and a pond guarding right back.

#6 - Par 4.
C: 391 yards
R: 386 yards
F: 361 yards

Plays long because it's uphill into west wind. Play tee shot left of two fir trees to stay away from water right.

#7 - Par 5.
C: 537 yards
R: 509 yards
F: 422 yards

Hit straight over crest down fairway lined both sides by trees. Beware pond in front of green, flanked left and behind by lake.

#8 - Par 3.
C: 168 yards
R: 158 yards
F: 141 yards

Fine short hole requiring tee shot across or along reed-covered marsh. If the wind is blowing from west hang tee shot out right.

#9 - Par 4/5.
C: 459 yards
R: 377 yards
F: 363 yards

Aim tee shot over or just left of taller of two trees in front of tee boxes. Be prepared for small pond in centre of fairway just beyond 150-yard markers.

#10 - Par 5.
C: 567 yards
R: 536 yards
F: 421 yards

A character builder. Shoot right of visible left fairway sand on a hole swinging right and uphill. And there's more sand on both sides 150 yards out from green. Solid hole.

#11 - Par 4.
C: 398 yards
R: 374 yards
F: 313 yards

Watch for pond 220 yards out beyond right side hummocks. There's sand in the middle about 230-250 yards out depending on tee box. Big-time sand right and back of green.

#12 - Par 4.
C: 337 yards
R: 311 yards
F: 243 yards

Malibu Beach. Sand all the way left and right. There's none in the middle! Oh, and there's sand all round the green.

#13 - Par 3.
C: 140 yards
R: 127 yards
F: 77 yards

Pretty hole. Water right with mini-Stonehenge effect provided by sandstone boulders behind green.

#14 - Par 5.
C: 478 yards
R: 454 yards
F: 422 yards

Aim tee shot right of left fairway trap. Long hitter's second, Mr. Average's third or so, will have to carry pond, plus sand into green.

#15 - Par 4.
C: 322 yards
R: 299 yards
F: 248 yards

Distinctly driveable because of sharp downslope into green. Ideal is draw round large boulder and trees on left. But there is sand front left of green.

#16 - Par 4.
C: 302 yards
R: 287 yards
F: 243 yards

Uphill sliding left. Solid sand right and various traps left. Best advice – stay centre.

#17 - Par 4/5.
C: 447 yards
R: 421 yards
F: 366 yards

Downhill beauty, fading right. Tee shot should be aimed down right but watch those moguls out there. Sand front right of green.

#18 - Par 3.
C: 221 yards
R: 205 yards
F: 179 yards

Strong hole. Water both sides, and trees off right fairway. And watch the driving range way left.

80 Wheatland Trail
Strathmore, Alberta, T1P 1A5
Telephone: (403) 934-2299

The 475-yard, par 5, 5th hole

Sundre Golf Club

"Where narrow is the norm..."

Par 72/73

This superb track is one of those rural jewels whose existence you want to scream at Alberta visitors and those less-adventurous Albertans unwilling to try pastures new. Only a tee shot away from the foothills town of Sundre, the course was first set up as a nine-holer back in the early '60s and then upgraded to a full 18 ten years ago. This one really does, as they say, require every club in the bag. Discretion is the sensible way to approach many of these fine holes meandering through the treescape. At least think of an iron option on each tee box even though you finally go for the driver or fairway wood. It's a course where being long really counts for little and in fact can spell trouble. Accuracy and position should be the bywords. Watch out too for the variation in green sizes. There are some with acreages large enough to graze a goodly herd of cattle and others as small as postage stamps. This one hones the skills.

#1 - Par 4.
C: 405 yards
R: 387 yards
F: 318 yards

Narrow but mostly straight. And it's made narrower by isolated trees intruding, especially on the left, along the way. Tee shot left centre is good because green "hides" round to the right. Watch hidden water on the right for the approach starting about 130 yards out. Mounded green has sand to the left.

#2 - Par 3.
C: 231 yards
R: 186 yards
F: 170 yards

Starts out from narrow chute of trees and then opens up further up with a small dip in front. Favor the right side of the green for shot because of sharp drop-off on left and behind.

#3 - Par 4.
C: 349 yards
R: 325 yards
F: 238 yards

Tee shot has to be fired down the centre away from continuous line of trees all the way left and another one starting out right up towards the green. Fairway then rises slightly towards an elevated pond, hidden if the fountain isn't on, immediately before the green. Live or die by your lofted approach.

#4 - Par 5.
C: 562 yards
R: 543 yards
F: 430 yards

Tee shot centre left on dogleg left has to negotiate water intruding from the left in front of tee box. Keep going but watch major dip in front of the green which is heavily trapped on both sides. Each side has one fearsome St. Andrews-type steep-walled bunker. Green has front end tilt and tends to fall off to the left too.

#5 - Par 3.
C: 130 yards
R: 130 yards
F: 125 yards

Should be straightforward but there's potential for major sand grief on both sides. Green slopes drastically from back to front so below the pin is best.

#6 - Par 4.
C: 384 yards
R: 384 yards
F: 335 yards

Dogleg right where tee shot should be hit centre or centre right. Starts out open enough but avenue of trees narrows things down considerably on the way down a gentle drop to the green. Ridge causes front third of green to be much lower than the rest.

#7 - Par 5.
C: 491 yards
R: 472 yards
F: 418 yards

Highest handicap hole. Hit tee shot straight out with idea of landing somewhere right of tall pines on the left. The noose begins to tighten again with the neck into the green narrowing threateningly. Putting can be tricky on green with more rolls than a roller coaster.

#8 - Par 4.
C: 367 yards
R: 347 yards
F: 326 yards

Slight dogleg left so tight it could choke you. There's the usual avenue of trees but individual pines and spruce popping up on both sides have their say too. Remember the advice on the irons option. There's sand on the left of the green when you get there.

#9 - Par 4.
C: 360 yards
R: 339 yards
F: 321 yards

Centre left is good here with water tucked away right of the landing area. Anyway a large tree and sand front right of the green really dictate an approach from the left. There's also a trap on the left side.

#10 - Par 4/5.
C: 425 yards
R: 418 yards
F: 405 yards

A fine hole requiring a tee shot aimed towards the right of the lone pine on the left edge of the fairway. This fairway narrows and widens as you go and has a marked right to left lean. Sand guards both sides of the green.

#11 - Par 5.
C: 483 yards
R: 470 yards
F: 434 yards

A dogleg right. Hit tee shot centre right to take advantage of the turn. Just one point. This *is* a dogleg. The eventual target is not the green straight ahead, but one tucked away right. It has a severe, that's severe, back-front slope, a trap left and big drop-off behind.

#12 - Par 4.
C: 374 yards
R: 356 yards
F: 333 yards

Nice but narrow. The trees funnel in ever tighter down towards the small green. Just be straight and do you really need a wood?

#13 - Par 4.
C: 328 yards
R: 311 yards
F: 267 yards

Another strong iron recommendation on a hole that drifts gently right. Be straight is the motto here too. The green has a marked left to right slope.

#14 - Par 3.
C: 205 yards
R: 191 yards
F: 161 yards

Long and narrow requiring an accurate shot to avoid heavy sand penalties on the left of the green.

#15 - Par 3.
C: 124 yards
R: 112 yards
F: 103 yards

Short therefore easy? Wrong. You've really got to hit this elevated green to get par or better. And look out, it plays longer than it looks.

#16 - Par 4.
C: 414 yards
R: 400 yards
F: 317 yards

Magnificent. Fairway widens and narrows down the usual avenue of trees and progress is further complicated by two deep grassed gullies, one starting about 100 yards from the green, the next 40 yards out and climbing up to the green. Straight long iron or fairway wood off the tee sets up long iron or mid iron approach over them.

#17 - Par 5.
C: 551 yards
R: 540 yards
F: 462 yards

The signature hole and a thing of beauty. Straight but narrow with trees hugging both sides. Again deep grassy gullies provide the interest with one starting 200 yards from the green and another about 150. Just a thought. Two really solid five irons and an eight iron set up my birdie. A great, great hole, but then I'm biased.

#18 - Par 4.
C: 318 yards
R: 309 yards
F: 267 yards

This uphill dogleg left is tempting. It is possible to get near the green with an educated draw round the trees. But at least think about iron and iron again . . .
Box 440
Sundre, Alberta, T0M 1X0
Telephone: (403) 638-3510

The 349-yard, par 4, 3rd hole

Sylvan Lake Golf and Country Club

"Potential about to be realized..."

Par 72

Long-time general manager Rodney Klatt has a positive gleam in his eye at the moment. A change of ownership at the start of 1995 has suddenly meant an infusion of cash which will bring significant upgrading and improvement on a course which already has natural charm and challenge in abundance. Opening in 1996 is the spanking new clubhouse complete with turret to blend in with the Cape Cod-type houses on the nearby lakeside. And improved tee boxes, the addition of some sand here, water there... will mean that this course, its first and tenth tees almost in the vacation mecca's downtown will soon be able to take its place among the province's most pleasant. It's a pity former owner and operator Ellis Stone isn't around to see it. The man who ran the show from 1959 to 1975 is gone now but not forgotten. The Ellis Stone memorial rock in the ninth hole's fairway pays tribute to the man who died of a heart attack mowing the 14th.

#1 - Par 4.
R: 367 yards
F: 367 yards

A pleasant warm-up hole with open straightaway fairway. Enjoy it while you can, it's the widest on the course. Favor the right side slightly to open up the approach to a flattish green.

#2 - Par 5.
R: 419 yards
F: 419 yards

It's a shortish par 5, but the fairway between the trees is narrow. Aim centre left and you want to be up on top. The creek makes its presence known, sneaking in from the left right across about 220-230 yards out in a dip. Careful, this one bites.

#3 - Par 3.
R: 180 yards
F: 180 yards

Tricky and pretty. Tee shot crosses creek in front of elevated tee box. Green slopes dramatically up back right.

#4 - Par 4.
R: 315 yards
F: 315 yards

Slight dogleg left and things are definitely getting tighter. Now you might fancy a draw shot with a three wood or something similar. I did. But think about it. Isn't it wiser to hit a mid iron halfway for accuracy and probably the same club into the green? Just a suggestion.

#5 - Par 5.
R: 509 yards
F: 495 yards

Aim tee shot straight out through funnel of trees. Then start manoeuvring into position for approach from right of green. That should keep you away from houses on the left. There's talk this green might be moved slightly more right in the next few years.

#6 - Par 3.
R: 142 yards
F: 142 yards

Should be simple. Nice big green in attractive treed amphitheatre setting. Just be straight.

#7 - Par 4.
R: 313 yards
F: 313 yards

Dogleg left. A tee shot hitting ground centre left is just about ideal.

#8 - Par 4.
R: 349 yards
F: 349 yards

A mounded fairway demands a tee shot down right side. But anything too far left or right will tend to introduce tree trouble on either side. Best to play your second short and then pitch and run. This is one tiny green which drops sharply off the back.

#9 - Par 4.
R: 394 yards
F: 380 yards

Highest handicap hole around here. Ideal landing area for tee shot is about six or seven metres either side of the Ellis Stone memorial rock tucked right at the start of the dogleg right. It's about 170 yards out. The new configuration round the green has mounds immediately behind and a railway-tied trap back right. The fence behind is OB. Excellent front-nine closer.

#10 - Par 4.
R: 334 yards
F: 334 yards

#1's twin. A welcome wide open fairway. Let 'er rip straight down the middle, but don't let it lull you to sleep for what's to come.

#11 - Par 4.
R: 382 yards
F: 382 yards

A good drive is a necessity here. The uphill slope on the landing area has a left-to-right lean, so centre left is good. And this is another small green.

#12 - Par 4.
R: 295 yards
F: 295 yards

It almost looks like a good drive centre right can hit the green on this one. But it does narrow and those trees are sneaking in from the left for any errant hook.

#13 - Par 5.
R: 569 yards
F: 555 yards

For my money the toughest on the course. Aim tee shot centre left. Only long hitters stand any chance of crossing the creek, 40 yards in front of green, in two, so why not lay up and go across in three (or whatever). There's a severe downslope at the back of the green.

#14 - Par 3.
R: 193 yards
F: 193 yards

Testing. Trees all left and green is tucked in tight beyond them. Either hit fairway wood or long iron draw to stick on green, or play safe with shot into big landing area right and chip and putt from there. Mmm. Really makes more sense.

#15 - Par 4.
R: 311 yards
F: 311 yards

Maybe an iron is best off the tee here aiming over the creek in front of the tee box for big landing area in the centre. Watch it! For some reason or another, the ball tends to go right on this one.

#16 - Par 3.
R: 223 yards
F: 223 yards

A challenge. There's only been one hole-in-one here in the last 16 years. I'd say it's the second hardest on the back nine despite the huge green. Go for it and try and hug the trees right. If a hook enters the equation there's a huge landing area left.

#17 - Par 4.
R: 365 yards
F: 365 yards

Nice dogleg left with a strong right-to-left slope on the fairway. Sensible tee shot is centre right. This one has a very shallow green.

#18 - Par 5.
R: 476 yards
F: 424 yards

Careful, there may be some water around that wasn't there when I passed through. Manager Klatt was drooling at the thought. But until then a good tee shot centre will avoid the present landing area water right, and set up a chance at a second across the creek to the green. The creek winds in front of the green and down its left side.

5331 Lakeshore Drive
Sylvan Lake, Alberta, T0M 1Z0
Telephone: (403) 887-2811

Typical terrain

Taber Golf Club

"Where corn is king..."

Par 72

This southern Alberta town of around 6 500 people is famous for one product, corn. Each fall, the local growers reap their harvest and spread out over the province selling their wares. But there's nothing corny about their local golf course on the western edge of town. Bit by bit it's becoming one of the more respected tracks in the south of the province. I say bit by bit because there's still work going on and some of the newer fairways had not filled in as they should and will when I paid a late summer visit in 1995. The parkland track's design however is sound and maturity will take its natural course.

#1 - Par 5.
C: 513 yards
R: 499 yards
F: 427 yards

A good opener doglegging right around the water with OB left. Yes, it can be cut with a solid drive of about 260 yards. But maybe it's best to hit an iron or fairway wood into the turn. Approach is along narrow fairway to an elevated green with a back-right, front-left slope and severe drop-off behind. Birdie is chirping.

#2 - Par 5.
C: 573 yards
R: 563 yards
F: 492 yards

No foolin' around, back to back par 5s and this one's a monster dogleg left round the pond with more water straight out right. Aim draw tee shot towards the big trees right of the clubhouse and that should set up slight uphill approach towards the green. This one has a nasty bank dropping off left.

#3 - Par 4.
C: 435 yards
R: 424 yards
F: 350 yards

Not much respite here. A long par 4 dogleg right with water on the outside of the turn. Aim tee shot centre right for safety. This green has daunting traps front left and front right.

#4 - Par 4.
C: 362 yards
R: 346 yards
F: 340 yards

I found myself already looking forward to a short hole break here, but it didn't come on this one. A draw down centre left is good to set up approach into green which will take water short right of it out of play. Big left to front right slope on this one.

#5 - Par 3.
C: 191 yards
R: 174 yards
F: 152 yards

Ugh! Call this a short hole? And look at the mounds. All it takes is the right club, a straight hit and watch the wind and . . .

#6 - Par 4.
C: 347 yards
R: 347 yards
F: 310 yards

A testing tree-lined dogleg left from elevated tee boxes. It's best suited to a draw tee shot aimed down a line just right of the distant elevators. That leaves mid or short iron approach into a green which has a leftish tilt at the front.

#7 - Par 4.
C: 397 yards
R: 388 yards
F: 379 yards

Straight but drive should go down the centre left, even left, to best open up a green tucked away right in trees at the end. But on approach watch two things. There's a large tree with overhanging branches sneaking in on the left and there's a nasty dip in front filled with rough when I passed through. It cost me too! Best to fly it in case it's still there.

#8 - Par 3.
C: 213 yards
R: 201 yards
F: 188 yards

Heck, don't they know what short means around here? A tough par 3 with a distant green shaded by surrounding trees. There's a nasty ditch all the way left and major fall-offs both sides of the green. Tricky.

#9 - Par 4.
C: 334 yards
R: 325 yards
F: 300 yards

You can get close to this one with a good tee shot. Trees tight left with a cart path just beyond them. The biggest and best landing area is centre right up near a green with substantial drop-offs left side and behind. Birdie time.

#10 - Par 5.
C: 493 yards
R: 479 yards
F: 438 yards

Straightaway hole with a much wider fairway than any of its predecessors. Go for it. Only problem is another rough-filled dip about 50 yards in front.

#11 - Par 3.
C: 193 yards
R: 182 yards
F: 172 yards

Reasonably straightforward hole but watch the sand front left and front right.

#12 - Par 4.
C: 400 yards
R: 384 yards
F: 322 yards

Centre right is best for tee shot on a tree-lined hole with OB all the way left. Don't lose your approach right though as there are nasty mounds and trees on that side of the green. This one has a noticeable tilt from back to front.

#13 - Par 4.
C: 392 yards
R: 370 yards
F: 340 yards

A beauty. Slightly downhill and straight. Aim drive for pyramid-roofed house in the far distance. Water creeps in from both sides in approach to green. Either use lofted approach or, if you're feeling lucky, use the widish land bridge between the water to hit a low bump and run on.

#14 - Par 4.
C: 378 yards
R: 340 yards
F: 330 yards

Straightforward hit straight out from elevated tee boxes across the creek 75 yards out and avoiding water skirting the right side.

#15 - Par 5.
C: 602 yards
R: 581 yards
F: 539 yards

Ideal spot for tee shot on this dogleg right around the water is centre right. It's a long hit to cut the corner. The approach becomes a narrow neck into the green which has fall-offs left side and behind.

#16 - Par 3.
C: 151 yards
R: 128 yards
F: 105 yards

Now that's what I call short. There's sand front right and left. When I passed through it was spongy going dead in front.

#17 - Par 4.
C: 452 yards
R: 436 yards
F: 390 yards

A nice dogleg left with sand behind the trees left to catch corner cutters. A draw down the centre does the trick to best open up the green here.

#18 - Par 4.
C: 432 yards
R: 417 yards
F: 382 yards

A solid home hole, but basically what you see is what you get on this one.

4909 - 44th Street, Box 484
Taber, Alberta, T0K 2G0
Telephone: (403) 223-2951

The 397-yard, par 4, 7th hole

Three Hills Golf Club

"They call the creek something else..."

Par 35/37

It's officially known as the Three Hills Creek, but regulars here have been known to call it other things. It's the golfer's constant companion, as it meanders to and fro through this course built in a valley on the community's original town site. The terrain is wide open and there are very few trees on the track. The testing lay-out is similar to inland moor courses in Scotland. It's "natural" golf with the creek the course's heart and soul.

#1 - Par 4.
C: 334 yards
R: 334 yards
F: 318 yards

A fine opening hole. Downhill tee shot with creek ambling along right and very accessible. Favor left side. And with the approach shot, note the creek has wound behind small green.

#2 - Par 3.
C: 175 yards
R: 150 yards
F: 150 yards

Testing. Tee shot has to negotiate creek loop about 30 yards in front of green right.

#3 - Par 5.
C: 444 yards
R: 444 yards
F: 417 yards

The creek goes all the way right, swings round green and heads back on left side coming into play on that side 150 yards out. Result? A challenging narrow landing area. Accuracy a must all the way.

#4 - Par 3/4.
C: 288 yards
R: 175 yards
F: 175 yards

A fine hole. Tee shot must hug hillside right to hit green tucked tight against slope. A left-hander's dream, this one.

#5 - Par 4.
C: 370 yards
R: 348 yards
F: 348 yards

Nervous because you can't see the creek? It's there, waiting to gobble up an errant approach shot left towards a plateaued green. The 12 foot high green requires finesse to hit and stick.

#6 - Par 3.
C: 153 yards
R: 150 yards
F: 120 yards

This one bites. Tee shot has to cross creek twice to reach safety on right-to-left sloped green. Aim right. There's all sorts of nastiness left.

#7 - Par 5.
C: 608 yards
R: 561 yards
F: 510 yards

The good news is creek is out of the way early. It crosses in front of tee box 75 yards out. Just keep playing straight, but make sure final shot into green stays below pin. Downhill and sidehill putts here are trouble.

#8 - Par 4.
C: 343 yards
R: 343 yards
F: 300 yards

The creek almost seems to say "I'm back!" It stretches all the way along right. There's a big tee shot landing area centre and left. A particularly small green this one.

#9 - Par 4/5.
C: 450 yards
R: 387 yards
F: 280 yards

A strong finisher requiring blind tee shot over creek, cart path and fairway crest. Hit straight. Creek bids a quiet, but threatening farewell, tucked down to the right of the double-trapped green.

P.O. Box 1004
Three Hills, Alberta, T0M 2A0
Telephone: (403) 443-5065

The 334-yard, par 4, 1st hole

Water Valley Golf Club

"A true golfing treasure..."

Par 72

If there was one moment that most justified my trek of '95, the travel, the time, the exploration, it perhaps came on the fourth tee box at Water Valley. It was the realization that a true treasure had been uncovered. The par 5, flowing down and then upwards to the distant green, takes the breath away. And it's only one of many great holes on this "secret" gem west of Cremona. Farmer Brian Setter likes golf and he has land. So just under ten years ago he started pacing it, imagining golf holes, how long they'd be, how they'd fit into the aspen, birch and poplar-filled landscape. He studied books on golf course design. He took this from here, that from there, borrowed an idea from that . . . and he built nine holes. In July 1995, he opened his second nine. What he's done is create a masterpiece, not only in terms of aesthetic beauty but in golfing challenge. With the new nine's fairways and rough settled as well as the old, he'll have one of western Canada's best.

#1 - Par 4.
C: 436 yards
R: 412 yards
F: 373 yards

A dogleg left. Aim tee shot centre right for good position opening up the green. One factor common on this course is that on every dogleg, the turn must be reached before progress to the green can continue. There are no shortcuts. This green, slightly downhill for the approach slopes back to front.

#2 - Par 3.
C: 125 yards
R: 106 yards
F: 90 yards

Pretty, but technically, the only real so-so hole here. Get your par or birdie and be grateful later. Huge green, sand front right, may require a two-club adjustment depending on pin placement.

#3 - Par 4.
C: 316 yards
R: 295 yards
F: 265 yards

Dogleg left with big landing area right. Aim tee shot to right side inside bunker right. That leaves a nice uphill mid or short iron into green with sand front left.

#4 - Par 5.
C: 514 yards
R: 475 yards
F: 410 yards

Stunning two holes in one. Play it like that. Stage one needs a drive down onto landing area left. It's too long a hit straight over the trees and creek in the dip, something like 330 yards. Your hopefully-second shot across the creek onto the "second" fairway is vital. A good one sets up an uphill approach for par . . . or better.

#5 - Par 4.
C: 420 yards
R: 405 yards
F: 387 yards

Imaginative hole requiring imaginative shotmaking. Hit downhill tee shot, maybe an iron, into general area of lone fir tree in turn of dogleg right, something like 200 yards out. But too far and you're up the proverbial creek which runs all the way along the left for the approaches to the green sloping down at the front.

#6 - Par 4.
C: 325 yards
R: 310 yards
F: 280 yards

Shortish but uphill. Aim for the three tall distant spruces all the way to the green. Watch for major hidden water problem, a small lake, right, starting behind tall spruce, 75 yards out from green.

#7 - Par 5.
C: 465 yards
R: 445 yards
F: 425 yards

Sharp dogleg right with downhill tee shot, again think iron, aimed to the right of two trees in the valley near that creek. Be as right as you dare but make that turn! Good position will set up fairway wood or long iron shot for chance at making it in two. Green, set in hill leaning right to left, has sand right. Gee, that was fun as well.

#8 - Par 4.
C: 350 yards
R: 325 yards
C: 305 yards

Dogleg left with left-to-right fairway lean. Good tee shot position is just inside mounds on outside of turn. Elevated green, sand front left, has ridge causing major front-end slope.

#9 - Par 3.
C: 170 yards
R: 155 yards
F: 135 yards

Demanding uphill shortie. There's major tree trouble all the way left and sand on that side of the green. But right is a vicious downslope from the green and sand in the bank. Moral? Hug the left, but pray you're straight.

#10 - Par 4.
C: 365 yards
R: 365 yards
F: 355 yards

Original nine opens with straightaway hole. All this picturesque tree-lined avenue demands of you is be straight. Oh and by the way, the greens are mostly smaller from now on, and it's hardly noticeable but there's a gentle right-left slope on this one.

#11 - Par 4.
C: 315 yards
R: 315 yards
F: 285 yards

Gorgeous dogleg left. Aim tee shot for area right of second spruce on left of fairway. That should give you a nice mid iron into another small green which slopes back to front.

#12 - Par 5.
C: 419 yards
R: 419 yards
F: 345 yards

Not to question owner Setter's measurements but this sure plays a lot longer. Aim drive centre left and then on approach take severe left to right fairway slope into account. Watch small hidden pond right about 70 yards out from green which has a severe back to front slope.

#13 - Par 3.
C: 195 yards
R: 195 yards
F: 145 yards

Strong, long shortie. More space left but hug trees right if you want to hit green first time. The green is like all others here, suffering the Valley Effect, leaning towards the lowest point on the course. In this case, right to left.

Southern 148 Alberta

#14 - Par 5.
C: 468 yards
R: 468 yards
F: 385 yards

Thinking golf again. Dogleg left. Aim tee shot centre, then favor right side (not too right) of left-to-right leaning fairway. This way opens up the green avoiding two large, tall pines guarding front left about 50 yards out.

#15 - Par 4.
C: 315 yards
R: 315 yards
F: 305 yards

Wondrous downhill dogleg right. Aim tee shot at the tallest of the trees, the one which splits near the top, about 230 yards straight out, and you'll either stick on flat plateau or hit dramatic downslope right towards the green. If you fancy a fade tight to trees right, be warned. There's "invisible" sand just around the turn.

#16 - Par 3.
C: 150 yards
R: 150 yards
F: 115 yards

A cathedral of golf. Amphitheatre hole requires straight tee shot along or over pond right which curls round front right half of green. There's a vicious back right to front left slope here.

#17 - Par 4.
C: 410 yards
R: 410 yards
F: 335 yards

Rated the toughest hole on the course. and it could well be. A dogleg left but the rolling fairway wants everything to go right. Closing on approach distance favor the left because the larger two-tiered green is sneakily tucked away right.

#18 - Par 4.
C: 375 yards
R: 375 yards
F: 320 yards

Reach for the Thesaurus! No superlative is enough. Unforgettable vista of great uphill and narrowish finisher topped surrealistically by arc of tall-trunked trees against the skyline. Oh, and another thing. What a great clutch hole. Straight up!

Water Valley, Alberta T0M 2E0
Telephone: (403) 637-2388

The wonderful 315-yard, par 4, 15th hole

Waterton Lakes Golf Course

"A masterpiece restored..."

Par 71/74

The genius of golf course architect Stanley Thompson of Banff Springs and Jasper fame is re-emerging in the open slopes and treed meadows of another of his mountain park masterpieces at Waterton. In recent years, the Waterton course, with its magnificent panoramas over the Prince of Wales Hotel and the lake to Glacier Park beyond, seemed sadly neglected, like a favorite, well-to-do relative fallen on hard times. The fairways and greens were almost taken back by nature, by the oft-present deer, elk, and moose, and the occasional cougar and bear. The good times have returned. The wildlife and grandeur remain but the course, with the care it cried out for, is reborn, its fairways lush once more and its greens restored to reclaim their position as being among the best in Alberta. And it's only the start because there is a five-year improvement plan, mainly involving tee box reconstruction, in place. With super-friendly staff and such unforgettable surroundings, golf just seems the natural thing to do around here.

#1 - Par 4.
R: 322 yards

A benign opener doglegging gently right, but beware the roughed downslope to the right. A fade tee shot down left centre will leave a wedge into a green heavily bunkered front right, back right, front left and back left.

#2 - Par 5.
R: 486 yards

A majestic dogleg right with mountains providing an awesome backdrop. Aim tee shot centre left for spot which leaves you able to clear sharp 25-foot upslope with your next shot. Green, sloping slightly from back to front, has sand back right and back left.

#3 - Par 4.
R: 309 yards

The green is invisible down a steep slope. It's driveable with a favoring wind but allow time for those in front to clear. The wiser shot is a right-side lay-up just beyond the 150-yard markers, then a wedge onto the green hugged by trees right, mounds behind and two traps left. Good birdie possibility.

#4 - Par 3/4.
R: 221 yards

Difficult par 3 with tee shot over preliminary dip in fairway to flat area climbing towards green guarded tightly by trees both sides. Wind, from the left, a factor. Make sure green is clear.

#5 - Par 3.
R: 166 yards

Shortish, straight, simple. Right? Wrong! Mid-iron tee shot is usually into headwind, which can vary from breeze to gale off the distant lake. The flattish green isn't the biggest target on this circuit either.

#6 - Par 5. **R: 508 yards**	This one spars with true greatness. Waterton's longest, and one of its toughest. Hit tee shot centre onto flat portion of open fairway. With a tail wind, your length might surprise you. Eventually a steep hill has to be negotiated to reach the green perched on top, with sand front left and front right. Par's an achievement.
#7 - Par 3/4. **R: 247 yards**	Another tough one. Local pro Ken Roome talks in awe of using his driver here off the elevated tee box and still being short of the green tucked in trees down the hill. Yes, the Waterton wind may have a hand in this one. Par? Lucky you!
#8 - Par 4. **R: 379 yards**	A pretty straightaway hole with trees coming more into evidence especially down right side in approach to green. This one is usually played all the way into a headwind. Aim tee shot slightly centre left to open up green perched on bluff's edge with panoramic lake and mountain vistas. Sand front left and right.
#9 - Par 4. **R: 383 yards**	Take wind, usually from right, into account for tee shot here. Fairway down the hill slopes dramatically left to right. But ideally you want to be centre for approach into clubhouse green covered by sand, front left, and a second small trap on the right.
#10 - Par 4. **R: 308 yards**	OB all the way right. Elevated tee shot, trees left, should be aimed centre right of fairway below. Hole driveable, but sand left and back left, trees front right, encourage more respectful approach.
#11 - Par 5. **R: 485 yards**	Tee shot between trees should land around bank on fairway with faint dogleg left. If still below the bank, you should aim at the pyramid peak. The flat green's back there somewhere! Trees left and right of it – and close behind.
#12 - Par 5. **R: 467 yards**	It's usually about here that the scale of Waterton's challenge begins to dawn. The second of back-to-back par-5s. Be leftside off tee box. Heavy left-right slope will drag too-right tee shot down into trees and bushes. Keep going!
#13 - Par 3. **R: 157 yards**	Truly one of Alberta's great holes. Thompson's genius for simplicity and mischief are here for all to see. Tee shot requires a hit across a 100 feet-deep, largely-fairwayed valley, to a tiny, shallow green carved tee-box level into the mountainside opposite. Watch the wind, don't be short. The trick is to hit *just* long enough to the semi-cut above the green and trickle back down and on. Honest. It's been known to work.

#14 - Par 4.
R: 337 yards

Ah, the trees make their presence more felt. Elevated tee shot should land centre right to allow for fairway slope, right to left. Second requires uphill shot into green with only flag top usually visible. The fir tree behind is a good line. Extra club advisable here.

#15 - Par 4/5.
R: 424 yards

Straightaway into prevailing wind and the start of a stretch of really testing golf holes. Elevated tee box give's bird's eye view of Thompson's propensity for narrowing treed fairways in landing areas, opening them up again and then narrowing the neck into the big green. Fine hole swings right to left. Remember mountain's natural slope.

#16 - Par 4.
R: 321 yards

An outstanding hole doglegging sharply left round high-banked, right-to-left fairway to green unseen round the trees. Environmental note – look for wildlife on the mountain slope. Ideal tee shot is centre right draw to take the ball down to the green. Gone now, unfortunately, is the tall elm that once guarded the left approach. The stump's still there though.

#17 - Par 3.
R: 188 yards

Treacherous. Tough uphill tee shot, usually complicated by wind from right, onto plateaued green. It's smallish, two-tiered, front and back, and slopes left to right. If the pin's right and you're left, it's like putting off the edge of the world.

#18 - Par 4.
R: 395 yards

Homeward bound. Drive from elevated tee box should be aimed to left side of fairway falling from left to right. A good one followed by mid or short iron approach will get you home to the large flattish green with chance of par or better for the clubhouse gallery. Watch those subtle breaks though.

Box 200
Waterton Lakes National Park, Alberta, T0K 2M0
Telephone: (403) 859-2114

Wintergreen Golf and Country Club

"A foothills delight on city's doorstep..."

Par 71

A mere half hour's drive from Calgary gives city golfers a splendid opportunity for a change of pace. At Wintergreen they can savor the pleasures and differences in the game provided by mountain golf or, more accurately in this case perhaps, foothills golf. The dramatic changes in elevation on this track sited beneath the Wintergreen ski slopes, give the player some severe tests in applying both uphill and downhill techniques on the fairways wandering among the pine and spruce. Architect Bill Newis knew what he was doing. But don't be fooled. Wintergreen's range of tee boxes does not mean the course is purely for the better than average. Substantial length differences from the front tees allows the beginner or fun player the opportunity to enjoy the game and the magnificent scenery too.

#1 - par 4.
C: 396 yards
R: 379 yards
F: 325 yards

Sorry to disagree but... one official guide says the way to play this fine downhill dogleg right is a tee shot aimed left. Not in my book, literally, and my fellow players agree. It's got to be down centre right landing in the fairway as near the sand right as possible to give you a comfortable approach into the green down by the lake.

#2 - Par 5.
C: 530 yards
R: 505 yards
F: 418 yards

Almost a horseshoe hole sweeping left around the lake. It's the highest handicapped hole on the course, but with care can be mastered. Requires an accurate tee shot over the water towards the landing area right of the forever-sand lining the opposite shoreline, then careful shots along a narrow fairway The final approach particularly requires a squeezed iron between the water left and trees right.

#3 - Par 3.
C: 154 yards
R: 131 yards
F: 86 yards

Looks simple and should be. But stray too far off straight and there's trouble left and right.

#4 - Par 4.
C: 423 yards
R: 395 yards
F: 344 yards

You can see this fine hole as you drive in. It's uphill and always plays longer than it looks. Tee shot should be aimed right of water starting about 150 yards out. Good one will land in fairway right of sand on the left setting up long or mid iron approach into a green, guarded left and right by traps, and with a vicious downslope.

#5 - Par 4.
C: 380 yards
R: 364 yards
F: 282 yards

Good drive centre makes this uphill dogleg left so much easier. Anything hooked or overdrawn will land in trouble in hidden water left in landing area. The green nestling on the significant upslope is guarded by sand left and front right. Best be below the pin on this one if possible.

#6 - Par 3.
C: 225 yards
R: 205 yards
F: 155 yards

Pin placement can change this one's complexion drastically. You've either got to fly the green over the water or safety first often dictates a draw down right side to hit slopes and run onto the green. Really this course's joint signature hole with #10.

#7 - Par 5.
C: 510 yards
R: 470 yards
F: 382 yards

Reminds me of Scotland's Gleneagles for some reason. Tee shot on this dogleg left through chute of trees should best land centre left near the fairway sand. Then it opens up for approach shots into green. Watch for hidden pond short right, about fifty yards out. This green with severe slopes particularly on the back end can cause nightmares.

#8 - Par 4.
C: 385 yards
R: 360 yards
F: 303 yards

Nice hole drifting left. But a good tee shot centre will set up a shortish iron into green protected by a creek about forty yards in front. This one slopes back to front too.

#9 - Par 4.
C: 375 yards
R: 358 yards
F: 295 yards

Uphill dogleg left which can be a bit of an ordeal. Tee shot across creek landing just right of the fairway sand in the left sets up an uphill approach to a hilltop green guarded strongly by chasms of sand in front. Warning: You can't run it on between the traps. It's got to be an aerial attack . . . and club up.

#10 - Par 5.
C: 535 yards
R: 516 yards
F: 450 yards

If they start you off here, it's the rudest wake-up call you could get. Downhill tee shot must be hit centre right to avoid long, ball-gobbling pond extending down left side. Then you have to negotiate a creek crossing fifty yards in front of green. Lay-up might be better for some. Green well covered by sand front left and back right.

#11 - Par 4.
C: 386 yards
R: 364 yards
F: 300 yards

Concentrate and ensure tee shot is aimed centre left. This one pulls everything right towards the water for some reason and it really shouldn't come into play. Good drive sets up mid iron into tree-shaded green guarded front left and back right by traps. This one bites.

#12 - Par 3.
C: 194 yards
R: 165 yards
F: 126 yards

A challenging par 3. OB all along the left and little or no fairway. Requires straight, truly-struck tee shot across the pond to a green guarded front left by sand and a creek right.

#13 - Par 4.
C: 421 yards
R: 393 yards
F: 303 yards

Dogleg left with slightly uphill tee shot requiring to be hit centre left to land between fairway traps on both sides. The large green is fairly open but that trap front right covers more of the front than it looks.

#14 - Par 3.
C: 193 yards
R: 178 yards
F: 125 yards

What you see is what you get. Anything right is wet trouble, there's sand front left and on the right side. One more thing. Don't be too long. It's not too far to more water back there.

#15 - Par 5.
C: 528 yards
R: 490 yards
F: 446 yards

A fine hole. First requirement is safely negotiating tee shot about 200 yards from the back tees across water to fairway. The mounded embankment to the right is fairly safe but can produce some devilish lies. Then it's a case of manoeuvring between sand left and right towards green. The best approach all the way, except the tee shot, is along the left.

#16 - Par 3.
C: 163 yards
R: 141 yards
F: 95 yards

An arena of trees. Short but green is protected by fronting creek, and sand front right, left and back left. Try and be below the pin on this one.

#17 - Par 4.
C: 410 yards
R: 365 yards
F: 327 yards

Good tee shot from elevated tee box on this dogleg left will be hit centre left and cross a ditchy creek about 220 yards out. Anything right is bringing the lake into play at least for the approach shot. The left side opens up a green guarded right by a tiny pot bunker and a back trap.

#18 - Par 4.
C: 412 yards
R: 375 yards
F: 290 yards

As tough a finisher as you'll find. Tee shot on this dogleg right should be aimed centre left. That leaves severe uphill approach to the green. Traps in the hill front left and front right. You can either fly into the green high or take the run-in approach on the right side. Anything too long can cause headaches in the bank behind.

P.O. Bag #2
Bragg Creek, Alberta, T0L 0K0
Telephone: (403) 949-3333

Woodside Golf Course

"Wide open spaces can cause problems too..."

Par 70/72

If ever there was a case of appearances being deceptive, Airdrie's Woodside track emphasizes the point. It's fairly open, but subtle placement of highly-visible sand and water make this a course which can rear up and bite in the most surprising places. Add a frequent breeze to the equation and your score can mount alarmingly quickly. This is a links course that is in the main reasonably forgiving but with a number of holes which probe the weaknesses in any player's game. It's one that long hitters and placement players can enjoy equally.

#1 - Par 4.
C: 323 yards
R: 313 yards
F: 293 yards

Nice straightaway hole with the fairway narrowing in the landing area and opening up again towards the green. Probably the best tee shot is one favoring centre left to take a large trap front right partially out of play for a mid, short iron approach.

#2 - Par 4.
C: 365 yards
R: 358 yards
F: 345 yards

Another testing hole with water running all the way along the right. Best tee shot here is centre. Anything too right dices with a bank down into the water, anything too left means approach has to fly mound hiding left side of green.

#3 - Par 3.
C: 231 yards
R: 161 yards
F: 137 yards

Tricky little hole with wind from left often a major player. There's water along the right and the long green can mean careful club selection depending on where the flag is. The front end of this green tilts sharply.

#4 - Par 5.
C: 526 yards
R: 520 yards
F: 497 yards

Long hitters beware water starting in your landing area over the mounds left. Best drive is centre, centre right. Some can make the green tucked left behind the lake in two, others best lay up centre for short iron, wedge onto a huge elevated green. This is one with teeth.

#5 - Par 3.
C: 151 yards
R: 141 yards
F: 127 yards

Short hole often played into a headwind. It's another long green that may mean a two-club difference. There's sand front left and more right on top of a nasty downslope. And the water right isn't far enough away to guarantee a dry landing. Some calling card putts on this one.

#6 - Par 4.
C: 319 yards
R: 308 yards
F: 297 yards

This green is driveable for big hitters. But, be warned, anything too right is going to be wet. Best for the rest of us is a drive centre left to set up approach to the right of the green doubling with #8 left.

#7 - Par 4.
C: 369 yards
R: 360 yards
F: 346 yards

This is one good golf hole snaking ever so gently right. Centre left is the place to be left of the mound on the right of the fairway. About fifty yards behind that mound is water. Centre left tee shot sets up ideal short-iron approach up to an elevated green with a front-end slope.

#8 - Par 4/5.
C: 371 yards
R: 355 yards
F: 341 yards

By now, any complacency created by these "wide open spaces" should have disappeared. Here's another one demanding accuracy off the tee followed by a sure approach. Aim tee shot down centre but watch the water right and a creek-filled hollow straight out about 280 yards from the back tees. Your approach needs to be pretty high to stick the right side of the elevated green doubled with #6.

#9 - Par 4.
C: 366 yards
R: 352 yards
F: 332 yards

A sweeping dogleg right with water all along the right. Ideal tee shot line is centre with a fade. Longish hit will set up short, mid iron approach to green which has a severe embankment down to the water right. This one's mounded too.

#10 - Par 4.
C: 369 yards
R: 351 yards
F: 335 yards

Birdie chance. Straightforward downhill hole, but it does play longer than it looks sometimes. Best tee shot is centre, even slightly centre left to take driving range fence right completely out of play. The green leans back to front.

#11 - Par 4.
C: 427 yards
R: 412 yards
F: 395 yards

One of those holes that makes you want to measure it yourself. It plays long. Long drive straight down the middle makes the approach that much more comfortable. This green rolls slightly as well.

#12 - Par 3.
C: 159 yards
R: 146 yards
F: 130 yards

A headwind can be the fifth player in your foursome here. It's slightly downhill but you may still have to think about clubbing up to reach the tiered green!

#13 - Par 4/5.
C: 420 yards
R: 406 yards
F: 389 yards

Did anyone bring the measuring tape? Another one that plays long. Best idea here is a fairway wood off the tee to land about 220 yards out centre left avoiding the fall into an evil grassed gully crossing the fairway around the bridge on the left. Then it's a long iron or long-mid iron onto a green sloping dramatically back to front.

#14 - Par 4.
C: 355 yards
R: 340 yards
F: 325 yards

A great par 4 dogleg right from elevated tees round water right. OK, it's driveable, just, with a favoring wind. But is it worth the chance? Safe way is iron or fairway wood straight out centre right to reach the turn setting up short iron approach into waterside green.

#15 - Par 4.
C: 359 yards
R: 337 yards
F: 327 yards

Immensely difficult driving hole doglegging left and uphill. There's water left all the way to the turn and water straight out on the other side about 260 yards out. Go for upslope with your driver. Or, I've found best results with a three-wood, say, straight along the edge of the liquid left to land in the land bridge between the two stretches of water. Then club up for blind approach to the hilltop green. Good hole!

#16 - Par 3.
C: 139 yards
R: 127 yards
F: 101 yards

Attractive downhill hole needing a shot across a new fountained pond bang in front. Club down. It's nine iron or wedge time for most.

#17 - Par 4.
C: 351 yards
R: 332 yards
F: 309 yards

Fairway leans right to left sloping down to water semi-hidden behind mounds left. Centre right then is the best tee shot. Good one will leave a short or medium iron onto the large green doubled with #14.

#18 - Par 5.
C: 521 yards
R: 500 yards
F: 485 yards

Ideal tee shot is a long draw hit down centre to start round the gradual bend. Fairway straightens up after that and it's case of being straight avoiding a downslope falling away right and OB left. This green has a marked back to front lean too.

525 Woodside Drive
Airdrie, Alberta
Telephone: (403) 948-7224

Northern Montana

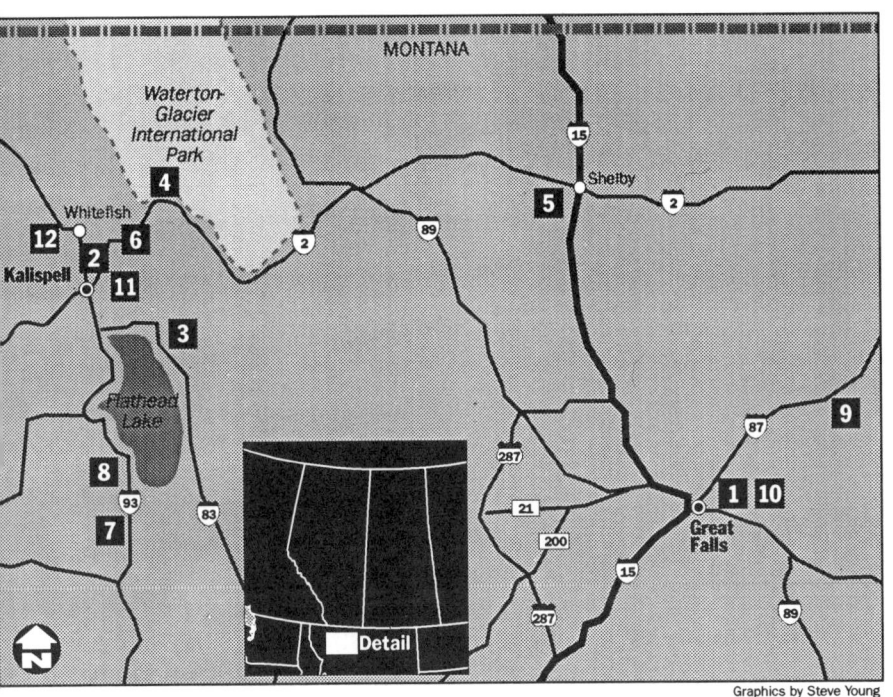

1. Anaconda Hills Golf Club
2, Buffalo Hill Golf Club
3. Eagle Bend Golf Club
4. Glacier View Golf Club
5. Marias Valley Golf and Country Club
6. Meadow Lake Resort
7. Mission Mountain Country Club
8. Polson Country Club
9. Signal Point Golf Club
10. R.O. Speck Golf Course
11. Village Greens Golf Club
12. Whitefish Lake Golf Club

Anaconda Hills Golf Club

"The best of both worlds . . ."

Par 69

This attractive course in Great Falls' northeast section of Black Eagle epitomizes what is happening at many smallish North American courses nowadays – a new nine of completely different character being added to a perhaps traditional and long-established older nine. Here a somewhat short but tricky treed front nine has been augmented by a full-out "desert" style links track complete with warning signs declaring "Be Alert for Snakes." The original holes require accurate shotmaking up, down, through and along narrow and rolling treed chutes. The new nine, longer, with larger greens, more sand and water requires tee shots over wastelands to come to earth on sometimes-distant landing areas. It's fun requiring a nifty gearshift at the turn.

#1 - Par 4
C: 352 yards
R: 335 yards
F: 322 yards

Pleasant downhill hole played through avenue of trees. With a fairway lean left to right, favor centre-left tee shot.

#2 - Par 3.
C: 217 yards
R: 200 yards
F: 159 yards

Tee shot needs to negotiate uphill chute of trees to a green higher than the tee box. Club up here.

#3 - Par 4.
C: 316 yards
R: 301 yards
F: 292 yards

Tee shot on this dogleg left has to be hit across the valley to top of slope on far side. Good target line is just right of trees in left of turn about 170 yards out. Success will mean a nice mid iron into green surrounded by trees. Noticeable back to front slope on this one.

#4 - Par 3.
C: 205 yards
R: 189 yards
F: 155 yards

Downhill with the fairway slope sending the ball left, so aim centre right just left of large fairway tree about 100 yards out.

#5 - Par 4.
C: 295 yards
R: 278 yards
F: 251 yards

Uphill dogleg right. Fade round or loft over the tall trees on the right. Success either way will set up short iron into hidden green tucked left of the white building in the hollow. But listen for the "All-clear" bell before making your approach to the green which has a severe back to front slope.

#6 - Par 4.
C: 264 yards
R: 248 yards
F: 222 yards

Yes, it's driveable. But it's uphill with OB down into the coulee right and there are trees all along the left. Sensible tee shot and best chance at birdie is a lay-up centre left.

#7 - Par 4.
C: 340 yards
R: 324 yards
F: 267 yards

Tricky, subtle. Downhill, sharp dogleg right with a steep immediate drop to the green at the turn 200 yards out. There's water on the inside of the turn too. Long hitters can cut corner and land close. But newcomers may want instead to aim iron or fairway wood at tall trees at eighth tee box and hope to drift down.

#8 - Par 3.
C: 151 yards
R: 133 yards
F: 120 yards

Nice shortie. Shot from elevated tee box should be aimed just right of green shelved on hillside falling right to left. Club down for this one.

#9 - Par 5.
C: 509 yards
R: 497 yards
F: 457 yards

What a great golf hole, toughest on the front nine. It's decision time at the tee box again. Dogleg right with a very early turn. Sensible way is mid iron out into turn. But adventurous souls may favor cutting the corner by aiming a drive across the water between the huts to land, hopefully, in the steep fairway.

#10 - Par 4.
C: 415 yards
R: 372 yards
F: 258 yards

Don't get snakebit! Downhill and uphill with heavy rough both sides. Aim tee shot centre left for best position for approach into green elevated maybe 30 feet above the landing area. Hey, a big green and grass bunkers.

#11 - Par 4.
C: 355 yards
R: 322 yards
F: 247 yards

Hope you've shifted gear OK. Dogleg left with ideal downhill tee shot aimed centre left to ready for uphill approach to another elevated green with a distinct back to front slope.

#12 - Par 4.
C: 338 yards
R: 315 yards
F: 273 yards

Cunning little so-and-so, this one. Dogleg left, becoming downhill, with green invisible from tee box. Try and hug a draw round the hill left but beware unseen water on left downslope about 70 yards from the green. This is another one where you wait to hear the bell before hitting.

#13 - Par 3.
C: 169 yards
R: 148 yards
F: 89 yards

Ever-so-slightly downhill so watch club selection. There's a nasty pond in dip in front of the green. Be safe unless you're sure. Aim to right side of green.

#14 - Par 4.
C: 386 yards
R: 360 yards
F: 264 yards

Elevated tee shot should be aimed down the right to have any hope of finding a level platform for approach shot into a large welcoming green.

#15 - Par 3.
C: 146 yards
R: 134 yards
F: 99 yards

Super-attractive par 3. There's water on the left front and side of the long narrow multi-tiered green. There are some area code putt possibilities here.

#16 - Par 4.
C: 364 yards
R: 317 yards
F: 211 yards

Unusual set-up with back-tee hitters having to negotiate bank of other tee boxes going uphill. There's big rough and coulee problems right. A good tee shot, aimed right of hilltop building, will land centre left for approach into green.

#17 - Par 5.
C: 488 yards
R: 459 yards
F: 357 yards

Great links hole. Downhill dogleg left with water in front of tee box. Ideal tee shot is aimed toward cart path disappearing over hill in the distance right. The huge green is set on a peninsula with creek and gulch trouble all around.

#18 - Par 4.
C: 356 yards
R: 339 yards
F: 289 yards

Good testing finisher. There are trees all along the right on this uphill hole, with serious coulee problems all along the left. Still, the tee shot landing area is large and safe if you hit centre left. The green has a severe front-end slope.

24th Street & Smelter Ave
Black Eagle (Great Falls), Montana 59414
Telephone: (406) 761-8459

The fairway on the 415-yard, par 4, 10th hole

Buffalo Hill Golf Club

"Magical Mystery Tour..."

Par 72/74

In no small way, this amazing municipal golf course in the north end of Kalispell finally convinced me the book you are reading now may be useful to some people. It was during a recent spring tour here with the Eagles that we found ourselves wandering around the woods as lost as Hansel and Gretel. The course is not, even locals agree, the easiest for strangers to negotiate. It's one of the toughest on the Montana circuit with blind tee shots, hidden ponds, invisible greens, narrow, treed, often doglegged fairways, and major elevation changes. It's a real test of stamina and patience – and of shotmaking golf. In short, it's a delight. But at Buffalo Hill, rightly rated one of the best in the state, it really does help to know where you are going.

#1 - Par 4/5.
C: 429 yards
R: 401 yards
F: 373 yards

Welcome to the first of the toughest one-two combination openers you'll find. The fairway's invisible tucked uphill beyond avenue of trees on left. Aim drive just right of them with a 3 wood or long iron and, ideally you will hit about 220 yards out. You'll have long to mid-iron approach into treacherous green sloping off back and front and with a tilt to the right. Sand left and right.

#2 - Par 5.
C: 598 yards
R: 587 yards
F: 497 yards

A monster. Dogleg right. Tee shot across valley to upslope or plateau favoring centre left. Trees down both sides. There's another deep valley to negotiate before a steep climb to a green on top. If you're playing from the bottom, club up! If you are leaving here only two over, you're in great shape!

#3 - Par 4.
C: 341 yards
R: 332 yards
F: 298 yards

Strong hole, but you've got a possible birdie chance. Downhill tee shot centre right will keep you away from tree trouble left and set you up with mid iron into tree-flanked green tucked up on the hill left. Don't be right of the green or behind it!

#4 - Par 4.
C: 330 yards
R: 321 yards
F: 266 yards

Fabulous hole. Downhill tee shot needs to clear narrow chute of trees down to dogleg left. The turn starts about 190 yards out. The banked fairway will help the ball round. Ideal shot might be a feathered fairway wood or long iron aimed centre to draw towards the unseen green close round the corner. Believe me, this is a good birdie chance too.

#5 - Par 3.
C: 225 yards
R: 195 yards
F: 147 yards

Spectacular, especially from the elevated back tees tucked just behind the previous green, the others down the hill. Anyway the river has to be negotiated with a tee shot that has to find its way down a long avenue of trees to a green with sand left and right.

#6 - Par 4.
C: 392 yards
R: 377 yards
F: 323 yards

Decision time. Dogleg left with the river all the way. If you've led a sheltered life and err on the side of caution, hit an iron or fairway wood about 180 yards out left centre. If you feel bold cut the dogleg through or over an area where the trees visibly thin. An unhindered 220-yard carry sets you down safely. Sand left and right fronts.

#7 - Par 5.
C: 485 yards
R: 470 yards
F: 412 yards

Start this long one cautiously. A straight hit of just over 200 yards puts you in the ideal situation in dogleg left turn to start going for it. There's river and trees all the way left. Cutting the corner is watery suicide! The green has sand right, and quite a slope from back to front.

#8 - Par 4.
C: 361 yards
R: 334 yards
F: 307 yards

Water right for tee shot, so aim right of the willow tree left for good position for approach. But beware the water on left side of green.

#9 - Par 3.
C: 203 yards
R: 178 yards
F: 153 yards

Good short front nine finisher. There's major sand and mound problems left and right. But the real headache is provided by tremendous slope from the left down to the front end. Putting can be a perplexing affair here.

#10 - Par 4.
C: 418 yards
R: 403 yards
F: 344 yards

Big hitters can carry tee shot over huge sand left on this dogleg left. But most should aim left of twin willows remembering there's water straight out for tee shot but a long way. Sand front left and back left. Again the problem is putting. The green has a curious basin back left. A pin placement in this vicinity is trouble.

#11 - Par 5.
C: 531 yards
R: 518 yards
F: 430 yards

A splendid par 5. Unleash the cannon. There's a big landing area out there but be wary of water well right. The next job is to get into good position to shorten the crossing over water left in front of green. A good target to achieve that placement is the two round pines towards the next tee box in the distance. The green has sand right and behind.

#12 - Par 3.
C: 106 yards
R: 106 yards
F: 83 yards

Attractive shortie. Tee shot is 90 feet down to large green below covered by sand at every corner. Club could vary two or three depending on wind. Club down. Target golf just doesn't come any better.

#13 - Par 4/5.
C: 445 yards
R: 420 yards
F: 353 yards

This one gets my vote as the most difficult on the course. Tough, tough hole. Everything about this one is narrow, the magnificently treed fairway, even the green. Not that it's really wide enough to have a left, a centre and a middle, try to favor centre left all the way.

#14 - Par 4.
C: 326 yards
R: 311 yards
F: 257 yards

Time for an iron or fairway wood off the tee towards the goalpost trees about 200 yards straight out. Warning: there are two hidden ponds in trees left about 50 yards in front of green. Another tough one.

#15 - Par 5.
C: 466 yards
R: 450 yards
F: 369 yards

Play this fine hole down the right. You'll have to hit approach in from that side if you want unobstructed entry to green tucked in left. This green is well trapped.

#16 - Par 3.
C: 129 yards
R: 120 yards
F: 80 yards

Good par 3 across the river and across sand in front. Green slopes back left to front.

#17 - Par 4.
C: 412 yards
R: 401 yards
F: 309 yards

Send out a scout! Tee shot onto big upslope should be as near the big ponderosa left as possible. And when you get there, just believe there really is a green and a hole that you can hit with a good second shot. It's down over the hill with a severe right to left slope running down onto it. Use the slope to run it on. But make sure it is clear.

#18 - Par 4.
C: 328 yards
R: 324 yards
F: 257 yards

Lovely finishing hole. Aim downhill tee shot just left of poplar trees on fairway's right. Downslope will carry you in close enough for short iron or wedge approach. Don't overshoot this green!

Box 1116, North Main Street
Kalispell, Montana 59901
Telephone: (406) 756-4545

Eagle Bend Golf Club

"Where the Golden Bear played..."

The name Nicklaus is synonymous with this fine course set down so impressively on the northeast shore of Flathead Lake near the cultural colony of Bigfork. The legendary Jack hangs out round here during his frequent Montana forays. And nine new holes in the upgraded 27-hole layout inaugurated by the great man himself in '95, were designed by Jack Nicklaus II. They are integrated with the old Ridge nine to form as challenging an 18-hole championship track as you'll find, but they still retain tee-boxes ensuring comfortable enjoyment for the more casual player. The old Lake nine, especially loved by locals, still exists to give visitors a seaside feel to rounds in and around the boating marina. The Flagship of the Flathead was tough. It just got tougher.

Par 72

Ridge Course

#1 - Par 4.
C: 418 yards
R: 393 yards
F: 356 yards

Dogleg right to unseen green calls for immediate decision. There's water straight out about 260 yards. Choice is a straight-away 220-yard hit into the turn, or a 250-yard shot cutting the corner over the trees to the hidden landing area. The green, sloping back to front, has sand front left.

#2 - Par 5.
C: 546 yards
R: 494 yards
F: 406 yards

First example of Jack Jnr.'s handiwork. Tee shot is hit over marsh-waste area onto distant upslope. Ideal tee shot is hit just right of large tree left to land somewhere on the plateau. The well-trapped green is tucked away right behind water right in the approaches. Can be reached in two but Mr. Average best lay up left for wedge into green.

#3 - Par 4.
C: 370 yards
R: 343 yards
F: 281 yards

Uphill dogleg right round lake. Two large traps guard landing area right and there are large grass bunkers beyond them. Tee shot should favor left side, setting up a mid iron into a flat green with sand left and behind.

#4 - Par 3.
C: 191 yards
R: 167 yards
F: 155 yards

Lovely treed par 3, elevated tee box, elevated green. Green slants left to right towards banked drop-off on that side. It also has a back to front slope with a crescent ridge creating an increased front end slope. Be below pin.

#5 - Par 4.
C: 300 yards
R: 289 yards
F: 281 yards

A personal favorite. The excruciatingly narrow avenue of trees doglegging up, then down left, is intimidating. If you've a well-trained draw in your arsenal, it can be reached with a brave shot skirting the trees left. The wiser way is a fivish-iron into the turn 180 yards out.

#6 - Par 3.
C: 166 yards
R: 145 yards
F: 128 yards

The signature hole hereabouts marked by a vertical drop of about 100 feet. Keep a sharp eye on the flag for deceptive wind unfelt on the sheltered tee box. Flattish green has sand, with a grass island, front left and a massive trap on the back.

#7 - Par 4.
C: 372 yards
R: 363 yards
F: 354 yards

Pretty straight, trees both sides, with large traps in the left landing area starting about 235 yards out from the regular tees. Centre right is a good line. Green is guarded by traps front left and right side.

#8 - Par 5.
C: 518 yards
R: 470 yards
F: 416 yards

A challenge requiring a 270-yard tee shot from the back to clear rightside fairway traps. At the end of the day, a high approach is best to avoid trap left and deep bunker front right. A mound in the centre of this one means both front end and back end slopes.

#9 - Par 4/5.
C: 461 yards
R: 452 yards
F: 431 yards

Highest handicap hole, certainly tough. Plays *long*. Give the group in front time to move on. It requires a drive of at least 220 yards to reach the top of the hill and get a chance of a decent roll on the other side. A front slope on the green almost begs a run-on shot between the traps.

#10 - Par 5.
C: 532 yards
R: 513 yards
F: 418 yards

Long ball hitters can carry the leftside traps with a 250-yard drive. Others best aim to land alongside them. For the final approach the ball should be in a position that allows you a shot into the green from the left. There's a steep-walled trap front right and a big bunker back left.

#11 - Par 4.
C: 340 yards
R: 316 yards
F: 244 yards

For some, it's driveable with a long hit liable to roll onto the green from the left. Left on this two-tiered fairway, with the left higher than the right, is best anyway. It's a 235-yard carry over the huge fairway-middle trap. Flattish green has trap back left and steep bunker right.

#12 - Par 3.
C: 211 yards
R: 164 yards
F: 130 yards

Pretty hole and really it should be pretty straightforward too. But there's a very large trap on the front edge and a huge one on the back.

#13 - Par 4.
C: 386 yards
R: 355 yards
F: 308 yards

Go for it on this dogleg right. The traps right can be reached, the first starting 235 yards out, the second 275. Centre is good and keep heading for the cedar log home where the Golden Bear has stayed. Watch the traps around the green including the one 15 feet below it. Sticking is tricky because everything tends to roll away from the centre.

#14 - Par 4.
C: 446 yards
R: 409 yards
F: 360 yards

With your drive from an elevated tee box watch the four traps guarding the left side of the fairway, the first starting 230 yards out. There's also a trap 285 yards out on the outside of the

	dogleg left. Water hugs the green's left and then, of course, there are the traps guarding the front.
#15 - Par 4. C: 377 yards R: 305 yards F: 275 yards	Big hitters can drive it from the regular tees, but it's uphill. Two large traps guard left side of green and there are fairway bunkers on the right around the 250-yard mark. Ideal tee shot would carry them and set up high approach into flattish green.
#16 - Par 3. C: 211 yards R: 182 yards F: 106 yards	A character-builder. Tee shot has to be hit over water-waste area although there's a bit of room for a dry landing left and behind is wide open. The water extends three-quarters of the way across green's front. Be long rather than short!
#17 - Par 4. C: 379 yards R: 370 yards F: 323 yards	Gets my unqualified support as the toughest here. Tee shot is hit towards water starting 240 yards out on the left and wandering across to a point 290 yards out on the right. Centre right makes sense then, but either way two stretches of water and bridges have to be crossed to hit the back-left, front-right sloping green. Be below the pin! Superb!
#18 - Par 4/5. C: 500 yards R: 459 yards F: 380 yards	If you're in the zone, treat yourself to a birdie here. There are three traps guarding the right about 240 yards out so target tee shot centre left. There's a trap front left, one back right, and the green is lower in the front.
Par 36	**Lake Nine**
#1 - Par 4. C: 405 yards R: 350 yards F: 299 yards	Slightly uphill and usually into a headwind off the Flathead, so this one tends to play long. Favor centre left tee shot if you can because there are landing area traps right 240 and 272 yards out. But watch sand left 200 yards out too. Green has serious trap front left and one back right.
#2 - Par 3. C: 191 yards R: 167 yards F: 115 yards	Always plays a bit longer than it looks (the wind again?). Warning: The green is 36 yards long so club selection can vary by two or three clubs depending on wind and pin placement. Very large trap front left and one back right.
#3 - Par 5. C: 532 yards R: 472 yards F: 386 yards	A distinct birdie possibility. But watch the proximity of water on the right in the trees and two traps at 260 and 300 yards. Centre left tee shot is good. There are sizeable beach areas front left and back right.
#4 - Par 4. C: 402 yards R: 372 yards F: 267 yards	Fine hole with tee shot across water. The sand on the right is reachable and there's a small hidden lake huddling in the trees about 295 yards out too. Tee shot centre left makes sense. Watch major trap immediately behind the green.

#5 - Par 4.
C: 434 yards
R: 410 yards
F: 354 yards

Another hole screaming "Don't ignore the Lake Nine." There's water out there on the right and there's two traps penalizing the "over-fade." There are three traps guarding this big green right. Depending on pin placement, now might be the time to practise that bump-and-run technique you've been working on.

#6 - Par 3.
C: 200 yards
R: 175 yards
F: 127 yards

Superlative golf hole. This one down by the lake inlets can play a lot longer or shorter depending on the wind. There's water down the left, huge sand in front and more beach back right. There are some bail-out possibilities right for a chip on to secure par.

#7 - Par 4.
C: 412 yards
R: 363 yards
F: 313 yards

An impressive hole sweeping left round the marina basin. Ideal tee shot is aimed just right of (or over) lone willow on the left. Two traps on the right 260 yards out front water just behind. The back-to-front sloped green has sand guarding front left and right side. A major ridge, parallel to cartpath, causes left side to be lower than right.

#8 - Par 5.
C: 532 yards
R: 466 yards
F: 399 yards

A marvellous, marvellous hole reminiscent of Pebble Beach's famed 18th. Play down the left and you're flirting with water, but the right side adds clubs to your approach. Your choice. Long hitters can hit this peninsular green in two. Others lay up into the neck for a wedge onto a green sloping back to front.

#9 - Par 4.
C: 389 yards
R: 350 yards
F: 314 yards

Two solid shots on this straightaway finisher could give you a last-gasp birdie chance. But there's OB right, a trap 220 yards out left, and water 300 yards out left hugging the approach to and side of the green. Tricky one has mainly back-to-front slope but rolls off the back too.

279 Eagle Bend Drive
Bigfork, Montana, 59911
Telephone: (406) 837-7300

Jack Nicklaus looks down 2nd fairway at Eagle Bend. The two spectators between Nicklaus and Lon Hinkle, leaning on club, are known to the author.

Glacier View Golf Club

"Fun in a hidden valley..."

Par 68

There's a hidden valley nestling on the western fringe of the Glacier Park mountains that hosts a perfect venue for family golf. Glacier View is a short golf course – it plays just over 5 000 yards from the men's tees and amazingly enough in this terrain, it's flat. It's not a difficult course by any standards, though it does have its problems. Its charm lies in the fact that while the family can relax and enjoy a comfortable round in superlative surroundings, it affords the family's big hitter and it may not be Dad after all a great opportunity of "going for it." Many of the holes are driveable, but watch the water lurking here and there. A fun outing for all.

#1 - Par 4.
C: 396 yards
R: 366 yards
F: 290 yards

Dogleg left with a tree 230 yards out in the middle of the fairway. A tee shot right of it opens up the small green best.

#2 - Par 4.
C: 275 yards
R: 260 yards
F: 233 yards

The first of the "go-for-it" holes. But there are trees right and it's a fairly narrow entrance into green. Be long if you like, but more important, be straight.

#3 - Par 4.
C: 434 yards
R: 336 yards
F: 315 yards

Good golf hole. Most demanding here. A slight dogleg left with all sorts of unpleasantness left in the form of trees and rough. It's open in the right landing area so why mess around? Bushes and trees immediately behind the green which has a ridge running diagonally back left to front right.

#4 - Par 4.
C: 350 yards
R: 343 yards
F: 335 yards

Dogleg right with a serious dip in the right landing area for shorter hitters. Good tee shot target is red 100-yard marker visible on left side of turn. If you can fade it all the better. Green has back left-front right slope and trees behind that might cause nasty lies.

#5 - Par 3.
C: 155 yards
R: 132 yards
F: 107 yards

What you see is what you get, but green has two-way slope falling off left and front right.

#6 - Par 4.
C: 318 yards
R: 309 yards
F: 300 yards

A good bang with Big Bertha in a tailwind and you're there on this dogleg right. But, if your game plan is less ambitious, watch the fairway sand 220 yards out on inside of turn.

#7 - Par 4.
C: 325 yards
R: 296 yards
F: 285 yards

Dogleg right with plenty of encouraging open spaces. This too is in that "I think I can, I think I can" category, especially off the regular tee.

#8 - Par 3.
C: 153 yards
R: 144 yards
F: 130 yards

No problem on the face of it unless you land somewhere in the vicinity of the beach right or the troublesome tree immediately behind the trap.

#9 - Par 4.
C: 383 yards
R: 370 yards
F: 358 yards

Dogleg right. Aim tee shot right of the fairway tree on the left. Mid to long iron approach should do the rest from there.

#10 - Par 4.
C: 284 yards
R: 266 yards
F: 248 yards

Dogleg right. But beware water starting about 180 yards out on the right and in the rushes immediately round three sides of the green. Short but good, this one. It's driveable on a good day, but is it worth the chance?

#11 - Par 4.
C: 285 yards
R: 260 yards
F: 240 yards

Lead us away from temptation... water on right stretches more than halfway from tee to green so be cool.

#12 - Par 3.
C: 122 yards
R: 116 yards
F: 110 yards

Straight forward short hole unless you count sand front left and front right and a strategically placed lone tree immediately behind.

#13 - Par 4.
C: 274 yards
R: 266 yards
F: 257 yards

Straight, driveable. But beware the dry pond on front right and side of green (at least, it was dry when I passed through).

#14 - Par 3.
C: 203 yards
R: 188 yards
F: 142 yards

Solid par 3. A clump of trees right and rough trouble left. And this rolling green makes for some tricky putting practice. Not an easy one.

#15 - Par 4.
C: 254 yards
R: 244 yards
F: 234 yards

Tempting again, but let discretion be the better part of valor. Three big trees on inside turn of dogleg right come into play on this fine hole. Best to aim tee shot centre left, maybe with an iron or fairway wood, to set up easier approach into green, treed behind.

#16 - Par 4.
C: 241 yards
R: 231 yards
F: 222 yards

Tee box set in middle of dry pond – and I wasn't there during a drought. Sand front left of green. Let it all hang out at this one. Enjoy!

#17 - Par 4.
C: 389 yards
R: 371 yards
F: 269 yards

Fade tee shot round trees right. Water starts making its presence felt about halfway along the right and wanders up alongside green. Undulating green again makes for difficult putts.

#18 - Par 4.
C: 304 yards
R: 296 yards
F: 288 yards

Dogleg left with water on the right, houses and pretty gardens on the left. A ball that lands centre right is in ideal position for mid to long iron approach hit into green.

P.O. Box 185
West Glacier, Montana, 59936
Telephone: (406) 888-5471/72

The 284-yard, par 4, 10th hole

Marias Valley Golf and Country Club

"A hidden gem on the high plains of Montana . . ."

Par 36

Four miles south of the northern Montana railway and grain town of Shelby and west of Highway 15 is a little piece of golfing paradise which is only too easy to slip by. This nine-hole, soon-to-be-eighteen, layout is snugly positioned deep in the picturesque cottonwood-filled Marias River valley, and it is a challenge. It's been there, scarcely noticed except by knowing Montanans, for more than a quarter of a century now, but with fine fairways and some of the biggest bentgrass greens in the state, it's high time the secret was out. The new nine, integrated with the old, may well be in play by the time you and this golfbag caddie arrive, but I included it anyway to encourage you to make an enjoyable stop for a game in a remarkable setting.

#1 - Par 4.
C: 406 yards
R: 401 yards
F: 381 yards

Ideally you want to cut over the cottonwoods about 200 yards out on the right and leave yourself a nice mid or short iron into a green with sand front left and front right. On this one, like most greens hereabouts, it's best to be below the pin because of the back to front slope.

#2 - Par 3.
C: 141 yards
R: 125 yards
F: 121 yards

Stay below the pin on this one as well. This green has a distinct back to front grade. Just be straight and those big cottonwoods shouldn't come into play.

#3 - Par 4.
C: 370 yards
R: 344 yards
F: 269 yards

A short dogleg right, a creek 40 yards in front of tee box, with fairway sand in left landing area about 260 yards out. Green, with another back to front slope, is guarded by sand front left and front right.

#4 - Par 4.
C: 405 yards
R: 339 yards
F: 319 yards

Be straight off the tee because there are serious mounding problems left and right. On this double-tiered green, you're going to encounter some interesting putting situations.

#5 - Par 5.
C: 600 yards
R: 581 yards
F: 500 yards

A great golf hole. A dogleg left with a creek crossing the fairway after the turn about 130 yards out from the green. Ideal tee shot landing is in the turn which would leave the choice of laying up to the creek or flying it into long, narrow green with back to front slope.

#6 - Par 4.
C: 360 yards
R: 329 yards
F: 309 yards

Lots of potential tree problems left and right, and there are mounds on both sides of the fairway too. There's sand front left of the green. But the important thing on this hole is being below the pin. It'll cost you if you're not.

#7 - Par 3.
C: 195 yards
R: 195 yards
F: 135 yards

Just a great par 3, that's all. Trees all around and the Marias River's on the left. It's a double-tiered green so land the ball below the pin.

#8 - Par 5.
C: 460 yards
R: 446 yards
F: 400 yards

"Lay up" tee shot short of the water in the middle of the fairway about 250 yards out. There's fairway sand right about 30 yards short of the green too. This green slopes sharply from right to left so rightside landing is best.

#9 - Par 4.
C: 412 yards
R: 402 yards
F: 382 yards

Nice finisher with fairway sand about 230 yards out bang in the landing area but you want to lean to that side with your tee shot. The green slopes back to front and has sand front right.

Shelby, Montana 59474
Telephone: (406) 434-5940

Meadow Lake Resort

"Resort golf at its finest..."

Par 72/73

Tucked away in the pines north of Columbia Falls, Montana, is the Meadow Lake golf and skiing resort, a haven for those who like to spend their off-time – time-share or vacation – on the golf course, literally. Resort golf can be an acquired taste because in some cases, sadly, the courses do not match the accommodation or other facilities. That's not the case here. The 18-hole circuit, with its wide variety of tee boxes provides a leisurely game for the less accomplished player, or a good challenge for those who fancy themselves a bit. The course has contrasts too because it meanders in an out of the forest on truly rural holes, while others are played among the condos and ponds that make up a resort. A good place to stay and a good place to play.

#1 - Par 4.
C: 418 yards
R: 399 yards
F: 249 yards

Slight dogleg left. Tee shot is hit over creek which then winds down left side of fairway. And watch pond well right. Tee shot should be hit centre right to open up narrow green to mid-iron approach.

#2 - Par 3.
C: 159 yards
R: 150 yards
F: 127 yards

A personal nemesis this one. I can't figure out why, so why listen to me? It's a straight hit to a large green guarded front left by sand. The problem is the green has a killer back-to-front slope. All I'll say is be below the pin (I think!).

#3 - Par 5.
C: 579 yards
R: 569 yards
F: 518 yards

This tree-lined giant is a classic par 5. Hit tee shot centre left as there are trees on the inside of the gentle dogleg right that have to be avoided eventually. Sand intrudes across the right front of the green which slopes back left to front.

#4 - Par 4.
C: 310 yards
R: 310 yards
F: 255 yards

Tough... and unusual. Dogleg left with second leg up dramatic hill to plateau green on top. Trees left make direct strike to green virtually impossible. So safe way is to hit fairway wood or iron tee shot as close as you can to foot of slope. Club up for your uphill approach.

#5 - Par 3.
C: 170 yards
R: 149 yards
F: 76 yards

Stunningly picturesque, and a good golf hole, too. Tee shot window from tiered tee boxes is narrowed by trees intruding left and right down the slope. Then there's the matter of the creek just in front of the smallish green far below. Good tee shot will give you a good birdie chance.

#6 - Par 4.
C: 432 yards
R: 432 yards
F: 358 yards

Demanding dogleg left. The further left you dare the better as long as you make the turn. There's sand on the right outside of the turn. A longish drive will still leave you a mid to long iron approach into a difficult green trapped in front and with a ridge running back to front.

#7 - Par 5
C: 526 yards
R: 502 yards
F: 462 yards

Shotmaker's par 5. Patience and positioning are important. It's a double dogleg left and right. Tee shot should be hit centre left. A good one may tempt long hitters to go for the green, just visible through the trees right, in two. (Good luck, you're on the verge of a triple bogey). The rest of us play a sensible shot down towards a large landing area where there's a full view of the green up the slope through the trees. Par is good going here.

#8 - Par 4.
C: 363 yards
R: 363 yards
F: 315 yards

OB left, hidden sand in the fairway landing area left, and water right. Keep tee shot centre left for "dry" approach into green which has water right, and sand front left and front right. The green slopes back left to front right.

#9 - Par 4.
C: 369 yards
R: 339 yards
F: 316 yards

Houses and OB left on this dogleg right. Aim fade between two copses of tall trees favoring left side. Tricky approach is then over creek to green with a serious back left-front right slope. It shouldn't come into play, but also be aware of water off to the left of green.

#10 - Par 4.
C: 352 yards
R: 335 yards
F: 291 yards

Uphill on a fairway with a serious right-to-left lean. The fairway sand right is 140 yards from the green, trapped left and right, for approach shot.

#11 - Par 4.
C: 377 yards
R: 377 yards
F: 230 yards

Dogleg right. Down, then up. Fairway trap on outside of turn is 250 yards out. Right of it is a good line to try for off the tee. Take at least one club extra for difficult approach up steepish slope to green set atop hill. Aim to hit right side of green if possible.

#12 - Par 3.
C: 156 yards
R: 146 yards
F: 114 yards

Proceed with care. Putting can be a treacherous affair here. The green on this seemingly simple hole is sloped heavily back to front. It's well-trapped too.

#13 - Par 5.
C: 611 yards
R: 509 yards
F: 447 yards

Excellent long hole. Fairway sloping severely left to right demands tee shot centre left. But after that, it's best to be in position centre or right for easier final assault on elevated green tucked high and left at the end of the trip.

#14 - Par 5.
C: 503 yards
R: 480 yards
F: 427 yards

No rest for the wicked. Another attractive par 5. Good target line for elevated tee shot is left of left edge of leftmost fairway trap on the right about 250 yards out from back tees. A good drive here will help set up a good birdie chance but watch that water lurking near the green front right.

#15 - Par 4/5.
C: 449 yards
R: 437 yards
F: 411 yards

Interesting hole. A large tree in the centre of the fairway guards the green in a dip about 30 yards behind it. I prefer going in from the right with my approach shot so I try for a tee shot favoring that side.

#16 - Par 3.
C: 179 yards
R: 165 yards
F: 130 yards

Straight forward hit across water, between trees, to an elevated green. Simple, right? Hmm . . .

#17 - Par 4.
C: 348 yards
R: 340 yards
F: 307 yards

Although it has a dogleg right feel about it, this one is actually pretty straight. Tee shot should be down centre left, probably over the highest crest in the fairway.

#18 - Par 4.
C: 339 yards
R: 328 yards
F: 245 yards

This finisher requires some care and thought. My way is to hit iron out towards trees on outside of dogleg left turn. Beware the water just beyond them about 195 yards out. Cross-water approach often made more difficult by shadows on green from trees surrounding it.

100 St. Andrews Drive
Columbia Falls, Montana 59912
Telephone: (406) 892-2111

The picturesque 170-yard, par 3, 5th hole

Mission Mountain Country Club

"*Majestic links with mountain views . . .*"

Par 72

Mission Mountain, the southernmost course on Montana's Flathead Valley circuit, is situated in beautiful rolling hill country west of the town of Ronan. In reality, this is the Mission Valley. Folk round here boast, with some justification, that the track, built eight years ago on seven feet of top soil, has some of the state's finest fairways and largest and truest greens. The fifteenth, a creek-split-fairway par 5, is said to be one of Montana's, maybe the country's, toughest long holes. I'm not arguing. With protected wetlands and their wildlife inhabitants forming part of the natural landscape, and stunning views of the Mission Mountains range to the east, it is an idyllic place to play.

#1 - Par 5.
C: 543 yards
R: 520 yards
F: 449 yards

A stiff test to start. They say it can be reached in two. For the rest of us, patience is a virtue. Just be straight down through the young trees to a flat green guarded by sand left and right.

#2 - Par 4.
C: 352 yards
R: 342 yards
F: 267 yards

Aim the downhill tee shot centre right to open up another flattish green to a lofted approach. This one is guarded by sand at every corner.

#3 - Par 3.
C: 190 yards
R: 185 yards
F: 155 yards

Elevated tee shot from back tees, flat from front. This big green sits pretty flat too but is well guarded by sand front right and back left, and those trees are tucked in fairly tight behind.

#4 - Par 4.
C: 391 yards
R: 385 yards
F: 302 yards

Dogleg right with water on the left coming into play about 300 yards out from the blues, 290 from the whites and 220 from the reds. Favor rightside tee shot for approach into green with water sneaking in on left front and on left side and with major beach problems right.

#5 - Par 4.
C: 331 yards
R: 324 yards
F: 213 yards

A crafty iron tee shot hitting large landing area centre right beyond the end of the water can pay off bigtime here. That sets up a lofted shot over dangerous creek, 256 yards out from blue tees, in front of green.

#6 - Par 5.
C: 485 yards
R: 485 yards
F: 360 yards

Yes, this one can be reached in two so there's a birdie chirping. But it takes two good accurate shots between OB left and trees right to get there. And watch out. The elevated green is surprisingly shallow, not much room front to back. Big sand problem front left.

#7 - Par 4.
C: 360 yards
R: 341 yards
F: 250 yards

Sharp dogleg right with trees inside the turn. It's about a 280-yard carry to the green cutting the turn and there's some strategically-placed sand there to discourage it. Sensible play may be long iron or fairway wood into turn and go from there.

#8 - Par 3.
C: 165 yards
R: 149 yards
F: 106 yards

Birdie time. A huge, flat green is guarded by sand front right.

#9 - Par 4.
C: 413 yards
R: 406 yards
F: 319 yards

Plays long. Flat tee shot requires only being straight into generous landing area with trees scattered left and right. Green, guarded by beach front right and left side has a sharp slope front end.

#10 - Par 4.
C: 399 yards
R: 390 yards
F: 304 yards

Lovely hole but it can drastically adjust your scorecard. OB left and right with protected wetlands inside dogleg right. Hit tee shot to flat area just before the turn about 250 yards out from blues. That sets up ideal approach over deep dip in front of green with wetlands front right

#11 - Par 3.
C: 170 yards
R: 161 yards
F: 111 yards

Downhill tee shot from championship and regular tee boxes must fly OB-protected wetlands to hit large green with tree trouble left and nasty rough right behind.

#12 - Par 4.
C: 395 yards
R: 357 yards
F: 341 yards

Shortish dogleg left with no serious problems if you're straight. Aim tee shot centre-centre right to set up hit into green covered left by sand and right by trees.

#13 - Par 4.
C: 387 yards
R: 382 yards
F: 332 yards

Nasty little par 4 with trees right and a very long green which may vary approach shot selection by two clubs depending on pin placement. Also, hit this green, protected by trees right and behind and sand left, on the right side to take advantage of right-to-left slope.

#14 - Par 4.
C: 288 yards
R: 282 yards
F: 278 yards

On a good day, this large two-tiered green on the hill is maybe, just maybe, driveable by long hitters. There's sand in front and a grass bunker right front. Lay up and hit lofted shot in is my way.

#15 - Par 5.
C: 563 yards
R: 557 yards
F: 423 yards

Ain't life grand? Choose left or right of the creek that dissects the fairway. Go left and it's 284 yards to the bridge from the blues, 262 from the whites. My whim is right over the lone pine. Then it's a hit of about 180 yards through trees into next landing area to set up approach. If you hit green too far right you'll end up in the water. Wow!

#16 - Par 3.
C: 160 yards
R: 156 yards
F: 123 yards

Some relief after the rigors of the fifteenth? Not a chance. Tough par 3 with traps on the left and water on the right.

#17 - Par 4.
C: 393 yards
R: 384 yards
F: 380 yards

Long-playing hole. Unless pin is right, tee shot should favor right side for access to green tucked in tight left.

#18 - Par 5.
C: 495 yards
R: 495 yards
F: 412 yards

Locals say this is a give-away finisher. Hmm. Aim tee shot left onto left-to-right sloped fairway. Good second and third and maybe there is a birdie chance after all.

640 Stagecoach Trail
Ronan, Montana, 59864
Telephone: (406) 676-4653

The green on the amazing 563-yard, par 5, 15th hole

Polson Country Club

"A challenging lakeside charmer..."

Par 72

Perched on the southern shore of the western United States' largest stretch of fresh water, Flathead Lake, are the holiday town of Polson and its intriguing 18-hole golf course. The fine track comprises a newish first nine providing open links-type golf with large greens, sand and water, and its older back nine, a colossus of a parkland course, with huge trees, smallish, sloping greens and climbing and dropping fairways. The back nine is nearly sixty years old, the maturing front less than ten. Advice. If shooting a good score is the be-all and end-all of your game, you better lay a good foundation on the new front nine. This is a serene place to play with breathtaking views of the Flathead and the Mission Mountains to the southeast.

#1 - Par 4.
C: 404 yards
R: 363 yards
F: 327 yards

A downhill dogleg left off elevated tees. A good drive aimed leftish over mounds on inside of turn sets up a shortish iron into green for a good starting birdie chance. There's sand right and there's a ridge halfway across the green from the left.

#2 - Par 4.
C: 355 yards
R: 314 yards
F: 293 yards

This elevated tee shot should favor centre right for better approach into a narrow elevated green with water right and behind. Green has left-to-right front slope.

#3 - Par 5.
C: 608 yards
R: 565 yards
F: 441 yards

Take your stamina pill. Tee shot from back requires 100-yard carry across water in front and then it's all slightly uphill from there. Tee shot centre right somehow feels better with trees and road left. The green has a gentle ridge across the middle of the green affecting putts from back to front and vice versa.

#4 - Par 3.
C: 195 yards
R: 148 yards
F: 112 yards

Slightly downhill, so watch your club selection. The green, with sand front right, slopes back to front.

#5 - Par 4.
C: 432 yards
R: 375 yards
F: 305 yards

A good golf hole. OB left and a mini double dogleg, left and then right. There's water straight out from tee box about 300 from the blue tees, and 250 from the white. Favor left with tee shot because the approach has to flirt with water hugging fairway right, and the right front of the green.

#6 - Par 4.
C: 428 yards
R: 365 yards
F: 307 yards

Straightaway hole but there's a 40 foot climb to the green to be negotiated at the last minute. Be leftish off the tee despite OB left, otherwise that daunting sand on the right front comes into play.

#7 - Par 4.
C: 382 yards
R: 342 yards
F: 296 yards

Good dogleg right. The green is hidden by mounds on inside of turn. Just over the mounds or just left of them is a good spot to set up approach into rolling green. You putt what you get on this one.

#8 - Par 3.
C: 205 yards
R: 160 yards
F: 119 yards

Downhill slightly, so watch club selection. The green has a severe ridge running across causing sharp downslope across its front third.

#9 - Par 5.
C: 528 yards
R: 471 yards
F: 422 yards

Tee shot landing just right of mounds on inside of dogleg left is ideal spot. But be careful, there's a slight climb towards the green so think of clubbing up for approach. There's major sand guarding the two-tier, back-to-front sloped green with left and right banks funnelling down into the middle.

#10 - Par 5.
C: 495 yards
R: 467 yards
F: 454 yards

Glorious downhill opener to the original nine. Huge trees provide avenue down which to hit centre tee shot towards the lake. Downward incline first steepens and then flattens towards a smaller green which rolls gently from back left to the front.

#11 - Par 3.
C: 192 yards
R: 182 yards
F: 165 yards

Club down for this downhill shortie. The impressive Flathead is immediately behind and there are trees left that can provide some problems for a hook or pull. There's a slight slope back to front so below the pin is good.

#12 - Par 4.
C: 290 yards
R: 280 yards
F: 247 yards

Good hole. What it lacks in yards it makes up for in challenge. Tee shot must be hit centre left onto left-to-right leaning fairway to set up approach dealing with sand in front right of green.

#13 - Par 4.
C: 328 yards
R: 284 yards
F: 247 yards

Slight dogleg right. Try to ignore tall trees left and right close to the tee box and hit a centre-left tee shot. Good one will leave a short iron over fringe of water to green with severe left to right lean.

#14 - Par 4.
C: 395 yards
R: 359 yards
F: 350 yards

The pressure is building. Another good hole. A dogleg left where you really have to favor rightside tee shot. Aim at tall pine on outside of turn. Anything left runs a serious risk of hitting steep embankment which will run it down onto road and OB. Back to front sloped green has serious drop-offs left and behind.

#15 - Par 5.
C: 495 yards
R: 472 yards
F: 370 yards

Mind-blowing. Just a great, great hole. Uphill dogleg right with trees both sides. Be left, left, left all the way. Fairway slides left to right and that lean increases all the way up to the plateau

#16 - Par 4.
C: 436 yards
R: 413 yards
F: 318 yards

#17 - Par 4.
C: 418 yards
R: 365 yards
F: 310 yards

#18 - Par 3.
C: 170 yards
R: 154 yards
F: 132 yards

green. And guess what? There's a near-cliff of a drop-off on the right side of it. Par is a major achievement.

What goes up must come down. Downhill dogleg left down through trees both sides. Good tee shot will be a centre-aimed draw down the slope. Success will leave a comfortable iron into green.

What goes down . . . Straight hit sets up approach to green. Optical illusion here. The huge pine that appears to be in front of the green isn't, it's an ideal target for approach to green lying in front of it. The green is a staircase with three distinct levels back to front.

Unusual to finish with a shortie, but it's a good one. There's a noticeable right-to-left fairway lean and there's sand five yards off the left side. Green has a diagonal ridge running through it roughly back centre to front right.

111 Bayview Drive
Polson, Montana 59861
Telephone: (406) 883-2440

The 192-yard, par 3, 11th hole

Signal Point Golf Club

"A five iron from ol' Shep's grave..."

Par 36/37

The intrepid Lewis and Clark and the ever-faithful collie cross 'ol Shep passed this way before us. They've all got statues in this historic outpost, once the last stop for Missouri riverboats and the start of the Whoop-up Trail, to prove it. Shep, who won the locals' hearts by keeping vigil at the station every day for five years after his master had been shipped back east for burial, is buried on a bluff overlooking the town and a mid iron from the first tee. This place, 40 miles northeast of Great Falls is historically special, and the course is one of the most enjoyably challenging I found during my own expedition of '95. Serious advice. Anyone heading south, instead of making a near-automatic first stop in Great Falls, should make a detour and play a twilight nine or eighteen on this course overlooking the spectacular Missouri River valley. It's worth the trip.

#1 - Par 4.
C: 421 yards
R: 402 yards
F: 383 yards

A nice straight opener with OB left and sand just off the fairway right in the landing area. The mid or long iron approach gives you your first encounter with one of this course's main characteristics, a semi-elevated green, with sand front left and front right. There's quite a downslope on the front end.

#2 - Par 5.
C: 526 yards
R: 510 yards
F: 444 yards

OB all along the left and trees right. Tee shot should favor centre right as the fairway has a sharp right-to-left lean developing closer to the green. It is another raised one, has a vicious front end downslope, and sand both front edges.

#3 - Par 4.
C: 376 yards
R: 364 yards
F: 352 yards

A superb dogleg left with a huge high plains cemetery all along the left. Aim tee shot centre left round the three fairway-edge trees. There's only tough prairie grass right and water just right and short of the raised green nestling in a courtroom of trees. Sand front right, left and behind. Another cruel front-end downslope.

#4 - Par 3.
C: 162 yards
R: 152 yards
F: 142 yards

Enjoy the moment. This one's picturesque in the extreme. Shot is over or along water right to a two-tiered green huddled in surrounding trees. Sand front left and another steep slope on the front edge. (It's maybe about here that you're starting to wonder why you're not scoring better.)

#5 - Par 4.
C: 388 yards
R: 373 yards
F: 358 yards

This is a straight one eventually reaching a mounded green again surrounded by trees with sand guarding both front edges. Here too they should erect a steep grade sign on the front.

(It's the greens! They're tough to stick and tough to putt. Yeah. That's what it is. Yeah.)

#6 - Par 4/5.
C: 447 yards
R: 436 yards
F: 426 yards

Dogleg left. A good draw down centre left will give the best approach into yet another elevated green guarded by sand front left and right. Surprise! A severely two-tiered green with a tricky front-end grade.

#7 - Par 3.
C: 218 yards
R: 200 yards
F: 157 yards

The bloody nerve! As if the hole's not long enough, the green's a staircase. Three tiers, substantial drops between, run from back left to front. (Aach! Maybe just pocket the scorecard this time round and enjoy the walk.)

#8 - Par 4.
C: 390 yards
R: 376 yards
F: 362 yards

Dogleg right. Favor centre right with tee shot. Long hitters can cut the corner. Mid or long iron approach takes you into narrow green with a twist. This time there's a depressed (depressing?) basin in the front. Sand front right and front left.

#9 - Par 5.
C: 529 yards
R: 514 yards
F: 499 yards

Uphill dogleg left, the Missouri valley down along the left. Aim tee shot at clump of three trees over the crest of the hill. After the turn, the fairway leans seriously right to left. The elevated green, sand front left and side right, has, surprise, tricky downslope at front. (Wow! How low's the sun? Can we do it again?)

Fort Benton, Montana 59442
Telephone: (406) 622-3666

The beautiful 162-yard, par 3, 4th hole

R.O. Speck Golf Course

"A parkland setting above the Missouri ..."

Par 72/73

Great Falls residents and visitors alike are lucky that in the city's two public courses, they have been given, by design or accident, two contrasting styles of golf. At Anaconda Hills, target golf is very much the name of the game. Here at R. O. Speck, the golfer can let it out on the sometimes-open, sometimes-treed track measuring nearly 7 000 yards from the back tees. The combined parkland-links setting is named after a former parks superintendent in the city and is perched on a high bluff overlooking the Missouri River. With major differences between back and front tees, R.O. Speck is an ideal spot for family golf.

#1 - Par 4.
C: 390 yards
R: 368 yards
F: 348 yards

A solid opener doglegging right slightly uphill through an avenue of trees. Aim tee shot slightly left of tree that looks as if it's in the right of the fairway. In fact it isn't, it's further on. A fade would help greatly. Green has heavy slope back to front.

#2 - Par 3.
C: 164 yards
R: 140 yards
F: 140 yards

Slightly uphill to green which drops off sharply on back half. A semi circle of trees covers sides and back closely.

#3 - Par 4.
C: 406 yards
R: 388 yards
F: 334 yards

This one sweeps hard left with trees down both sides. Good tee shot centre right sets up a strong birdie opportunity here.

#4 - Par 5.
C: 540 yards
R: 525 yards
F: 471 yards

The first of four monster par 5s measuring well over 500-plus from back tees. This one doglegs right with the ideal tee shot hitting ground centre right. Beware mounds and banks on both sides which can throw ball alarming distances either to your benefit or your chagrin. Green slopes heavily back to front.

#5 - Par 3.
C: 166 yards
R: 161 yards
F: 131 yards

Basically, you have a choice. Play either over or through trees about 50 yards in front of green. Over looks nicer. Elevated green, sloping back right to front left, has severe drop-offs behind and on both sides. Tough to stick.

#6 - Par 4.
C: 409 yards
R: 396 yards
F: 349 yards

Swings gently left and uphill towards green. Tee shot centre left sets up good approach into green which has heavy slope on the front end.

#7 - Par 5.
C: 502 yards
R: 484 yards
F: 423 yards

The shortest of the giants, not that that is much consolation. Starts flat and then climbs to green which has drop-offs back and sides and slopes to the front.

#8 - Par 3.
C: 141 yards
R: 117 yards
F: 117 yards

Last of three shorties on front nine. Enjoy. There's only one on the homeward nine. Straight forward but watch cart path and trees right.

#9 - Par 4.
C: 422 yards
R: 389 yards
F: 357 yards

Dogleg right. Good hole. Aim tee shot at rightmost floodlight pylon at distant ballpark. Reasonable length will land you in turn for mid or long iron approach into green.

#10 - Par 4.
C: 416 yards
R: 393 yards
F: 346 yards

A nice golf hole. Fairway through avenue of trees has a greater right-to-left slope than it looks, so centre right is a good tee shot idea. Tall trees ring the green threateningly.

#11 - Par 5.
C: 546 yards
R: 529 yards
F: 475 yards

Glorious Titan with epic view of wide Missouri across the highway left. You guessed it. The trouble lies left. The fairway subtly swings left then right towards distant green with back to front tilt. Consistent shotmaking will set up very solid birdie chance though.

#12 - Par 4.
C: 432 yards
R: 414 yards
F: 336 yards

Things begin to get like Piccadilly Circus around here with various greens and tee boxes clustered on top of the hill. This one is a dogleg right slightly uphill to an elevated green wedged on the hillside. The 17th green is immediately behind and slightly higher. Carts badly parked between the greens can easily cause target confusion.

#13 - Par 4.
C: 399 yards
R: 389 yards
F: 356 yards

Good dogleg left drifting down through another daunting funnel of trees. Best tee shot will land centre left leaving long-mid iron approach down to green with sharp drop-off at rear. Birdie time?

#14 - Par 4.
C: 329 yards
R: 312 yards
F: 269 yards

Sweeps left and uphill. Watch your target here too. Green is tucked away on the left, not the one visible on the right. Club up for your approach to elevated platform. Nice hole, this one.

#15 - Par 4/5.
F: 456 yards
R: 445 yards
F: 406 yards

Aim tee shot centre right on this seemingly long trek and keep going.

#16 - Par 5.
C: 541 yards
R: 524 yards
F: 439 yards

All the major trouble lies left with the railway tracks right there to hammer the point home. But despite that, you don't want to be travelling this road too far right as the green is tucked in tight right at the end of the sweep. Centre, centre left is the way to go.

#17 - Par 3.
C: 171 yards
R: 159 yards
F: 159 yards

Time for a breather? Okay, but be careful. Club up for this uphill shortie. It's best to aim at left side of green funneling down into the middle from both sides. Any trouble lies rightside.

#18 - Par 4.
C: 400 yards
R: 392 yards
F: 361 yards

Aim right of rightmost floodlight pylon and if you can do it with a slight fade all the better for a comfortable mid iron approach into the green. Good opportunity to wrap things up with a birdie.

29 & River Drive North
Great Falls, Montana 59401
Telephone: (406) 761-1078

The 416-yard, par 4, 10th hole

Village Greens Golf Club

"It's a lot tougher than it looks . . .

Par 70

Like many other golfers, I really should know better by now than to pre-judge a course by its cover. As I drove into the parking lot at this club on the north side of Kalispell, thoughts of the course looking "quite attractive" and "all right" drifted through my mind. An hour later I'd changed my mind, significantly rethinking the mis-assessment. And I swear I did it before the cheery woman member who had inquired what I was doing told me: "Well, make sure you give us a good write-up. It's a lot tougher than it looks." Yes, Ma'am, I am and it is. Village Greens is an estate-type links course, young but settling, and with holes often demanding the best of the best. Tee box maps here show traps on various holes. In some cases they do contain sand. But most as yet remain deep and tricky grass traps. I know which I prefer! This is a serious links course, with superb greens and fairways, that is only going to get better.

#1 - Par 5.
C: 589 yards
R: 550 yards
F: 530 yards

No messin' here. You're standing on the tee box of the course's highest handicapped hole. So let's get to it! It's a dogleg right around water. It's approximately 260 yards to the sand on the outer edge of the turn straight out. Then the way into the green is threatened by fairway sand left and right 80 to 100 yards out. Green slopes front to back. Tough opener.

#2 - Par 4.
C: 417 yards
R: 400 yards
F: 375 yards

Tee shot should favor left side of fairway with a generous landing area. Water right. Green has fairly severe downward slope at front.

#3 - Par 4.
C: 311 yards
R: 300 yards
F: 265 yards

Late dogleg left with traps both sides in the landing area. The turn comes after the left traps. Green is well-trapped with front downslope and back right fall-off.

#4 - Par 3.
C: 150 yards
R: 140 yards
F: 105 yards

No sand in the traps yet, but you'll maybe wish there was. This rolling green can make putting miserable.

#5 - Par 3.
C: 140 yards
R: 125 yards
F: 97 yards

Another shortie. That's nice . . . or is it? Water begins immediately in front of front tee box. *Deep* grass traps.

#6 - Par 4.
C: 422 yards
R: 412 yards
F: 355 yards

Dogleg left. Just in case the fountain's not on, you should know hole turns round water which starts about 200 yards out. Big grass traps on outside of turn and approach has to run gauntlet of large fairway mounds and grass traps round the green. Front half of green slopes sharply down.

#7 - Par 5.
C: 490 yards
R: 480 yards
F: 445 yards

Dogleg left with mounds and grass traps lining both sides of landing area and in approach. Safety off the tee is as near centre as possible. And there's sand right on the approach into the green which has a ridge running back to front.

#8 - Par 3.
C: 172 yards
R: 161 yards
F: 127 yards

It's straight, but there's a major sand headache stretching almost entirely across the front of the green from the right. Adding to our woes is the fact the green is wide but very shallow. Tricky.

#9 - Par 4.
C: 342 yards
R: 335 yards
F: 286 yards

Testing front nine finish, a dogleg left with fairway sand inside the turn. It's a threat, but right of it is a good target line for tee shot. Or, you can cut the corner . . . green is elevated, has a downslope front and a grass trap front right.

#10 - Par 4.
C: 402 yards
R: 382 yards
F: 362 yards

Go for it on a straightaway hole where the only major problems are mounds along the fairway and grass traps around the green.

#11 - Par 3.
C: 140 yards
R: 123 yards
F: 89 yards

Tee shot across water. Think *big* green, but it funnels into a little dip in the front end so there are some pretty interesting putts to be had on arrival.

#12 - Par 4.
C: 351yards
R: 331 yards
F: 285 yards

Dogleg right with water starting along that side early. Aim tee shot to the traps at the side of the green which has a bit of a right-to-left slope.

#13 - Par 4.
C: 407 yards
R: 370 yards
F: 354 yards

Attractive hole with water along the right landing area so favor centre left off the tee. In addition there are problems all the way up with grass traps and mounds which make for interesting lies. The green, sloped back to front, nestles at the foot of a hill.

#14 - Par 4.
C: 387 yards
R: 360 yards
F: 320 yards

What a great hole! Dogleg right with water along the inside of the turn. At the end of the water is a high ponderosa pine, about 250 yards out from the back tees. All this means an elevated tee shot aimed to right of trap on the left about 230 yards out, followed, hopefully, by a short or mid iron to green.

#15 - Par 5.
C: 500 yards
R: 482 yards
F: 453 yards

Go leftside with tee shot because there's water in the right landing area. Phew! it's a long one if it's into a headwind and there are mounds and traps long the left. The green has significant right-left front slope.

#16 - Par 3.
C: 135 yards
R: 120 yards
F: 110 yards

Getting there's probably the easiest part. Putts can be interesting on this big rolling green with heavy-duty sand front right.

#17 - Par 4.
C: 375 yards
R: 340 yards
F: 325 yards

Water left early and water right in the landing area. Best to stay left and try to hit the landing area beyond the end of the water left. That should leave a comfortable mid iron approach to the green.

#18 - Par 4.
C: 350 yards
R: 340 yards
F: 325 yards

Shoot centre right from this tee as there's nothing but headaches left in the shape of traps and water. Again, all being well, a medium iron will take you into a green marked by its strong back-to-front tilt.

500 Palmer Drive
Kalispell, Montana 59901
Telephone: (406) 752-4666

The 140-yard, par 3, 5th hole

Whitefish Lake Golf Club

"Contrasts in character..."

The old and the new... that's the tale of this long-established club on the fringe of town and overlooked by Big Mountain and its visible-for-miles ski slopes. The older North course sets out from beside the lovely old log clubhouse and restaurant; the new South course, open for three years now, begins in the shadow of the Grouse Mountain Lodge across the Eureka highway. This is the only 36 hole facility in the Flathead Valley. The North course has a "natural" feel with fairways and smallish greens melding into the contours, hills and trees of the landscape. It's old and established, but it's still a test, particularly the back nine containing some glorious holes which bite. The South course has a modern "design" approach with more sand, water and larger tiered greens. Of the two, it's the toughest, but players who prefer traditional courses will still enjoy the North track most.

Par 72

North

#1 - Par 4.
C: 392 yards
R: 381 yards
F: 342 yards

Straightaway opener with trees down both sides. Seems to play longer than it looks for some reason. Back left to front right slope on green protected by bunker front left and back right.

#2 - Par 4.
C: 329 yards
R: 319 yards
F: 291 yards

It's really straight ahead although it has a "left feel" about it. Again green slopes back left to front right with sand left, right and 25 yards in front right.

#3 - Par 4.
C: 435 yards
R: 411 yards
F: 374 yards

Another straight one but the trees are always close, especially on the right. Green with front half sloping down at the front has sand on the right side.

#4 - Par 3.
C: 194 yards
R: 170 yards
F: 138 yards

A quality par 3. Water intrudes all the way along the left and partially in front. But what water? There's a big green waiting up there!

#5 - Par 5.
C: 550 yards
R: 531 yards
F: 473 yards

It just feels like forever. An endurance test. The only advice here is to be as straight as possible every time and eventually the green is attainable. The green slopes back to front.

#6 - Par 3.
C: 142 yards
R: 132 yards
F: 122 yards

Seeming relief after #5, but be careful at this pretty little hole. There's big sand with a grass island front left, sand right, and there are not too many easy putts on this rolling green which has a big drop-off behind it.

#7 - Par 4.
C: 353 yards
R: 353 yards:
F: 338 yards

There's a slight right-to-left slope on this fairway and fairway sand right so tee shot should favor centre right. On the approach, beware the trees hugging the green pretty closely right. Green slopes back left to right front.

#8 - Par 4.
C: 361 yards
R: 351 yards
F: 273 yards

Elegant but tough dogleg left. Aim uphill tee shot at high point of fairway as it crests. Anything in that area will give you a nice mid iron shot down into green nestling among trees and trapped left and right. Again it slopes back left to front right. A good golf hole.

#9 - Par 5.
C: 565 yards
R: 559 yards
F: 462 yards

A tough closer to the front nine. A blind tee shot should be aimed straight between avenue of trees starting over the crest. Then it's full steam ahead to the distant green which slopes slightly back right to front left and is guarded front right by trap.

#10 - Par 4.
C: 280 yards
R: 270 yards
F: 243 yards

A fun opener to the back nine. Drastic dogleg right with a tree in the middle of the fairway turn. If you can hit a controlled fade a long way you might make the green. But the way to go is a creative mid iron towards the tree followed by a short iron up to the elevated green trapped right and behind.

#11 - Par 3.
C: 205 yards
R: 200 yards
F: 167 yards

A challenge. Tee shot is hit slightly down over depressed fairway to green only slightly lower than tee box. Anything short means tough uphill wedge to green with a trap behind to catch the over-enthusiastic shot.

#12 - Par 4.
C: 396 yards
R: 387 yards
F: 346 yards

Good, testing hole. It's a dogleg left with fairway dropping away left to right, so be bold and aim tee shot down left. Then it's an uphill approach, preferably to the left side of the green. Even if you stray a few feet too far the bank may carry it back down onto the green.

#13 - Par 4.
C: 355 yards
R: 342 yards
F: 312 yards

Simply a magnificent hole. Check in the mirror behind the tee box to make sure it's all clear before hitting. It's a steep downhill tee shot to the green maybe 80 feet below, half hidden by mounds and trees right. It's best to aim drive at clump of tall trees left or towards the one visible greenside trap. (There are two others hidden on right of green). Long hitters could make this one . . . but please check that mirror.

#14 - Par 4.
C: 373 yards
R: 361 yards
F: 348 yards

Aim blind tee shot, favoring centre left, over crest. That should leave you a comfortable iron into a back-to-front sloped green with sand front left and front right.

#15 - Par 3.
C: 164 yards
R: 143 yards
F: 121 yards

Tricky uphill tee shot to green maybe 40 feet above tee box. There is a desert in front and two more traps behind the narrow green. Par here is good.

#16 - Par 5.
C: 542 yards
R: 512 yards
F: 472 yards

Sweeping dogleg left requires tee shot hit centre right to avoid water starting in landing area left. Stay rightside all the way because it opens up green tucked away left at the end of the trip. Final approach needs care because of sentry tree left and sand front right. Green slopes back left to right front.

#17 - Par 4.
C: 371 yards
R: 345 yards
F: 312 yards

Another fine hole, a slight dogleg right. Aim tee shot just right of trio of tall pines on left side . . . but watch water left.

#18 - Par 5.
C: 549 yards
R: 530 yards
F: 422 yards

Warning: this hole is a potential destroyer of anything good that has gone before. Aim drive centre right down roller-coaster fairway, through narrow funnel of trees. The green is hidden in a dip at the end of the fairway. The final approach should be aimed at the centre of the end wall of trees directly behind the green. The two-tiered green slopes back to front. A killer.

Par 71/72

South

#1 - Par 4.
C: 427 yards
R: 400 yards
F: 354 yards

The tee shot should be aimed centre right as that big tree on the fairway's left can be a major annoyance. That leaves a slightly uphill mid iron approach to a green guarded left and right by sand and with a distinct slope, back left to front.

#2 - Par 4.
C: 401 yards
R: 376 yards
F: 332 yards

Dogleg right. Aim drive right of two large trees straight out. If all goes according to plan, a short-to-medium iron will take it into a green sloping severely down at the front, and from right to left on top.

#3 - Par 3.
C: 174 yards
R: 153 yards
F: 124 yards

Just be straight. Tall tree guards left front and traps cover the right front and side. Green falls away from flat rightside top to left and front.

#4 - Par 4.
C: 407 yards
R: 367 yards
F: 321 yards

Good tee shot target on this dogleg left is the brown building tucked in trees on outside of turn. A slight draw will help bring the ball around for a mid or short iron into green running back right to front left in downward layers.

#5 - Par 4.
C: 389 yards
R: 368 yards
F: 301 yards

Uphill tee shot on sharp dogleg left should ideally come to earth between fairway sand left and trees around the 150 yard markers. That still leaves a toughish mid iron up to a flattish green with sand front left and back right. Hope your insurance is okay if you *really* overshoot this one.

#6 - Par 5.
C: 470 yards
R: 470 yards
F: 404 yards

A toughie. Elevated tee box requires a hit through narrow chute of trees with OB all the way left. A stony-banked pond crosses starting about 220 yards out. A good position is the flat just across the water but the uphill approach is toughened by potentially big sand trouble right and a major ridge across the green in the back left corner. Good luck!

#7 - Par 3.
C: 207 yards
R: 187 yards
F: 131 yards

Picture postcard time. It's pretty all right, pretty wicked. There's water, petrified trees, reeds and rushes all the way left and partially in front of the bunkered green. Big landing area though. If you've got a high draw shot in your arsenal, draw!

#8 - par 4.
C: 402 yards
R: 364 yards
F: 323 yards

Squeeze play. Drive has to hit narrow fairway between watery reeds left and line of trees right. This might be the time for an iron off the tee. Just a suggestion! Green, sand left, slops back right to front left. Good hole.

#9 - Par 4.
C: 317 yards
R: 317 yards
F: 272 yards

Too late to order a power cart now! Uphill and how. But it is short. The dance floor, with sand front left, front right and behind, slopes surprisingly gently back to front. Just as well there's a halfway house to replenish breath and lost perspiration.

#10 - Par 5.
C: 514 yards
R: 491 yards
F: 447 yards

Not much respite though. This is a tough par 5. Hit tee shot over or just right of fairway sand left. Favor upside of the fairway as much as you can en route to the long, narrow green which has sand on its left. It slopes back to front.

#11 - Par 4.
C: 429 yards
R: 396 yards
F: 348 yards

Breathe in again for this one, a narrow chute of trees with heavy right-to-left slopes on fairway. Aim tee shot centre right, it'll come left no matter what. Green has natural back left-front right slope.

#12 - Par 5.
C: 548 yards
R: 520 yards
F: 467 yards

A testing downhill dogleg left. Be as left as you dare off the tee as there are traps in the rightside landing area. Your way into green tucked in left is uphill with four traps threatening final approach on right. Two-tiered green slopes back to front.

#13 - Par 4.
C: 354 yards
R: 315 yards
F: 286 yards

Challenging short par 4. Downhill tee shot has to take water starting about 60 yards in front of green into account. Land short and leave a short-to-mid iron through sentry trees guarding green's left and right fronts. Well-bunkered green drops away back left.

#14 - Par 4.
C: 348 yards
R: 338 yards
F: 259 yards

Good target here is furthest left of trees on left side. That negotiated, a short-to-mid iron will take approach round or over water right front of green. Testing.

#15 - Par 3.
C: 204 yards
R: 173 yards
F: 144 yards

Tricky little so-and-so. Water along first half of fairway and immediately right of green. Best shot is fade just right of greenside tree on left. Green is ridged in the middle with fall-off back left and front right.

#16 - Par 3.
C: 146 yards
R: 136 yards
F: 115 yards

So soon? Another shortie. This time two trees guard green left thirty yards from front. With traps at every corner, over the top is as good a shot as any here if the pin is left at all.

#17 - Par 4.
C: 361 yards
R: 336 yards
F: 322 yards

Aim tee shot at big, dark pine on left side and slope should carry you down slight dogleg dip. You should have a nice view of green, treed behind and trapped at both front edges.

#18 - Par 4/5.
C: 465 yards
R: 437 yards
F: 408 yards

A majestic finishing hole sweeping down a slight gradient and then up again towards the green, trapped left, right and behind. What you see is what you get.

Box 666, Highway 93 North
Whitefish, Montana 59937
Telephone: (406) 862-4000

The amazing South Course 207-yard, par 3, 7th hole

South-East British Columbia

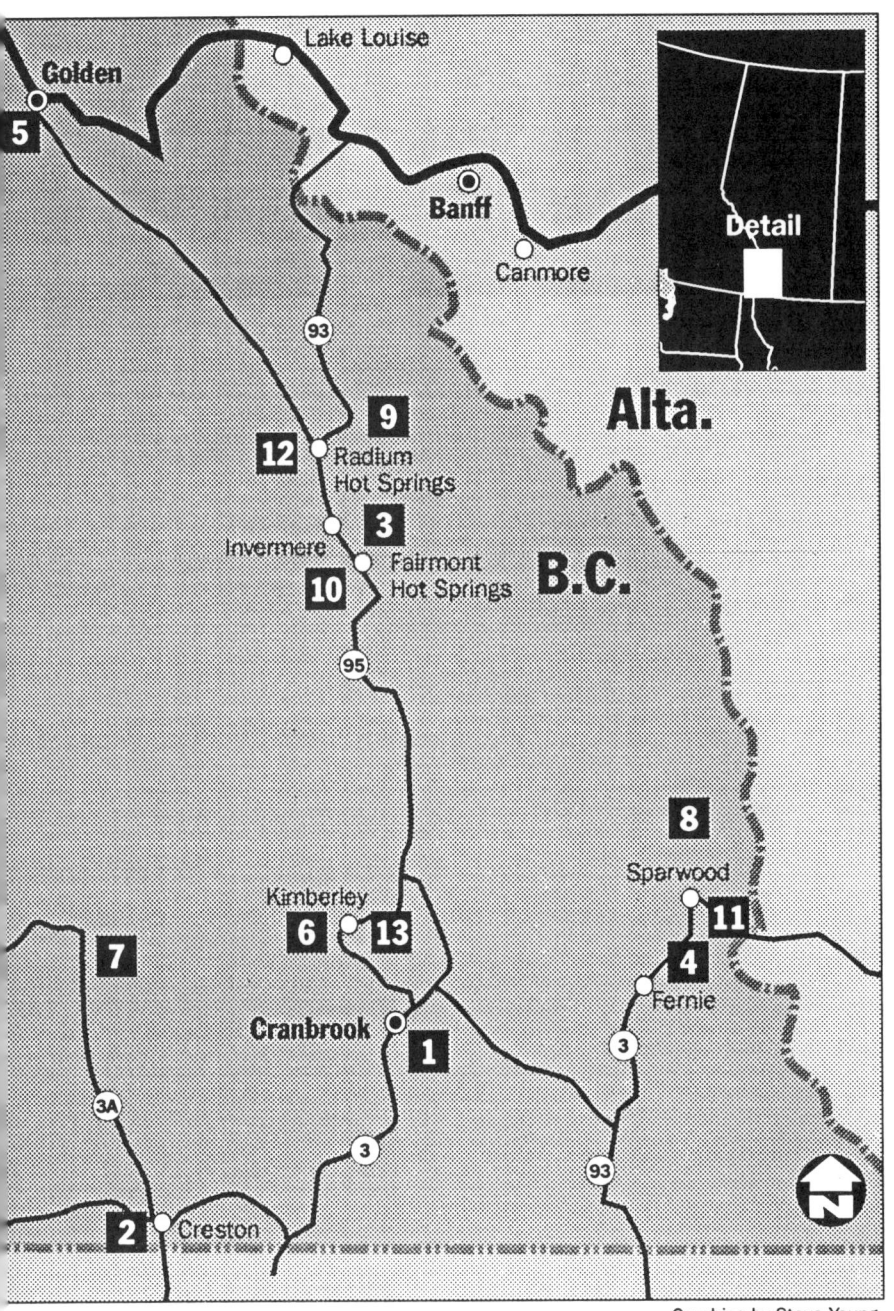

Graphics by Steve Young

1. Cranbrook Golf Club
2. Creston Golf Club
3. Fairmont Hot Springs Resort
4. Fernie Golf and Country Club
5. Golden Golf and Country Club
6. Kimberley Golf Club
7. Kokanee Springs Golf Resort
8. Mountain Meadows Golf Club
9. Radium Hot Springs Resort
10. Riverside Golf and Country Club
11. Sparwood Golf Club
12. The Springs Golf and Country Club
13. Trickle Creek Golf Resort

Cranbrook Golf Club

"Magnificent trees provide parkland serenity..."

Par 72/73

Cranbrook probably provides players with some of the purest parkland golfing pleasure they can ever get. Of its type, it's one of the best around. Its superb sloping and at-times narrow, fairways and truest of true greens, are set among magnificent mature trees making a round here just a delightful country outing though it's a mere stone's throw from the British Columbian city's downtown. I think it's fair to say also that the club boasts one of the largest and most striking clubhouse-pro shop complexes on the circuit. From the back tees, the course measures some 6500 yards and from the front 5900, so the range is there for golfers of every calibre to enjoy the challenge and sublime scenery.

#1 - Par 4.
C: 363 yards
R: 358 yards
F: 346 yards

A straight narrow starter where accurate centre tee shot is required. Mid or short iron approach has to carry a diagonal dip running away right to left in the fairway some fifty yards out from the green which has a slight back to front left slope. Two pot bunkers guard the front left and there's a trap front right. Lovely opener.

#2 - Par 4.
C: 377 yards
R: 359 yards
F: 341 yards

Slightly more open, so tee shot centre right is best to open up a green tucked away downhill and left. A cluster of trees left could provide approach problems if you're not careful. The elevated green, traps front left and front right, slopes heavily from back to front so be below the pin if possible.

#3 - Par 4.
C: 365 yards
R: 347 yards
F: 329 yards

Uphill, tree-lined and swinging away left. A 220-yard tee shot centre left is by far the best because a line of three trees guard the right approaches into the green. There's sand front left and on the right side. Nice hole.

#4 - Par 3.
C: 177 yards
R: 173 yards
F: 165 yards

Picture-pretty and tree-lined. It's fairly level and the green is fairly flat. There are potential problems though with sand front left and behind for the overhit. Be careful with club selection.

#5 - Par 5.
C: 489 yards
R: 478 yards
F: 423 yards

Fairly roomy but challenging par 5 with a fairway inclining very slightly right to left. Best tee shot is centre right to allow for the slope and setting up approach line into a green tucked tight left to the trees. Anything lost to Rush Limbaugh territory right could end up in the pond back right. Two-tiered green slopes left-right and is well-trapped.

#6 - Par 4.
C: 406 yards
R: 392 yards
F: 371 yards

Another elegant hole drifting round to the left. There's a fairly substantial landing area for a tee shot down centre left for approach into another well-trapped green. It has a back-front slope with a left-right lean on the front end.

#7 - Par 5.
C: 502 yards
R: 498 yards
F: 487 yards

A fine long hole doglegging gently right on a slight downslope. Tee shot centre, centre right is best here because if you're going for it in two, another cluster of trees impedes the approach on the left side. Green is trapped left and right and has a pot bunker more or less dead in front. Green slopes from back left to centre and back-front from there.

#8 - Par 3.
C: 188 yards
R: 180 yards
F: 150 yards

Picturesque to say the least. Mid-iron tee shot has to negotiate expanse of water intruding front left and trees tight right. There's also sand front left between the water and two-tiered green, right and behind. Go in high or if the pin's on the front think of dropping a shot short front right and running down slight bank onto the green.

#9 - Par 4.
C: 369 yards
R: 363 yards
F: 337 yards

Sharp dogleg right with a healthy landing area 170-200 yards out. An iron may well be the club to set up a comfortable shot onto a green ringed by traps. It has a front-end slope and kind of basins out in the middle up top.

#10 - Par 5.
C: 523 yards
R: 516 yards
F: 506 yards

Cracking back nine opener. It's a dogleg left but a drive straight out will do the trick if you watch a big grassy hollow about 270 yards out. The approach is slightly downhill and there's a sharp drop-off at the back of the big flat green, so be careful with approach club selection.

#11 - Par 3.
C: 179 yards
R: 172 yards
F: 162 yards

Reasonably straightforward but the big green is about 25 or 30 feet below the tee boxes so club down one or two. Green has front-end tilt and sand right.

#12 - Par 4.
C: 421 yards
R: 380 yards
F: 352 yards

If adjustments went as planned, this is going to be one superb golf hole from 1996 on. The new green is pushed back maybe fifty yards and further left on this latish dogleg left winding uphill. A centre right tee shot is best to line up approach into a green sloping back-to-front and guarded on both sides by bunkers.

#13 - Par 4/5.
C: 450 yards
R: 446 yards
F: 432 yards

It's nice to crest the hill about 200 yards out and use the downslope towards the green for extra length. But watch the trees immediately behind the green which has a front-end slope. This hole bites. It looks deceptively simple but it isn't the third-highest handicap hole around here for nothing!

#14 - Par 5.
C: 531 yards
R: 524 yards
F: 404 yards

Attractive par 5 which moves slightly right to left with a left to right fairway slope. There are potential headaches about 150-175 yards out from the flattish green in the shape of a deep gully crossing the width of the fairway, so be careful as you close in.

#15 - Par 3.
C: 156 yards
R: 149 yards
F: 140 yards

The trouble here lies right. The fairway funnels everything in that direction if you're not there, and there's a steep bank up to the green on that side with sand at the bottom. Smallish green has trouble at the back too with sand left and a severe drop-off behind.

#16 - Par 4.
C: 380 yards
R: 380 yards
F: 361 yards

Vying for inclusion in my favorite list. A picturesque downhill dogleg left. The challenge is provided by a deep trans-fairway valley about 150 yards out from the green. So don't be too long with your ideally-centre tee shot. Green is fronted by sand with a narrow entrance between and is surrounded by trees. Great hole.

#17 - Par 4.
C: 406 yards
R: 403 yards
F: 387 yards

And don't expect any respite here on the highest handicap hole for men. It's straight but complicated greatly by a fairway which drops sharply from right to left from the middle about 100 yards in front of a very shallow green. It has a marked back to front slope. Tricky!

#18 - Par 4.
C: 280 yards
R: 263 yards
F: 241 yards

Unusually short, but enjoyable finisher. This one is definitely driveable and as a consequence, birdieable. Have fun and go for it hitting across a depression with a slight fairway lean right to left. The green, fronted by traps, has a back-front slope.

2700 - 2nd Street S, Box 297
Cranbrook, British Columbia, V1C 4H8
Telephone: (604) 426-6462

Creston Golf Club

"The secret is getting out..."

Par 72

A couple of years back after a reasonably successful negotiation of this often amazing southern B.C. course, I was chatting smugly to a member in the clubhouse. Extolling the course's virtues, I remarked that none of our group had realized that such a gem was hidden in this gorgeous orchard-filled terrain. He looked at me, smiled knowingly and said: "Well maybe that's the way we like it." Far from unfriendly, just a matter of fact. This one is a personal favorite, its holes sweeping up and down the hilltops and pine-covered valleys south of the town. It has several simply stunning holes, including the unforgettable par 5 seventh, the challenging Spiral Staircase par 4 twelfth, and numerous other great ones. Sorry, my friend, but the secret is getting out. Power cart strongly recommended.

#1 - Par 5.
C: 489 yards
R: 477 yards
F: 421 yards

Great opener where tee shot should be hit down centre left. The reason is simple. Second shot must be hit left of large tree 80 yards out from the smallish green round which all the trouble lies right in the form of sand and downslope.

#2 - Par 4.
C: 418 yards
R: 395 yards
F: 357 yards

This hole plays longer than advertised because it's all uphill. Think about clubbing up for each shot. OB right and the green is trapped on both front edges. Maybe think of pitching just short of the green and running on between the two traps.

#3 - Par 4.
C: 382 yards
R: 367 yards
F: 312 yards

Aim centre or long left to clear the last tree on the inside of the turn. Watch fairway traps left too. A small two-level green can be hard to hit because it's semi-hidden. Always play to the right of the pin on this one. Big trouble left.

#4 - Par 3.
C: 178 yards
R: 160 yards
F: 104 yards

Take the elevation change into account when you go into your bag. The green slopes big-time right to left. Pin high left is your best birdie chance.

#5 - Par 4.
C: 326 yards
R: 297 yards
F: 250 yards

Iron time on a tough tight dogleg left. Ideal shot is centre left 190 yards off the white tee to land in the turn inside the traps on the outside. That leaves a wedge onto the cliffside green, a multi-tiered, well-trapped affair. Common sense says be below the pin for the best putts.

#6 - Par 3.
C: 117 yards
R: 102 yards
F: 80 yards

Downhill with a vengeance. Club down, I scream. The trick here is to land on the same layer as the flag and don't be long. The water is tight back left and behind. Wow!

#7 - Par 5.
C: 535 yards
R: 526 yards
F: 490 yards

Simply one of the great holes in Canadian golf. Hit the sweet spot on your hilltop drive and watch that ball soar out there forever onto the tree-lined fairway far below. Avoid the fairway trees and astounding length can be achieved with a nice, easy swing. You might even be able to reach in two, but the green can be tricky to hold. A lay--up might be best.

#8 - Par 4.
C: 347 yards
R: 333 yards
F: 303 yards

The large fairway tree centre-right is 225 yards out from the white tees. Drive short of it or past it on the left and you'll have a nice approach into a smallish sloped green. But trouble usually accompanies anything left of this one.

#9 - Par 4.
C: 337 yards
R: 312 yards
F: 271 yards

Either go over or around the stand of trees in front of the tee box on this fine dogleg left. This is another tricky green where it's best to be below the pin.

#10 - Par 3.
C: 227 yards
R: 207 yards
F: 176 yards

Long and tricky. Tee shot should really carry swail and pot bunkers in front. But another way is to lay up into the swail and chip on close for par. There are subtle inclinations on this green and traps behind!

#11 - Par 5.
C: 516 yards
R: 468 yards
F: 435 yards

A solid hit down the centre will hit the sloped fairway and drop the ball to an ideal position on the left. A careful second should be hit to avoid the swail on the left and give you best shot into whatever in placement there is on the day. No matter where it is though, be below it.

#12 - Par 4.
C: 353 yards
R: 343 yards
F: 295 yards

Another Creston spectacular. The mind-blowing Spiral Staircase. Downhill tee shot on this dogleg left must hit one of the two platforms in the turn. Think iron. That leaves a short iron or wedge onto an abundantly-trapped, two-tiered green. (Warning. Do not try to drive the hidden green. It's stupid and dangerous. I've been on the 'incoming' end.)

#13 - Par 3.
C: 161 yards
R: 147 yards
F: 137 yards

Tough downhill par 3 where club selection in an arena of trees is everything. Have a close look at the flag for wind indications. The tee box is sheltered. The green is very shallow on the left and there are traps over there too.

#14 - Par 4.
C: 334 yards
R: 318 yards
F: 296 yards

Make your mind up time. Options abound on this beautiful hole. Tee shot short, left or over the water in the turn. Respectively those are hits of roughly 175, 200 or 225. The closer to the green the better so it's a choice of easy tee shot, tough approach; or hard tee shot, easier approach.

#15 - Par 4.
C: 336 yards
R: 293 yards
F: 270 yards

Dogleg right where tee shot of 200 yards is bliss. That leaves a short uphill wedge onto a smallish green guarded left by a bunker. Believe posted distances on this one. It can look shorter than it is.

#16 - Par 4.
C: 447 yards
R: 396 yards
F: 330 yards

You really have to be brave. Anything too left gives a nasty approach line into a green with deep swail short left. So favor the right side with Mallory Road and OB right. An approach from over there is much more rewarding.

#17 - Par 4.
C: 391 yards
R: 381 yards
R: 308 yards

Narrow dogleg left where ideal tee shot will land 200-220 yards out centre left. The shorter your game, the further right you should be. There's major sand front left. Be warned. This one can ruin a thus-far respectable scorecard!

#18 - Par 5.
C: 539 yards
R: 508 yards
R: 469 yards

The second of a last pair with a knock-out one-two punch. It's a double dogleg right and then left. Best shot is centre, even centre left, to set up second onto plateau to be able to see the green tucked left, and guarded left and right by deep bunkers.

Box 2103
Creston, British Columbia, V0B 1G0
Telephone: (604) 428-5515

Fairmont Hot Springs Resort

"One of the great golfing destinations . . ."

Par 72

It's long been one of the premier venues for the travelling golf fraternity, especially from the Calgary area, and deservedly so. This resort with its challenging 18-hole championship layout, and the proximity of other fine tracks within an hour's drive in each direction, have made the valley in the Radium Hot Springs area one of western Canada's golfing hot spots. The course alternately rambles across hillside meadowland and then through the property used by vacationers using the fine resort and hot springs facilities. And of course, there is the Fairmontster, the never-ending 600-yard par 5 fourth hole to contend with. This course is all about challenge and fun and both can be had by golfers of all levels. A word of advice. Everything on this course tends to lean east-to-west off the mountainside. Any problems? Take a compass.

#1 - Par 5.
C: 495 yards
R: 485 yards
F: 445 yards

A fine opener. Take that mountainside effect into account and aim tcc shot centre left to roll down somewhere left of the fairway traps right. It can be reached in two but Mr. Average should lay up down right into the neck of the two-tiered green for a chip and a putt. Traps left and behind.

#2 - Par 4.
C: 400 yards
R: 390 yards
F: 330 yards

A tree-lined tester. The green is tucked away left, so ideal start off the tee is a drive down centre right to hit somewhere left of or just beyond those evil traps on the right. Another two-tiered green has bunkers front right and back left.

#3 - Par 3.
C: 160 yards
R: 143 yards
F: 123 yards

Short, but it has potential problems. It's fairly sheltered by trees in here, but watch out for the headwind coming up the valley into your face. It could knock any underhit shot down into the pond straddling the route in. There's major sand right and sharp drop-offs behind and back right.

#4 - Par 5.
C: 600 yards
R: 560 yards
F: 480 yards

The Fairmontster. Don't let length scare you. Concentrate on getting three solid shots and you'll be there. Favor the left all the way taking into account that left-right mountainside lean and avoiding OB right. Patience, and more patience, all the way to the narrow elevated green.

#5 - Par 3.
C: 190 yards
R: 180 yards
F: 165 yards

Simply beautiful. With Columbia Lake views dominating matters, try and concentrate hitting the right side of this green avoiding hideous chips from the left side. It's fairly exposed here so winds can be a factor in club selection.

#6 - Par 4.
C: 425 yards
R: 416 yards
F: 406 yards

Another demanding hole with open fairway start followed by trees crowding in on semi-invisible green towards the end. Centre-left off the tee box will set up a long mid-iron approach shot. Aim it down the right and that will avoid nasty trap front left. A really good golf hole.

#7 - Par 4.
C: 278 yards
R: 265 yards
F: 235 yards

Think this sharp dogleg right through and it's birdie time, folks. Yes, it's driveable at around 250 yards as the crow flies but it may cost you big. Best is iron or fairway wood out across the creek into the turn about 200 yards out. Then it's an uphill wedge and try to be below the pin.

#8 - Par 4.
C: 405 yards
R: 393 yards
F: 360 yards

Right. It's right all the way. Right? Hit tee shot on this well-treed challenge down centre right. Natural mountainside drift will carry it down left. And aim long mid-iron approach into the right side of this small high green too.

#9 - Par 4.
C: 425 yards
R: 413 yards
F: 378 yards

Down to the clubhouse. You can let 'er rip here provided you're confident it will go down right side. The mountain will drop it centre left. The high road is best to prevent approach having unfortunate close encounter of the watery kind left, right and in front.

#10 - Par 5.
C: 460 yards
R: 432 yards
F: 391 yards

It's possible to start the back nine with a birdie on this one. Tee shot across the water and down the middle will set up a nice position to go for the green or lay up short right of it. Chip and a putt . . .

#11 - Par 4.
C: 440 yards
R: 425 yards
F: 346 yards

OK. This one's tough. Tee shot on this undulating fairway must favor the left to set up fairway wood or long iron approach aimed at the heart of a hidden green. Miss it either side and you're in trouble. Walk out of here with a par, you deserve a medal.

#12 - Par 3.
C: 139 yards
R: 129 yards
F: 110 yards

A treed arena hole. It's short but the ball must carry the pond from tee-box to green . . . and those holiday homes are pretty intimidating. There's nasty sand front left of this unusually flat green. Look out for fickle, swirling winds.

#13 - Par 5.
C: 480 yards
R: 465 yards
F: 375 yards

Forget the view, if you can. Concentrate on a solid drive down the centre which should hit downslope and give you a pleasant surprise lengthwise. Then it's go-for-it or lay-up time. It's a tricky two-tiered, back-front, green. But feasibly, it's a rare birdie chance.

#14 - Par 4.
C: 370 yards
R: 362 yards
F: 355 yards

They call this uphill struggle Cardiac Hill hereabouts. Nice, eh? Tee shot anywhere between centre left and centre right is more than handy for mid-iron, uphill, approach into the green. Best club up no matter what. It's deceptively steep. There are nasty drop-offs all around this one.

#15 - Par 4.
C: 323 yards
R: 310 yards
F: 250 yards

Loving it or hating it depends on how you play it on the day. This dogleg left has an almost impossibly narrow neck between slopes and trees. Ideal tee shot is long iron towards the cart path right. Too far though and the neck up to the elevated green starts narrowing again. I just don't know about this one . . . but play it well and it is fun. I suppose it's all about accuracy after all.

#16 - Par 3.
C: 151 yards
R: 144 yards
F: 138 yards

Elevated green across the creek. A fun hole if you get it right. Right as in centre right of green. A high score awaits left and behind.

#17 - Par 4.
C: 386 yards
R: 380 yards
F: 316 yards

The course's late clutch hole and it's a tester. Aim tee shot down the right and the slope will carry it down into centre-left. That's a good place to be for lofted mid-iron approach to an elevated green where most of the trouble lies to the left. Rightside incoming is ideal.

#18 - Par 4.
C: 395 yards
R: 375 yards
F: 310 yards

What a finish. Scenic closer where tee shot from elevated tee boxes should be aimed centre right if possible. The green is tucked away left behind ponds short left. Go in high or right.

Box 10, Fairmont Hot Springs
British Columbia, V0B 1L0
Telephone: (604) 345-6514

The Fairmontster – The 600-yard, par 5, 4th hole

Fernie Golf and Country Club

"Coal town struck gold with its golf course..."

Par 70

It was a man called Michael Phillips who, in 1873, wandered this way and discovered a coal basin. The township was soon named after William Fernie who first developed part of the basin in 1887. But it wasn't until the Crowsnest Pass was reached by the Canadian Pacific Railway that the seam was first really actively mined in 1898. The town boomed and over the years big money was made. As Fernie flourished, a golf course was begun on its southeastern fringes. The town continues to thrive on tourism and trade navigating the pass between Alberta and British Columbia and vice versa. The demanding 18-hole championship course, with water and sand aplenty, wends its way along the valley below the imposing mountain grandeur of the pass. It's a worthy match for Kananaskis and Banff.

Warning – This great course has undergone some changes in the close season between 1995 and 1996. Not only has the clubhouse been moved, the order of holes has been rotated. What follows below is the new configuration due to be introduced June 1, 1996.

#1 - Par 4.
C: 396 yards
R: 383 yards
F: 318 yards

The trouble here is saved up for the approach so prepare accordingly by hitting fairway wood or long iron off the tee down centre or centre left. There's substantial sand starting 98 yards out from the green right and major traps front left and middle right. This green tilts from 1 p.m. to 7 p.m.

#2 - Par 4.
C: 379 yards
R: 364 yards
F: 321 yards

Is it imagination or is the screw already tightening? This superb dogleg right around the lake supports the theory. Again a fairway wood or long iron is best off the tee. A good one down the left into the corner sets up best approach into two-tiered green running back left to front right. Local knowledge says the bottom tier is "wetter" than the top.

#3 - Par 3.
C: 218 yards
R: 187 yards
F: 143 yards

Long iron or fairway wood necessary to carry along the water right to a distant green surrounded by sand.

#4 - Par 5.
C: 528 yards
R: 503 yards
F: 428 yards

On this demanding course, the longest off the back tees. It's pretty much a straightaway but tee shot over the water should be aimed centre left. In the approach watch out for major trap right about 75 yards from the green. Sand front left and front right.

#5 - Par 3.
C: 169 yards
R: 144 yards
F: 96 yards

More target golf. This one's nice too. Shot has to fly the pond just in front of the green. It's trapped front left, front right and behind and has a marked back to front slope. Be below the pin.

#6 - Par 4.
C: 401 yards
R: 375 yards
F: 288 yards

A testing hole sweeping left to right. Be centre left off the tee to avoid evil humps and water on the right side. Another problem here, for the approach shot, is a huge bunker straddling the fairway about 65 yards out from the target. The green, sand behind, slopes back to front.

#7 - Par 3.
C: 182 yards
R: 144 yards
F: 121 yards

Tricky tee shot with water threatening left and right just off the tee box and with a substantial trap waiting to devour anything short left in the fairway. The green, sloping back right to front left, is guarded by a trap right.

#8 - Par 5.
C: 513 yards
R: 500 yards
F: 428 yards

It's not imagination! Things are heating up. Toughest here. This one requires an accurate middlish tee shot. But it's the approach you have to watch. It has to be channelled through narrow gap between water left and right and there are nasty mounds about 100 yards out left. There's sand front left and back left.

#9 - Par 4.
C: 438 yards
R: 395 yards
F: 329 yards

There's disconcerting water short right off the tees. Aim tee shot straight out but long hitters beware troublesome dip about 130 yards from the green on the left. This elevated green slopes back right to front left and has sand on the right.

#10 - Par 4.
C: 416 yards
R: 392 yards
F: 314 yards

A nice dogleg right. Drive from elevated tee box should be hit down centre staying away from water threat on the inside of the turn. Long, mid iron approach should take fairway trap 70 yards short left into account. This diagonal green has sand front right and back left.

#11 - Par 3.
C: 190 yards
R: 153 yards
F: 105 yards

A character builder. Shot has to cross water which then slides dauntingly all the rest of the way left. Major mounds threaten the green's right, and there's substantial sand front centre. A right-left slope adds to the fun.

#12 - Par 4.
C: 388 yards
R: 376 yards
F: 366 yards

Solid hole sweeps left to right. Tee shot should be hit centre left for best approach view of the two-tiered green which drops from back left to front right.

#13 - Par 4.
C: 430 yards
R: 410 yards
F: 329 yards

A really sound one sweeping right with OB all along the right. Watch the line of trees starting along the right fringe about 130 yards out. Centre left is perhaps best for the drive allowing a fairly free approach into a green with sand guarding left and right.

#14 - Par 4.
C: 368 yards
R: 368 yards
F: 351 yards

Dogleg right of varying severity depending on the tee box you're playing. OB right. Good drive from elevated boxes will be aimed left of large fir tree on the right side of the fairway. A huge trap runs diagonally left-right round the left and front-left of the green.

#15 - Par 4.
C: 426 yards
R: 412 yards
F: 306 yards

Long and it plays tough. Go down the right off the tee to set up best for difficult approach into the green. For the approach, there's water starting from the left about 100 yards out from the green. There's a little landing pocket for the lay-up just beyond. Sand left, right and behind.

#16 - Par 3.
C: 173 yards
R: 159 yards
F: 135 yards

This one could vary by three clubs depending on tee box you're using and pin placement. Shot has to avoid water short right and severe sand threats front left, back left and front right. Nice one.

#17 - Par 4.
C: 368 yards
R: 355 yards
F: 308 yards

A fine hole with water along the left early and then later in the right approaches to the green. Tee shot dead centre is best. There's major beach problems front left and that pond on the right is not too far away back right. Bushes are uncomfortably close behind too.

#18 - Par 5.
C: 521 yards
R: 493 yards
F: 416 yards

A late dogleg right and a great one. Favor the left side with your tee shot out over the creek. That's good for position and avoids nasty humps on the right. Then lay up short of the trap on the outside of the turn to set up wedge onto the green trapped right and behind and with water threatening left and right.
Box 1507
Fernie, British Columbia V0B 1M0
Telephone: (604) 423-7773

After June 1, 1996, the 430-yard, par 4, 13th hole

Golden Golf and Country Club

"A Golden gem..."

Par 72/73

Watch out for the eagles' nests dotted along the fairways. They're your best shot at eagle on this outstanding course which, I think it's fair to say, is one of British Columbia's best-kept golfing secrets. Its sloping fairways wandering through the pine and spruce amid the mountains southwest of town, make for all sorts of golfing challenge and delight the eye. And the course provides another opportunity to savor the skills of course architect Les Furber in the shape of his new back nine. Heck, even the drive to the course is a challenge. The signs on the fringe of town proclaim a five-kilometre run to the facility, but after a few minutes on Dogtooth Road along the Columbia River, you can't help wondering... "Keep on going," "Almost there," urge other notices. Do keep going. This one's well worth the trip. And despite a couple of serious climbs, the course is walkable.

#1 - Par 4.
C: 358 yards
R: 335 yards
F: 286 yards

A dogleg left veering round the trees along that side. Fairway has a noticeable left-right tilt, so best tee shot is a draw down centre left far enough out to avoid the trees and compensate for the slope. Layered green, with back-front slope, has sand left and right. Nice opener.

#2 - Par 4/5.
C: 475 yards
R: 440 yards
F: 382 yards

Highest handicap hole and it's a great one. Aim elevated tee shot draw down centre avoiding the steep bank on the left and staying away from the creek all the way along the right from the turn. Ideal landing area is on a line left of the rightside 150-yard marker rock. Then it's straight to a green sloped in front and, over a middle ridge, sloped at the back. Small traps guard each side.

#3 - Par 4.
C: 400 yards
R: 365 yards
F: 281 yards

A sharp dogleg left with a creek crossing about 200 yards out just before the turn. Straight out is the way to go to make the turn and open up the approach. Watch for two traps short left of the green and bunkers right and behind. Again a centre saddle causes a slope on the front end and a slight fall-off back left.

#4 - Par 3.
C: 217 yards
R: 191 yards
F: 152yards

It's not even a formality if you do manage to hit this huge, rolling green that can leave you long-distance putts. But getting there's a headache too, with major sand intruding from the right about 50 yards from the green, more immediately short right and a beach on the left. Get par and get outta here!

#5 - Par 4.
C: 383 yards
R: 367 yards
F: 327 yards

Straightaway, but no walkover. The river's on the left and there's fairway sand 200 yards out right. Trees hug the right of the green which has sand front left and behind. It slopes back-left to centre and then centre to front.

#6 - Par 5.
C: 533 yards
R: 513 yards
F: 455 yards

Challenging dogleg right. Water left and right off the tee with that on the left going all the way round the turn up to the green. Ideal tee shot is aimed left of the dead tree on the right near the turn. Then it's case of sensible approach(es) to a green with sand left and threatening mounds right. Fine, fine hole.

#7 - Par 3.
C: 163 yards
R: 130 yards
F: 97 yards

Unusual and fun. Aim towards the left side of the green no matter what on this two-tier fairway hole. Serious trouble lies right on the lower level with a railway tie wall short right of the green. End up against that and it's a horror show. Traps left, behind and front right. Diagonal ridge across the green causes two-way slopes off it.

#8 - Par 5.
C: 517 yards
R: 475 yards
F: 400 yards

Best tee shot is centre left down this straight left-right leaning fairway. Green has two traps right and one left. Another green saddle makes for a front end slope and a run-off back left.

#9 - Par 4.
C: 400 yards
R: 367 yards
F: 322 yards

Fairly steep uphill dogleg left with hidden hazards. There's one trap visible in the turn but there are two more unseen beyond and left of it round the bend. If you're long, a solid draw will carry them all. If you have doubts, play safe right of the visible trap. You'll still have a nice approach to green trapped front left, right, and behind. Good hole.

#10 - Par 4.
C: 412 yards
R: 372 yards
F: 320 yards

Into Furber territory. Steeply uphill with fairway sand right. Best to hit tee shot centre left to allow for left-right fairway drift. This green has a fearsome ridge across it. If the pin's on front and you're beyond it, it's very possible to putt off the dance floor.

#11 - Par 4.
C: 385 yards
R: 358 yards
F: 306 yards

Gorgeous hole with Holt Creek running all the way downhill right and then across the fairway immediately in front of the green tucked away right at the bottom. Hit down the left to give yourself a longer fairway and set up wedge approach into the well-trapped green. Nice, nice, nice.

#12 - Par 5.
C: 514 yards
R: 473 yards
F: 433F yards

Whoa! Here we go! Magnificent downhill par 5 set against a stunning backdrop of mountains and the Columbia. It's definitely reachable in two with solid shotmaking. Water all the way down the left so centre right is best line off the tee. The crested green, trapped left, short right and back right, has long putts galore on request.

#13 - Par 3.
C: 160 yards
R: 130 yards
F: 92 yards

Tricky one where club selection is all-important. The shot is across a small creek to a green sloped in front and with a right tilt back right. Oh, and those trees "immediately behind" the green? They're *over* the extremely fast-flowing Holt Creek. Cunning, eh?

#14 - Par 4.
C: 409 yards
R: 379 yards
F: 335 yards

This fairway's even narrower than most with sand in the left landing area and the Columbia on the right. Still, the landing area is fairly open. But on approach, watch out for the pond starting right of the green and going behind. The front end tilts, and the top leans right.

#15 - Par 4.
C: 400 yards
R: 370 yards
F: 317 yards

Uphill dogleg right so a fade tee shot centre right is your best bet. Heavy mounding surrounds a green with sand front right and on the left side. Fairly sharp front end slope on this one.

#16 - Par 3.
C: 198 yards
R: 159 yards
F: 139 yards

Downhill so maybe club down on a pretty hole distinctly more difficult than it looks. Holt Creek roars down the right, there are two traps left and another right overlooked by a troublesome tree.

#17 - Par 4.
C: 380 yards
R: 359 yards
F: 301 yards

A narrowish straightaway hole made narrower by the intimidating presence of a lone tree creeping in on the left about 100 yards out from the tee box. Centre is the route to a multi-tiered green bunkered left, front right and back right. Interesting putts to be had here.

#18 - Par 5.
C: 514 yards
R: 480 yards
F: 435 yards

Upslope dogleg left with the second leg steepening even more. Tee shot should be drawn inside fairway sand on the right. Approach should then be hit centre left away from another trap short right. The flattish green is flanked front left and front right by bunkers. Strong finisher.

Golden, British Columbia V0A 1H0
Telephone: (604) 344-2700

Kimberley Golf Club

"The original's a beauty too..."

Par 71/72

This course has been around much longer than its new neighbor, Trickle Creek, but don't dare neglect it if you're on a playing tour in the area of British Columbia's little piece of Bavaria. Make no mistake, it is a true mountain spectacular in its own right. Uphill and downhill, the fine championship track wends its way through some awesome, heavily-treed scenery and those trees can easily creep unwanted into play if you're not on top of your game. And special mention on a course riddled with special holes must be made of the fabulous number one with its elevated tee boxes set alarmingly in full view of the fine clubhouse's balconies and decks. A lone twilight game here was a serene highlight in my summer tour of 1995.

#1 - Par 4.
C: 299 yards
R: 299 yards
F: 299 yards

Mind-blowing. Downhill dogleg left off clifftop tees. Accuracy and spunk required. It's up to you, but my solid seven-wood draw down centre right hit the crest of the distant downslope and rattled down to within 40 yards of the invisible green. Honest! I have a deck-full of beer-swilling post-tournament revellers to testify to it! Anything too left off the tee will get hung up in trees down the left. Flat green has traps left and right.

#2 - Par 4.
C: 380 yards
R: 380 yards
F: 380 yards

Straight downhill with trees all the way both sides. A draw down centre right works well to take the ball down towards the green. It has a sharp Himalayan back-front slope on the back half but is flat at the front. Watch club selection on approach because an overhit shot could vanish in trees immediately behind. Whoa! This is going to be fun.

#3 - Par 3.
C: 164 yards
R: 155 yards
F: 146 yards

Looks simple. Medium iron, sand right. Wrong! Hidden water tucked out of sight maybe ten yards left of the green. Sneaky but good! (And hey, they even provide a tow rope up to the next tee box!)

#4 - Par 4.
C: 315 yards
R: 309 yards
F: 309 yards

Distinctly driveable. Downslope shot should be hit centre right to avoid off-putting copse of trees clustered short left of the green. It's a big rolling one where too-long putts could destroy sound approach work.

#5 - Par 4.
C: 359 yards
R: 333 yards
F: 307 yards

Bunker Hill they call it. Almost an optical illusion because it looks flat but the slope does exist. Stay as close to the bluff left as you dare to avoid two huge pines looming short right of the green for your approach. The green itself slopes left to right.

#6 - Par 5.
C: 516 yards
R: 499 yards
F: 479 yards

Allow me to introduce you to one superb golf hole. Daunting uphill tee shot through chokingly-narrow funnel between trees. When you get there it's a bit wider than it looked but still, it's iron time for accuracy. Then in the approaches it really does get narrow. The green's front end is flat but there is an upward slope back right. Unless you're dead accurate with woods, think iron all the way here.

#7 - Par 3.
C: 194 yards
R: 175 yards
F: 156 yards

Club down on this downhill "Illusion" hole. Major sand right. Hmm.

#8 - Par 4.
C: 341 yards
R: 327 yards
F: 308 yards

Good birdie opportunity on this one that goes uphill all the way. The green is heavily-sloped back to front and has a trap extending round the right and back-centre.

#9 - Par 5.
C: 478 yards
R: 468 yards
F: 459 yards

Another birdie chance and round here try and take 'em while you can. Downhill dogleg right. Another narrowish fairway with a large pine threatening the landing area for longer hitters expert in fading the ball round the curve. Good spot for Mr. Average is right of the other large tree on the fairway's left.

#10 - Par 3.
C: 202 yards
R: 192 yards
F: 178 yards

Testing, uphill and long. Major sand trouble right and left of a tiered-green drifting back to front. Good hole.

#11 - Par 4.
C: 286 yards
R: 277 yards
F: 264 yards

Visually stunning from a tee box sandwiched among the trees. The straight fairway dips then climbs up to the green perched at eye-level to the tees. There's sand left, right and behind. But be warned, the tiers *are* tiers. And yes, it is driveable if you hit the sweet spot. Wow!

#12 - Par 4/5.
C: 430 yards
R: 419 yards
F: 404 yards

Undoubtedly the toughest here. Tee shot is made tortuous by steep banks dropping in from both sides at different lengths. Oh and surprise! You wouldn't have known it was there until after you hit, but the hopefully straight-out tee shot has to carry deep ravine with road at the bottom. Survive and carry on. Double wow!

#13 - Par 4.
C: 310 yards
R: 300 yards
F: 273 yards

One good thing follows another. Slightly downhill tee shot from the elevated tee boxes should be straight down the middle. This green has a huge ridge across the middle. If the pin is in front, don't be on the back!

#14 - Par 5.
C: 524 yards
R: 504 yards
F: 482 yards

A dogleg left with a huge bank flowing down from the left. In fact, the fairway leans right disconcertingly sharply in places. The left side is best all the way if you can manage it. But watch out for hidden sand left over the crest about 90 yards out from the green. Sand front left, front right and back right on a green flat on top, tilted in front.

#15 - Par 3.
C: 151 yards
R: 127 yards
F: 108 yards

One of those memorable holes. Spectacular downhill beauty with two traps left and a bank sloping down onto the green from the right. Club down!

#16 - Par 4.
C: 459 yards
R: 424 yards
F: 263 yards

Ah, I wondered if we'd encounter that hidden ravine at #12 again. Here it is and from the back tees at least it has to be recrossed. But this time we can see it. Is that better or not? Aim tee shot to landing area on top of far upslope. Centre is good for approach into green hidden beyond.

#17 - Par 4.
C: 359 yards
R: 330 yards
F: 315 yards

Hogan's Alley is the name and it is an alley of trees. Elevated tee shot down the middle into treed valley below is good and then it's back up to a green on a severe upslope. Another two-tiered green where the back is to be avoided unless the pin is back there.

#18 - Par 4.
C: 373 yards
R: 343 yards
F: 318 yards

Coming Home is the name and yes, it's been quite a trip! Downhill dogleg left with a left-right leaning fairway. Ideal tee shot is a draw down centre right. Anything hit well but too straight is in real danger of making the bunker on the outside of the turn. The green is trapped left and right and has another small flat platform on top and a front end slope. Nice finisher with a reasonable shot at birdie.

159 - 305 Avenue
Kimberley, British Columbia
Telephone: (604) 427-4161

Kokanee Springs Golf Resort

"A classic in the Kootenay..."

Par 71/74

If only this course was a couple of hours nearer Calgary... but it's more than worth the occasional special trip for the weekend or vacation especially with the fine 26-room lodge on site and other accommodation available in the nearby hamlet of Crawford Bay due north of Creston on the eastern shore of Kootenay Lake or maybe you could use the private landing strip. Calgary oilman Ken Jennings started things here back in the 60s when he decided this idyllic spot was ideal for a golf course. He got one of the best to make the dream a reality too, world-renowned course architect Norm Woods. It wasn't all smooth going though because in 1970, all the greens died. The joke was the course was "Kootenay's million dollar hayfield." The joke's the joke now. This one's magnificent, but I recommend a power cart until the new hilltop clubhouse is built.

#1 - Par 4.
C: 439 yards
R: 413 yards
F: 379 yards

Right there with Kimberley for most spectacular opener of my trip. Tee shot from 100-foot high tee box should be hit from its right side out towards the left bird box (150-yard marker) with a fade. Hit it well and you'll never forget it soaring up and away and then down onto the distant fairway. Large, narrow green has two tiers and sand both sides.

#2 - Par 3.
C: 170 yards
R: 157 yards
F: 143 yards

Everything tends to fall right on this one. Tricky with trees hanging in on left and traps beneath them. The three-tiered green also has huge sand right. Club selection is the thing here to negotiate your way into the green.

#3 - Par 4.
C: 294 yards
R: 294 yards
F: 272 yards

Fascinating. Tree-lined fairway falls left to right and that slope increases down near the hidden but driveable green. The trick is to fly tee shot over the left bunker and ball will feed down into the green. Difficult putting green because of hidden breaks. Birdie chance though.

#4 - Par 4.
C: 321 yards
R: 296 yards
F: 272 yards

Downhill and driveable, but there's a multitude of traps down both sides of the fairway and the green has sand left and right. Good tee shot is a fade down the left and you might carry on down onto the green which has some serious undulations on the right. Don't be long with approach. A serious drop-off behind will carry overhit into the trees.

#5 - Par 4.
C: 462 yards
R: 421 yards
F: 390 yards

Breathtaking. Highest handicap. Elevated tee box is set in rock and log surrounds. Tee shot should be struck towards the smaller of two trees to the right of the bridge crossing the fast-flowing Crawford Creek. A good one sets up anything from a three iron to a seven iron across the creek to a very narrow green 50 yards long. Traps left and right.

#6 - Par 5.
C: 501 yards
R: 479 yards
F: 456 yards

Back across the creek. Don't worry, unless you're Daly your drive shouldn't reach it. Long hitters can hit green in two but more likely scenario is a second landing on the severe upslope to a huge tiered green, sand left and right. A too-casual approach could leave a devilish long putt. Feeling the exquisite pressure this great course exerts yet?

#7 - Par 3.
C: 183 yards
R: 157 yards
F: 139 yards

Hey! Reminders of Anaconda Hills in Great Falls. Climbing tiered tee-boxes have to be flown from the back. Trickily uphill hole with big slopes all around the three-tiered green and sand right. Far better off right than left.

#8 - Par 5.
C: 482 yards
R: 471 yards
F: 460 yards

Ah, memories of an Eagles trip. "Aim for the purple tree . . ." It's there and that's the direction for the blind tee shot on this right-left leaning fairway. In other words a draw up the right. Fairly easy to reach in two but a huge oak covers the left 100 yards from green, there's sand right and invisible trap left. The narrow green is 50 yards long.

#9 - Par 4/5.
C: 431 yards
R: 416 yards
F: 401 yards

The experts' advice on this one is a draw off the left side of the tee down the right to carry it down the hill onto the flat. I'm usually okay there. The problems come after that. But pro David Miles says it's a mere five or six iron across the creek into the shallow green watching the sand front left, back right and the pond right. Hmm. Don't be long!

#10 - Par 4/5.
C: 418 yards
R: 409 yards
F: 389 yards

Another stunning elevated tee box on this gentle dogleg right. Hit tee shot well down centre left and you'll have a mid iron into a relatively open, undulating green which has an uphill slope, sand left and right and trees on both sides.

#11 - Par 3.
C: 169 yards
R: 155 yards
F: 131 yards

A beauty. Downhiller requiring maybe a club less than normal. This is one difficult green sloping away from the tee box and left. There's sand front left and middle right. Pray the pin isn't back left. When it is, it should carry a health warning.

#12 - Par 4/5.
C: 408 yards
R: 396 yards
F: 384 yards

Dogleg right with a capital "D." It's a 90-degree turn. Ideally you'll pick a long iron out of the bag and hit it down the middle with a slight fade into the turn. Again a four-club variation for the uphill approach. Whatever your first reaction, at least think of clubbing up. Narrow rolling green has sand front left and traps on the right.

#13 - Par 4.
C: 416 yards
R: 391 yards
F: 368 yards

This dogleg right has an elevated tee with a very narrow chute of trees to shoot through. The hole's made for faders who can hit it accurately down the left side to stay clear of the trees on the inside of the turn. Another four-club green, leaning left-right, has sand on both sides.

#14 - Par 4.
C: 371 yards
R: 351 yards
F: 258 yards

The first problem of many here is the tee shot across the water bang in front. A good one down the middle, though, will hit the upslope of a fairway depression setting up a shortish iron into a narrow green with trees tight left and a rock wall and sand right. If it's any consolation it's the flattest green on the course. Maybe you're past caring.

#15 - Par 4.
C: 395 yards
R: 375 yards
F: 360 yards

Dogleg left where a drive down centre left gives you the best options. Here, your approach has to carry both the creek about 30 yards in front of the green, and then a nasty mound. You don't want to be left on this one. The rough is overwhelming.

#16 - Par 3.
C: 148 yards
R: 117 yards
F: 86 yards

Simple par 3? Should be. But it's amazing how many bogeys it accumulates. Problem is you have to fly over the edge of the elevated reservoir right to hit the flattish green. It's a big one and slopes back to front.

#17 - Par 5.
C: 556 yards
R: 543 yards
F: 524 yards

This giant, the longest here, deserves a chapter to itself. Shot from elevated tee box should be hit centre with a draw to avoid water in the landing area right. Very difficult to make it in two. There are big trees and a severe bank on the left and little apple trees in front. It's another narrow, tiered green where you could be wrestling with a four-club choice depending on pin placement. Wow!

#18 - Par 4.
C: 370 yards
R: 352 yards
F: 335 yards

Lovely finish. Downhill start where left is best but watch the creek in the fairway. Now, hitting the longest green on the course can present a five-club choice. You've got to negotiate the creek in front and miss the pond right. They've held putting clinics on the back of this 12 000sq. ft. green when the pin is on the front. I kid you not!

P.O. Box 96, Crawford Bay
British Columbia, V0B 1E0
Telephone: (604) 227-9362

Mountain Meadows Golf Club

"Where the bears and the antelope play..."

Par 36/37

A scenic 30-minute run along the Elk River Valley on Highway 43 north of Sparwood brings the golfing traveller to the little mining town of Elkford and its ever-so-pleasing nine hole course on its southern outskirts. Designed by brothers Reg and Roy Stone, the track is laid out on one of the rare flat pieces of real estate in the area. But don't be fooled. Strategically-placed trees, or rather trees left untouched in strategic spots, and elevated greens with at times startling drop-offs demand an accurate game. The valley location is super, the locals friendly, and nature lovers get plenty of opportunity to spot moose, deer, geese, the occasional bear and very appropriately, the elk after which the valley, river and town were named.

#1 - Par 4/5.
R: 432 yards
F: 423 yards

A nice straightaway hole with OB and Highway 43 disturbingly close left. Best tee shot on a hole usually played into a prevailing wind should be aimed between most distant fairway tree on the left and the rightside 150-yard marker. Your mid-iron approach will then have to tackle the first of the course's elevated greens. This one has a front-end slope.

#2 Par - 4.
R: 308 yards
F: 301 yards

Short, sharp dogleg left with trees on the inside. Yes, with a rare north wind, it's possible to cut the corner with a lofted tee shot and land close. But the percentage shot is a mid-iron draw into the turn and go from there. Mounded green has roll-offs all around. Good hole.

#3 - Par 3.
R: 164 yards
F: 157 yards

Exciting short hole. A row of trees strung across the fairway Your choice. Low and through with a punch shot or up and over. Watch out for a nasty invisible pond ten yards left of the green that will swallow up anything tending to drift that way. Mounded green has trap right too.

#4 - Par 4.
R: 304 yards
F: 299 yards

Solid dogleg left with tree and creek problems. Tee shot should be hit centre left across the creek 150 yards out avoiding scattered trees trying to make life difficult. Corner cutters beware, the creek continues all the way down the left side in the trees.

#5 - Par 3.
R: 184 yards
F: 119 yards

Not much room for error here on a fine par 3. Shot is usually into wind and has to be played through narrow chute between huge tree left and line of trees right. There's sand front left and absolutely no forgiveness behind if you're long.

#6 - Par 4.
R: 360 yards
F: 269 yards

Superb dogleg left requiring a tee shot through a narrow funnel of trees to carry a minimum of 150 yards to cross the creek. It's a 210-yard carry to the outside corner of the dogleg, so sensible shot for visitors is an iron out that way into the large landing area. Slight change here is a saucer green with sand front left and front right.

#7 - Par 4.
R: 389 yards
F: 293 yards

Great signature hole, a dogleg left with a tee shot from elevated boxes needing to carry the creek below. Trouble is the trees and an out-of-sight pond continue up the left side beyond that. So centre right for tee shot is safest. Problems continue because on the approach you have to dice with tall trees playing sentry to two-tiered green 60 yards out.

#8 - Par 5.
R: 462 yards
F: 445 yards

First of par 5 double act to finish. It's straight but shortish yardage means nothing most days because hole is invariably played into that headwind sent up from Sparwood. Just be straight and get there when you can.

#9 - Par 5.
R: 565 yards
F: 406 yards

Straight but the toughest here. The headaches are caused by a clump of large trees dead centre about halfway to the green from the back. And they can be reached easily with that tailwind. Pick your side and go for it. On approach, more tree problems with clumps left and right on the way into another mounded, elevated green. A fun finish.

P.O. Box 4
Elkford, British Columbia V0B 1H0
Telephone: (603) 865-7413

From the tee on the 389-yard, par 4, 7th hole

Radium Hot Springs Resort

"A mountainside jewel..."

Par 69

Just south of the Columbia River valley spa town of Radium is a rare golfing jewel hidden in the mountainside meadows surrounding the fabulous Radium Hot Springs Resort. This fine course, though not overly long at around 5 200 yards, is the perfect choice both for the discerning golfer and for the family that vacations and enjoys its playing moments together. The course drifts up and down the western side of the mountain slopes along magnificent tree-lined fairways which often demand a high degree of accuracy. In 1995, the men's course rating sat at 66.1, but post-season modifications to holes 1, 2, 10 and 16 suggest that guests at the resort's fine hotel and impressive condominiums and day visitors to the picturesque course alike will find the challenge even greater from now on. An idyllic place to play.

#1 - Par 4.
R: 335 yards
F: 324 yards

A tee shot centre, centre right, will keep you away from the OB left and leave you a comfortable mid iron into a hilltop green trapped front left, back left and front. The green itself undulates from left to right.

#2 - Par 3.
R: 103 yards
F: 93 yards

More of the green is visible now than before. A short iron or wedge will take you up onto it but beware traps front left and back left. It used to be possible to maybe hit the bank behind and roll back on. Not now. That ploy is prevented by a very small gully at the back.

#3 - Par 4.
R: 277 yards
F: 277 yards

A personal favorite. Driveable from the highly-elevated, tree-flanked tee box by going straight over the large pine straight out about 200 yards. Well-hit shot will carry on down slope towards the elevated green which has traps on both sides and slides from back to front.

#4 - Par 4.
R: 326 yards
F: 313 yards

This dogleg right is a challenge. It requires a drive down the left side to the turn about 240 yards out to best open up the green round the corner. A good one will leave short iron approach watching out for traps left. Green slopes left to right and back to front.

#5 - Par 4.
R: 295 yards
F: 282 yards

Good hole for the driver to emerge with a hit down the right hand side. That should leave a wedge to the green dropped in a hollow and sloping right to left. Leftside position will leave you a nice uphill putt on most occasions.

#6 - Par 5.
R: 484 yards
F: 460 yards

A fine dogleg left par 5. Hit fairway wood or long iron off the tee to the turn about 210 yards out. Ideally it will turn the corner and roll down the slope a bit further leaving another three wood or long iron approach to the green. But beware OB right. This green slopes left to right.

#7 - Par 3.
R: 181 yards
F: 176 yards

Tricky long or mid iron onto a smallish elevated green which slopes slightly right to left.

#8 - Par 3.
R: 130 yards
F: 100 yards

Picturesque tree-surrounded short hole. The green is fairly flat but has a nasty trap front right and there's nothing but trouble short left down in the gully. Green leans right to left.

#9 - Par 4.
R: 400 yards
F: 391 yards

A fine closer to the front nine doglegging first uphill then downhill. Ideal tee shot is squeezed between trees left and fairway tree just in the turn. It should run down the slope leaving a long iron into the green. Be warned. This green slopes front to back so if you don't produce a lot of backspin, it may be best to hit short and run on.

#10 - Par 4.
R: 339 yards
F: 335 yards

An already fabulous hole just got even more character. Hit a three wood through the neck of the tree-lined fairway. (Don't worry too much about going slightly off course as the steep slopes either side will generally bring her back down and on). The change is down at the now-elevated green with water back left. A short or medium iron should put you on.

#11 - Par 4.
R: 318 yards
F: 314 yards

A slight dogleg left requiring a three wood or long iron tee shot down the right. That should leave a comfortable medium or short iron into a relatively flat green with a trap front left.

#12 - Par 3.
R: 165 yards
F: 149 yards

Visually, the course's star. It's a 92-foot drop from the back tees down to the green. Club down one, possibly two, for this one. You don't want to be long or you'll be chipping back from the 13th tee box below the green. And there are traps left, front right and behind. Wow!

#13 - Par 4.
R: 385 yards
F: 350 yards

Downhill and open so drive it all you want down the middle. You should be left with a long or mid iron into an elevated green but watch OB all the way right.

#14 - Par 5.
R: 489 yards
F: 485 yards

Gorgeous dogleg right where ideal is to hit driver centre right leaving yourself a three wood or long iron approach to the green, a fairly flat one without any sand concerns.

#15 - Par 3.
R: 188 yards
F: 185 yards

Perfect shot here is a long iron with a slight draw into a green, trapped left and with an immediate bank right. Calling card putts available on request.

#16 - Par 5.
R: 451 yards
F: 450 yards

Ideal tee shot on this excellent hole is up centre with a slight fade. There's a trap right about 150 yards off the tee, and the visible one left is about 240 yards out. The big tree that used to cause approach headaches is gone but the green is now left of centre and tiered back to front. Watch traps front right, back right and a pot bunker left.

#17 - Par 3.
R: 126 yards
F: 115 yards

It's pretty but what you see is what you get. All it needs is a short iron or wedge across the water. Hmm.

#18 - Par 4.
R: 350 yards
F: 346 yards

Start thinking of dinner by aiming tee shot directly at the corner of the distant dining room. A good one will leave you a nice mid iron across the water onto a tree-shaded, two-tiered green.

Box 310, Radium Hot Springs
British Columbia, V0A 1M0
Telephone: (604) 347-9652

Riverside Golf and Country Club

"The mighty Columbia keeps you company..."

Par 71

I suspect there are hundreds of "Riverside" golf clubs on the world golfing circuit. What sets this one apart is the fact that here the river is the mighty Columbia within miles of its beginnings and the splendor of the mountain scenery through which it starts its fantastic journey to the Pacific. The superb 18-hole track is the newest of the two in Fairmont Hot Springs and although at times it threads its way through real estate development, at no time do the grandiose houses and condominiums intrude to the point of distraction. This is a fine course ranging from tough from the back to comfortable for the casual player or recent beginner from the front. Oh and by the way, by my count the Columbia comes into play on 13 holes, including several where it has to be traversed.

#1 - Par 4.
C: 393 yards
R: 372 yards
F: 344 yards

A nice gentle start with a dogleg left. Tee shot should be aimed centre right into turn to avoid traps left about 150 yards from the green and open up the rolling green for a long, mid-iron approach. It is trapped left, back left and right.

#2 - Par 4.
C: 355 yards
R: 338 yards
F: 311 yards

Straight but potentially deadly. Serious hookers can fly across the adjoining sixth fairway into the Columbia and there's hidden water on the right starting about 75 yards off the white tees. Centre then is good to set up a short iron approach. But don't lose it right as the water becomes a nasty pond short right of a green trapped at the four corners.

#3 - Par 3.
C: 150 yards
R: 138 yards
F: 130 yards

Gorgeous little hole with water short right off the tee box and requiring the first crossing of the Columbia. The two tiered green, higher right than left, is very shallow. It's bunkered front right, left and behind. And don't be too long or the trees come into play.

#4 - Par 5.
C: 560 yards
R: 525 yards
F: 420 yards

A sharp dogleg left with the Columbia on the right. Best to play the course here with a fairway wood or iron out into the turn although it's possible to fly the trees inside with a 235-yard carry. The dead tree right is 146 yards from the green so judge your approach from that. Green is tiered back to front with traps both sides and back right.

#5 - Par 3.
C: 180 yards
R: 167 yards
F: 146 yards

Don't worry. It's only from the blue tees that you have to cross the Columbia twice! Super hole with a green trapped all around the right, and with mounds, cart path and trees left. Do you think accuracy might be a factor?

#6 - Par 5.
C: 504 yards
R: 477 yards
F: 455 yards

Hit tee shot centre right across the Columbia to start off on this dogleg left. Watch trees right in the landing area for a slice and traps on the left about 230 yards out. On approach, beware hidden water short right of a green on which humps can give a variety of testing putts. Traps front right and back left.

#7 - Par 4.
C: 385 yards
R: 366 yards
R: 325 yards

Tricky dogleg right with water galore. Tee shot should be hit out into the turn avoiding traps right with pond behind them around the 150-yard markers. The Columbia threatens the approach. It loops round just short right of the green and then behind it. A nasty trap right in front of the right-left two-tiered green, makes for some difficult pin placements. More sand back right.

#8 - Par 3.
C: 193 yards
R: 173 yards
F: 147 yards

The Columbia is right there all the way right. Shot needs to be fired along it up to a green trapped front left, back left and front right. There's a front end slope on this one.

#9 - Par 4.
C: 386 yards
R: 368 yards
F: 332 yards

Difficult dogleg right to finish the front nine. Tee shot should be hit out through trees both sides to land centre left. To some extent that will take water front right out of play for your approach. Only to some extent. The shallowish green has a mean saddle across the middle with sand front left, back left and back right.

#10 – Par 4.
C: 316 yards
R: 301 yards
F: 242 yards

Tough! Uphill dogleg left where tee shot should be hit out towards the lone blue spruce. The approach is threatened by two large fir trees playing sentry. Jungle and the cart path left of the green and it's also protected by a treacherous trap front right and others back right and behind. The slope on this one can roll putts back down the hill.

#11 - Par 4.
C: 442 yards
R: 422 yards
F: 340 yards

Toughest here. OB right and your ball could end up in Kimberley if it lands on a truck on the highway left. Stay left, though, all the way on a fairway leaning heavily left-right. The tall fir on the left is ideal tee shot target. The slant increases inside the 150-yard markers. Humps left of the green and two large traps on the right. It slopes back-front, left-right.

#12 - Par 4.
C: 367 yards
R: 351 yards
F: 331 yards

This narrow downhill hole really requires a fairway wood or long iron off the tee for accuracy avoiding OB all the way right. Don't fade or slice around here! Play approach to left side of the green and it should roll down and on. Whole green tilts left-right down to three fearsome traps right.

#13 - Par 3.
C: 183 yards
R: 170 yards
F: 116 yards

Across the wide Columbia! Really the signature hole hereabouts requiring a shot across the river to a huge green trapped left, front right and behind.

#14 - Par 5.
C: 590 yards
R: 525 yards
F: 454 yards

Unusual to say the least. A horseshoe dogleg right. Playing the course is best! Cutting the corner(s) is suicide requiring two crossings of the Columbia. Some long hitters though hit short off the tee and then hit a fairway wood back across to fairway short of the green. Best is to keep hitting round the turn. The reward is a big flat green.

#15 - Par 3.
C: 152 yards
R: 127 yards
F: 106 yards

It's a medium, short iron across the river bang in front of the tee boxes to a green bunkered in front, left and right. The green drifts back-left to front-right.

#16 - Par 4.
C: 369 yards
R: 349 yards
F: 328 yards

Dogleg right with options.. Choice? Hit wood or iron out 200 yards or so out near the 150-yard marker. Or hit a 230-yard shot across the turn and land relatively safely. The second leg is uphill to a green with a severe back-front slope, and trapped front left, back left, and front right. Most days, be below the pin on this one.

#17 - Par 4.
C: 420 yards
R: 385 yards
F: 345 yards

Play the left side staying away from pond on the inside of this slight dogleg right, and landing short of the traps on the left. Long hitters could maybe clear the water with a perfect shot. The green, bunkered front left and front right, has no tiers but is undulating.

#18 - Par 5.
C: 562 yards
R: 548 yards
F: 477 yards

The Columbia's behind and left off the tee and three, that's three, ponds come into play. Best to hit five wood tee shot straight out to land left of first pond right. Then hit second up between pond left and another right about 140 yards out from the green. The green has a huge trap left and three more on the right. It slopes back to front. Wow!

Box 993
Fairmont Hot Springs, British Columbia, V0B 1L0
Telephone: (604) 345-6346

Sparwood Golf Club

"Splendor on the mountainside..."

Par 36/37

The spectacular pass country through southwestern Alberta into British Columbia is unforgettable for its magnificent and never-ending mountain scenery. Some members of the golfing fraternity already know that the territory is also home to some of the most scenic and satisfying tracks to be found. For those not already in the know, add the fine nine-hole Sparwood course to your list of destinations the next time you're in the Crowsnest Pass corridor. Visually, it's second to none, and the lay-out leaning off the mountainside is a real challenge. The course has a wide and mixed range of four tee boxes to ensure that eighteen holes played here provide enough variety and enough of a test to linger longer than a couple of hours. Splendid. Yardages listed below are simply longest to shortest.

#1 - Par 5.
C: 450 yards
R: 450 yards
F: 415 yards

Plays long into prevailing breezes along the valley. The fairway leans left to right down the mountain slope. Ideal tee shot then is played down left side to allow for a fall right. Downhill second, or eventual approach, has to negotiate a small pond left and another intruding on the right. Sand short right of a green with a back to front slope.

#2 - Par 4.
C: 342 yards
R: 320 yards
F: 285 yards

Hug the trees left as tightly as you dare with your tee shot on another severe right-leaning fairway. Another problem here is fairway sand about 40 yards short of the green right which will catch any long hitter's ball that rolls down too far. A slightly elevated green with sand left is difficult to stick.

#3 - Par 4.
C: 360 yards
R: 360 yards
F: 355 yards

Stick to the left again. On this one you have an approach shot choice. Hit high into a vast welcoming green or pitch and run down left side and on that way. There's a large trap left and a smaller one right.

#4 - Par 3.
C: 168 yards
R: 160 yards
F: 155 yards

A delightful uphill par 3 where a marshy pond has to be negotiated from the back tees. You've turned east now, so the slope runs right to left, and you'll likely have a tailwind. Mounds along the left and pines behind the green threaten the shot as well as traps left and right. Green has a right to left lean with the mountain.

#5 - Par 4/3.
C: 285 yards
R: 235 yards
F: 175 yards

Whichever tee you play from, remember the prevailing tailwind. From the back a tee shot down the centre is best, because a clean hit down the right could just about make contact with a strategically-placed trap front right. There's also sand to the left of the large green.

#6 - Par 4.
C: 385 yards
R: 360 yards
F: 258 yards

A lovely hole sweeping left through the pines to a green barely visible at fairway's end. There's also a creek (dry when I passed through) crossing the right-left leaning fairway about 250 yards out from the back. Best tee shot again is one favoring right side to allow for the mountain drift. Sand high on the right of the green and to its left. Front end tilts right to left but it's flatter on top.

#7 - Par 3.
C: 180 yards
R: 162 yards
F: 140 yards

A super little downhill hole. So taking grade and a prevailing left-right wind into account, club down one at least for the shot into a green with big-time trap left, another right and more behind.

#8 - Par 4.
C: 465 yards
R: 424 yards
F: 424 yards

Some say this is the toughest here but what's to come isn't too bad either! Still, one hole at a time. Fairway slope has switched back to left-right and it's usually into the wind again. Tee shot should be aimed down centre left keeping an eye on that (dry?) creek. Approach is complicated down the right by a small pond and a larger one further right that really shouldn't come into play, but watch sidehill lies.

#9 - Par 5.
C: 538 yards
R: 500 yards
F: 480 yards

Memorable! Ideal wind-driven shot should go down the left and a cautious second should be placed into the turn of this 90-degree uphill dogleg right. Then club up two or three to hit a three-tier, staircase green on top of the hill. The ridges between tiers are fierce so be below the pin. Sand at sides and behind further complicate things.

Highway 3, Sparwood, British Columbia V0B 2G0
Telephone: (604)425-2612

The 168-yard, par 3, 4th hole

The Springs Golf and Country Club

"A Columbia Valley challenge..."

Par 72

This fine Les Furber-designed course, opened in 1988, and set atop the high bluffs overlooking the mighty Columbia River and its marshlands below is as stern a golf test as you'll find. But plenty of tee box variations, four in all, mean that the more recreational golfer can enjoy the serenity of the mountain and river views in enjoyable fashion too. Some of the holes here verge on being unique, witness the uphill dogleg left second, and the short-but-stupendous cross-canyon par 3 seventeenth. That one brings a whole new definition to the words "short game." If you're looking for an indication of where your game is at in a valley riddled with good courses, The Springs is one that will give you a tough assessment.

#1 - Par 4.
C: 415 yards
R: 380 yards
F: 299 yards

A downhill dogleg left with a right-left leaning fairway sweeping round to the hole. Aim tee shot down centre right towards the distant trap and she'll roll down left. That leaves a comfortable short iron or wedge onto a back-front sloping green.

#2 - Par 4.
C: 396 yards
R: 370 yards
F: 313 yards

This dogleg left is fearsome first time round. But it's not so bad if you play with your head. Hit an iron or fairway wood down to land right of the fairway trap and gully left. Then it's a severely uphill mid or short iron up to the hidden plateau green trapped front right in the slope. Be bold with it. Short can be trouble and there's room behind.

#3 - Par 5.
C: 503 yards
R: 471 yards
F: 415 yards

A beautiful sweeping dogleg right with a fairway that climbs and then drops down towards the hole. It's one for patience. Centre-left tee shot will set up a second that really should be laid up short of the green for chip on and best shot at birdie on a flattish but severely-trapped green.

#4 - Par 3.
C: 185 yards
R: 149 yards
F: 90 yards

Don't be daunted by appearances. Forget the pin and aim for the open part of the green thus avoiding those layers of dangerous, railway tie-backed traps short right. (The only traps I have come across where they provide steps to get in and out). And be wary of the nasty pot bunker behind. Wow!

#5 - Par 4.
C: 431 yards
R: 403 yards
F: 342 yards

A dogleg left round a vast waste bunker in which you can ground your club if you find yourself in there. You won't need to though with a centre-left tee shot hit towards the trees on the outside of the turn. Club up, possibly, for your approach into an elevated rolling green.

#6 - Par 3.
C: 195 yards
R: 178 yards
F: 122 yards

A strong short hole requiring a hit across the valley to a green, lower left than right, with hideous sand trouble short right, and other traps left and back right. Stay well away from the right and be below the pin if possible.

#7 - Par 4.
C: 386 yards
R: 360 yards
F: 314 yards

A challenge. Tee shot should be hit straight out between waste bunkers left and right (again you can ground your club in there) to land near the turn 260 yards out from the tips. Your approach might vary two or three clubs depending on the pin placement on a long roller coaster green.

#8 - Par 4.
C: 355 yards
R: 330 yards
F: 280 yards

A thinker's hole. Put away the driver and instead go for a 200-yard iron or fairway wood into a large landing area short of the water left which creeps up to the green. A lofted approach should be aimed at hitting the green not the pin. There are some undulations on this one. Ahem!

#9 - Par 5.
C: 550 yards
R: 516 yards
F: 460 yards

Think three to get there. Tee shot should be hit straight out to land inside trap in the turn. Then a careful mid-iron lay up along the lake left will set up a pitch and putt for birdie. It's been done! The well-trapped green has predominant back-front slope.

#10 - Par 5.
C: 501 yards
R: 494 yards
F: 400 yards

Consider your options after a straight-out tee shot to land short of the water. Your approach is a choice of braving the lake in two or laying up into comfortable landing area right of it. Either way can work for birdie.

#11 - Par 4.
C: 352 yards
R: 326 yards
F: 272 yards

Safety first. It's iron time, folks. Hit mid iron out towards traps on the left and away from the water short right on this dogleg right. An accurate one will give you a second comfortable mid or short iron into a green, trapped right and behind, with pretty serious undulations.

#12 - Par 4.
C: 392 yards
R: 346 yards
F: 297 yards

Again it's a matter of placement and that's best with an iron. Hit tee shot centre, centre right to land inside the traps right. Leaves a mid-iron approach into a green heavily-trapped front left and back right. This green tilts back-left, front-right.

#13 - Par 5.
C: 500 yards
R: 473 yards
F: 428 yards

A left-right lean on this fairway will carry a leftside tee shot down into an area between the traps. The green can be reached by long hitters in two but an iron lay up down the right side for wedge on is safer bet. Stay below the pin on this sloping green if you can.

#14 - Par 3.
C: 189 yards
R: 174 yards
F: 85 yards

It's best to be below the pin on a back-front sloping green with traps front left, back left and back right. On a sheltered tee box, you can be fooled about swirling winds up in the target area. Look at the flag!

#15 - Par 4.
C: 428 yards
R: 406 yards
F: 345 yards

Tricky dogleg left where you don't want to be short of the turn but not too far because of the trap and creek through the fairway. It's about 250 yards to the trap. Then a nasty trap front left can cause avoidance problems in the approach which result in creek trouble right of the green.

#16 - Par 4.
C: 384 yards
R: 359 yards
F: 301 yards

Beware a nasty dip on the left side of the fairway in what would normally be the landing area. Best hit 200-yard iron or fairway wood short of it. The funnelled approach has got to be straight to avoid beach problems left and right. If in doubt lay up to this mounded green.

#17 - Par 3.
C: 149 yards
R: 124 yards
F: 101 yards

I won't bother saying it. Aw, shucks, I will. Don't be short! This spectacular trans-canyon hole is special, isn't it? Go for it!

#18 - Par 4.
C: 406 yards
R: 399 yards
F: 299 yards

The view? Try and forget it. This is as tough a finisher as you'll get. From the back it's about 230 yards to the left fairway trap on this dogleg left. But good spot for tee shot is just right of it. And strangely, you may need to club up to reach the trap-surrounded green.

P.O. Box 430
Radium Hot Springs, British Columbia, V0A 1M0
Telephone: (604) 347-6444

The awesome 185-yard, par 3, 4th hole

Trickle Creek Golf Resort

"A true wonder of the golfing world..."

Par 72

Word started trickling through, so to speak, a couple of years back that something special had happened in Kimberley, four hours southwest of Calgary. "I hear Trickle Creek is something else," the chat on the circuit went. "Have you played Trickle Creek, yet? Well I tell you..." What happened was the making of a masterpiece that golf course architect Les Furber is going to find almost impossible to top in years to come. The astonishing thing about this track on the slopes of North Star Mountain is that it will be only four years old in 1996. So mature, comfortable and natural in its spectacular Purcell Mountains setting, it looks and feels as if it has been there since The Creation. Its memorable holes are tough, but we lesser mortals shouldn't despair. Four tee boxes accommodate all grades of player. A power cart is recommended on a course where iron or fairway wood off the tee is often best. An unforgettable experience.

#1 - Par 4.
C: 328 yards
R: 298 yards
F: 229 yards

Shortish, testing opener with, get used to it, trees tight on both sides. It sneaks left with ominous moguls down the right. A draw tee shot down centre left is ideal to set up short iron approach across a 2ft.-wide creek 36 yards out from the green's heart. It has a slight back-front slope and a tricky little basin in its front end.

#2 - Par 4.
C: 403 yards
R: 362 yards
F: 299 yards

Hit tee shot centre or centre left down funnel of trees ensuring it carries the hollow pushing in from the left side. There's a nasty gully about 130 yards out from the green too and two trees and heavy mounding guard the rightside approach across another dip just in front. Sand front left, front right and back left. Green runs off front right.

#3 - Par 3.
C: 210 yards
R: 170 yards
F: 108 yards

A superb arena for golf. Try and forget the huge expanse of sand front left and front right. Think positive. The huge green is a massive landing area for a well-hit shot. A gradual back-front slope means below pin is best.

#4 - Par 5.
C: 530 yards
R: 507 yards
F: 446 yards

Here we go! Hope you're warmed up. A great long hole requires a tee shot aimed left of the lone fairway tree on the right 220 yards from the green. Then it's a case of a lay up avoiding fairway sand left and landing just alongside or just beyond fairway sand right. That's the best side to approach a bunkered green with a slight back-front slope.

#5 - Par 4.
C: 451 yards
R: 422 yards
F: 351 yards

"Hit all you've got" advises the sign and it makes sense on highest handicap hole drifting right. Ideally, you need a long fade down centre right to avoid a sunken fairway basin left. An approach is playable from down there but the view's much better from top right. Diagonal green slopes back right-front left, is trapped left, front right and behind.

#6 - Par 4.
C: 386 yards
R: 351 yards
F: 277 yards

One beautiful hole. Accuracy is the maxim. Tee shot, which has to run gauntlet of moguls and mounds, should be aimed towards visible greenside trap. But beware. The right side of a hidden creek starts about 250 yards out on the right and wanders across to a point 300 yards out left. If that's not enough boulders run its length and could cause drastic direction changes. Green trapped right slopes back to front.

#7 - Par 4.
C: 409 yards
R: 372 yards
F: 295 yards

A more open feel to this one, but don't be lulled to sleep. It's a dogleg right with mounds both sides and major fairway sand on the right. Try and keep tee shot centre left. Two things to watch around the green, a nasty dip in front and a troublesome half-ridge on the rightside putting surface.

#8 - Par 3.
C: 209 yards
R: 183 yards
F: 108 yards

If you're going to err, err left. Steep embankment left will at least bring it down to safety on the green or just short of it. Anything right here is beached or history down the bank on the other side. Warning: Anything too short can hit cart path and then watch it fly!

#9 - Par 5.
C: 531 yards
R: 502 yards
F: 424 yards

The main trouble is left with fairway sand in the landing area and mounding all the way on that side. A centre-right draw is best on a fairway falling to the right. There's heavy mounding short left of the green which is also trapped both sides. Green leans back to front with a small ridge at the back to throw the ball left or right.

#10 - Par 4.
C: 333 yards
R: 318 yards
F: 226 yards

Monumental hole requiring a tee shot centre right across ravine avoiding nasty ponds fifty feet down short left and fairway sand on the left of the hillside facing you. The 150-yard markers are on top on the other side so judge your carry from those. Go into this two-tiered green in the valley from the right. There's nothing but tree trouble left and a shot landing on downslope short right will carry ball on.

#11 - Par 3.
C: 174 yards
R: 152 yards
F: 107 yards

Phenomenal signature hole. The green is 100 feet below the tee box so club down accordingly. Anything short will hit severe upslope landing area and cause chipping nightmares. Sand behind, front left, front right. Be careful with club selection and a back-front ridge across the middle. Ah, holes like this make life worthwhile.

#12 - Par 4.
C: 438 yards
R: 438 yards
F: 340 yards

No let-up here. Severe dogleg left with sand trap in the middle of the bend about 260 yards out from the back tees. Note: it is in the middle atop a mound, not on the right as it appears. A tee shot just left of it is ideal for approach into a narrow, back-front sloping green with gargantuan mounds on both sides.

#13 - Par 5.
C: 527 yards
R: 489 yards
F: 425 yards

Don't panic! Yes, it's a challenge but think it out. The creek on this sharp dogleg right crosses the fairway about 200 yards out. Fairway wood or iron just short of it or a well-hit fade just over it round the bend sets up severe uphill approach to hilltop green guarded by, count 'em. seven traps. Club way up and go in high!

#14 - Par 3.
C: 216 yards
R: 171 yards
F: 117 yards

Everything falls away right towards a long beach all the way short right. There is a trap left of the diagonal green, but there's also a good landing area short left. Left is the way!

#15 - Par 4.
C: 417 yards
R: 402 yards
F: 240 yards

Elevated tee shot across sometime pond, sometime dry pond, onto a climbing fairway sweeping right to out-of-sight green on hilltop. Best tee shot is a hard fade aimed inside fairway trap left. A for-once flattish green has sand front left.

#16 - Par 4.
C: 404 yards
R: 380 yards
F: 321 yards

Best tee shot possibility on this fine dogleg right is straight hit over the left edge of the fairway trap right or if you're shorter than that, short and left of it. That sand is 170 yards out from elevated green with three bunkers left and one in the mounds short right. This green has a front-end slope.

#17 - Par 5.
C: 523 yards
R: 494 yards
F: 444 yards

A majestic fairway sweeps left on this tough par 5. Best tee shot is straight out between slopes dropping down from left and right. With luck you'll land to the left of the fairway traps to prepare to lay up. Lay up because of a unique feature. A creek with a boulder wall immediately behind, 12ft high right, 4ft high left. On top is a 50-yard long landing "strip." Traps left and right of a sloping green.

#18 - Par 4.
C: 407 yards
R: 378 yards
F: 325 yards

Best tee shot here is one centre past solitary pine on left of fairway about halfway to the green. Approach then has to negotiate creek 50 yards in front and various traps scattered among the mounds. And do watch that sand and water immediately back left. What a finish! What a course!

P.O. Box 190
Kimberley, British Columbia, V1A 2Y6
Telephone: (604) 427-5171

Trickle Creek's stunning 174-yard, par 3, 11th hole

South-West Saskatchewan

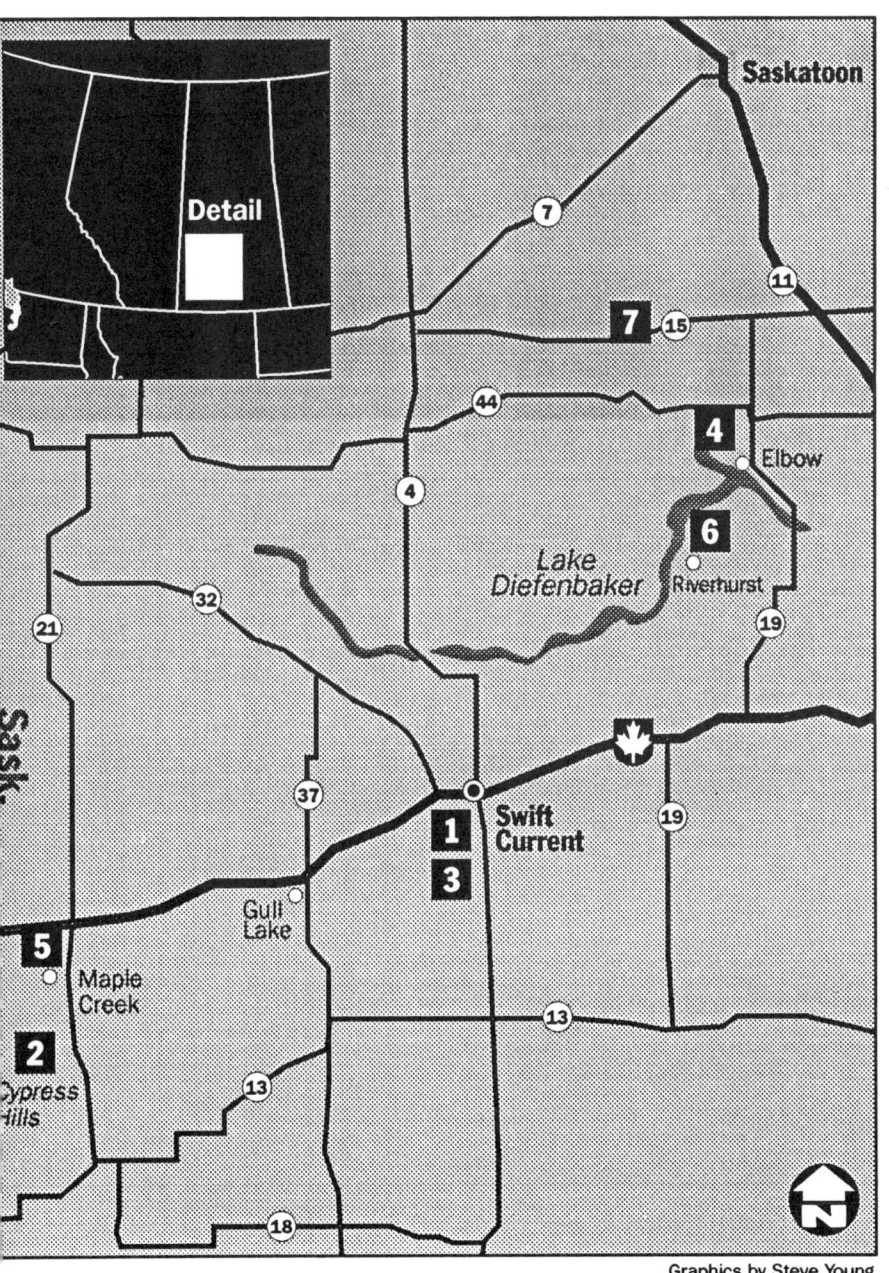

Graphics by Steve Young

1. Chinook Golf Course
2. Cypress Hills Golf Course
3. Elmwood Golf and Country Club
4. Harbor Golf Club and Resort
5. Maple Creek Golf Club
6. Riverbreaks
7. Riverview Golf Club

Chinook Golf Course

"A challenging alternative..."

Par 36

This is one of two courses in Swift Current. It may be a nine-holer, but this challenging track is in no way a poor cousin to the 18-hole Elmwood. Rather its links lay-out is a welcome alternative to the other's parkland style, giving the city's lucky locals and visitors alike an opportunity to play golf with a different feel. Don't be fooled by Chinook's more open look. With water and sand hazards abounding players have to choose their spots with care. With an attractive format, friendly staff, and good company on the course, this was a fun stop on my tour.

#1 - Par 4.
R: 405 yards
F: 405 yards

A nice dogleg left round water on the inside of the turn. A centre-right draw aimed at the last evergreen on the outside of the turn is ideal to set up a mid or short iron approach into a biggish green.

#2 - Par 4.
R: 337 yards
F: 305 yards

Another dogleg left with water threatening again on the inside. This time however your draw tee shot can favor centre rather than right. This green is guarded by sand front left and front right which really shouldn't bother a lofted short iron approach too much.

#3 - Par 5.
R: 450 yards
F: 436 yards

A really nice late dogleg right that's really a par four-and-a-half. It should be birdie time. A drive down centre left will set up comfortable approach into a green trapped left and right and with a sharpish back left-front right slope that can make putting interesting.

#4 - Par 3.
R: 161 yards
F: 138 yards

Good short, downhiller. A troublesome little dip in front of a flattish green will devour anything short. And there's major sand front left and two traps at the back. Be high and get there!

#5 - Par 4.
R: 427 yards
F: 414 yards

A hole to match the best anywhere. A dogleg right along the creek. Aim fade tee shot just left of the factory roof and you should have happy landings beyond the creek. Then it's downhill through an avenue of trees onto a side-trapped green, tucked right, and with back-front slope. I'd guess regulars are fairly happy with a bogey on this one.

#6 - Par 5.
R: 471 yards
F: 452 yards

Another short par 5. Early dogleg right with creek threatening right side all the way. Ideal drive is a centre-left fade. This green, very reachable with two solid shots, also has traps on each side.

#7 - Par 3.
R: 171 yards
F: 150 yards

Nice short hole with creek crossing in from about 140 yards out from the back tee box. There's sand front right too. Ideally, you'll take them out of play with a high fade.

#8 - Par 4.
R: 387 yards
F: 367 yards

Ninety-degree dogleg right. Yes, the corner can be cut with a solid 250-yard tee shot across the creek. But be warned. There is out of bounds and sand inside the turn. Then it's pretty straight up to a green which fades left from front-right to back left. There's a trap front left.

#9 - Par 4.
R: 366 yards
F: 350 yards

Time for finesse. Hit a mid-iron lay-up to the water about 200 yards out. Then it's another mid iron across the lake onto a green severely sloped back to front with a trap front right and one middle left. Good finisher.

Swift Current, Saskatchewan
Telephone: (306) 778 2776

The 471-yard, par 4, 6th hole

Cypress Hills Golf Course

"The magnificent setting is real . . ."

Par 36

Artificial greens! I can hear the protests of the purists already. But relax guys, it's hard to imagine a finer place for the game of golf than this course meandering through lodgepole pines and white spruce in the heart of Saskatchewan's scenic pride and joy, the Cypress Hills Provincial Park. Anyway, how often do you get the chance to putt on turf said to have been rescued from the hallowed ground of Taylor Field, Regina? Get over your phobia, grab the family and enjoy ultimate target golf in a setting second to none. Anyway, with a lack of natural irrigation, winter rules apply all season long!

#1 - Par 4.
R: 380 yards

Really testing double dogleg left and then right. Aim tee shot as left as you dare along the trees to open up any chance of an approach into a green tucked right and guarded front right by a screen of trees. Assuming you eventually make the greens, I'll leave putting to you on this course.

#2 - Par 3.
R: 142 yards

A huge spruce guarding the right approach begs the question, fly it or left of it? Trees down both sides but it's open up at the turf, I mean green.

#3 - Par 5.
R: 463 yards

Wide open. Put it down and let 'er rip. A good aiming line is just right of the two small spruces. Trees creep in on the green from the right so centre left is good all the way.

#4 - Par 4.
R: 296 yards

A great hole. Straight but a ravine and trees sneak in from the left just in front of the green. If you are left and short off the tee, there is a narrow gap to negotiate your approach shot. But best is long and right to open up clear shot into green.

#5 - Par 5.
R: 487 yards

Virtually due west into the prevailing wind. This wide fairway leans left to right so tee shot should favor the left to compensate. There's a huge dip about 100 yards out from the green that can produce tricky lies. Make sure you hit final approach to the right of the pin. A drastic embankment left spells disaster.

#6 - Par 3.
R: 180 yards

Tee shot basically has to be a draw down the right even though there's a large, disconcerting spruce about 70 yards out. But trees close in from the left hiding the left of the green.

#7 - Par 4.
R: 286 yards

Hit uphill tee shot just left of solitary spruce on the right as you look out. A good one will leave you a short wedge onto a green with a nasty ridge running from back to front.

#8 - Par 4.
R: 382 yards

Trees all along the right of this open fairway with the green tucked in tight against them at the end. Aim tee shot towards two small trees lurking in the middle of the left-right leaning fairway and you should be all right for approach.

#9 - Par 4.
R: 357 yards

They saved the toughest for last. Things suddenly feel tighter with trees all the way left round the dogleg left. Safest way is a three-wood or long iron straight out into the turn. There is room to absorb a 230-yard shot. A tree bang in front for the approach is disturbing and what's this? There's sand behind a back-front sloping green.

Box 1994
Maple Creek, Saskatchewan S0N 1N0
Telephone: (306) 662 4422

The 296-yard, par 4, 4th hole

Elmwood Golf and Country Club

"A parkland gem on the prairies..."

Par 71/73

The golfers of Swift Current are blessed with one of the best parkland-type courses it was my pleasure to play during my summer journey. And I promise I would have still felt that even if I hadn't posted a 77 on my scorecard the hot prairie day I chose to stop by. The course must have inspired me. It is at times nothing short of magnificent. The variety is endless with treed avenue fairways, more open holes where natural and manmade water hazards come into play, and more than one blind tee shot to make life more than interesting. Pop in and have a look at the wonderful ninth hole sweeping along the valley floor to the pond-protected green below the clubhouse and you'll get the idea. A gem.

#1 - Par 4.
C: 375 yards
R: 368 yards
F: 364 yards

Stunning opener doglegging left from an elevated tee box. Tee shot out over the trees below should favor the right side but avoiding the fairway trap over there. Good position will set up a comfortable mid iron into a tiered green with traps left and right.

#2 - Par 3.
C: 197 yards
R: 182 yards
F: 166 yards

Longish, with sand trouble front left, front right and back left. The trees huddle close and there's another major ridge running across this one. Tee shot too right brings problems. It might even be an idea for some to come up short and chip on for par chance.

#3 - Par 4/5.
C: 388 yards
R: 377 yards
F: 365 yards

Par 5 for the women? It's the killer hill up to the green that does it. Tee shot ideally hit towards centre left will hit flat landing area then bring out the oxygen masks for the climb. You'll maybe need to club up two or three to reach the formidable hilltop green they call The Fort.

#4 - Par 5.
C: 510 yards
R: 500 yards
F: 480 yards

From The Fort to The Cellar. Tee shot from elevated tee box has to be struck down middle of avenue of trees. There's nasty creek and marsh trouble over them left. Then continue the careful approach to a sharply-mounded green that can be difficult to stick on.

#5 - Par 3.
C: 207 yards
R: 200 yards
F: 193 yards

A strong short hole. You've got to be straight here with a tee shot through a chute of trees. Miss the elevated green and you'll have some nightmarish chips from slopes on both sides.

#6 - Par 4.
C: 378 yards
R: 363 yards
F: 348 yards

Great-looking golf hole which bends right along a line of trees and the creek on the left. Hit tee shot centre left and that'll give you your best line into a narrow green which is guarded by a trap left and two right.

#7 - Par 4/5.
C: 437 yards
R: 430 yards
F: 420 yards

Phenomenal dogleg right requiring blind tee shot up over the hill. Check mirror to ensure all is clear then go centre right with the tee shot. Unless you've got prodigious length, there's a chance the approach will be blind too. Traps front-left, front-right and back-right.

#8 - Par 3.
C: 128 yards
R: 118 yards
F: 111 yards

I hope heights don't bother you. Club down for this attractive hole requiring a drop shot down onto the green laid out far below. Get it right and it's birdie time!

#9 - Par 4.
C: 354 yards
R: 348 yards
F: 338 yards

The Glen's a gorgeous hole and the toughest for women. Tee shot should be hit down the avenue centre right. Good one will set up lofted mid or short iron into green covered front by fountained pond, sand right and an imposing tree slap bang behind. This one tilts back to front.

#10 - Par 4.
C: 334 yards
R: 324 yards
F: 310 yards

Straight tee shot down the chute of trees will set up wedge or short iron into green. Only problem is that the approach is often blind because it's played from down in major dip about 120 yards out from green. A good birdie chance.

#11 - Par 3.
C: 196 yards
R: 190 yards
F: 163 yards

Waterloo they call it. Could be appropriate. The creek in front requires a 120-yard carry and it's best to go for the right side of the green on the hill. Anything left is liable to cause migraines.

#12 - Par 5.
C: 475 yards
R: 465 yards
F: 430 yards

Good hole veering left towards the green with the creek threatening right and a roughed hill left. Elevated tee shot is best hit down centre left. The approach must avoid a five-foot-deep grassed gully about 120 yards out from green which has traps left and nothing but rough trouble right.

#13 - Par 4.
C: 365 yards
R: 350 yards
F: 298 yards

Another nice one. Fairway wood or iron time to lay up down left side towards creek crossing about 70 yards in front of the green. And best be below the pin on this sloping green guarded front left and on the right by traps.

#14 - Par 3/4.
C: 250 yards
R: 240 yards
F: 230 yards

Among the longest par 3s of the odyssey. Straight downhill requiring a three-wood or even a driver to hit the narrow green. And watch that creek all the way left.

#15 - Par 5/4.
C: 460 yards
R: 448 yards
F: 360 yards

Men must negotiate disconcerting line of trees crossing the fairway from the right about 200 yards out. Your call. Round, through or over. Good tee shot lands centre right and gives you a good chance to make the hillside green tucked left in two. Do it all right and pencil in a birdie.

#16 - Par 4.
C: 365 yards
R: 355 yards
F: 307 yards

Fine and fun. Blind tee shot (unless laying up into turn) needs a carry of 220 yards over the hill to land in fairway of this dogleg right. There's a stake on the hill to give you your line. Good one will leave a short iron or wedge into green guarded heavily by traps and water short right.

#17 - Par 4.
C: 355 yards
R: 345 yards
F: 332 yards

Deceptively steep uphill straightaway hole maybe needing some careful club-up selection especially on the approach. Good birdie chance though.

#18 - Par 5.
C: 480 yards
R: 470 yards
F: 420 yards

Last Chance they call it and it does give you one for a birdie. Good straightaway tee shot gives you the opportunity to make it on in two using downhill slope onto green guarded left and right by traps.

Swift Current
Saskatchewan
Telephone: (306) 773-2722

The downhill 128-yard, par 3, 8th hole

Harbor Golf Club and Resort

"Majesty above the lake..."

Par 71

Roughly in the heart of the triangle of Swift Current, Saskatoon and Regina is the remote hamlet of Elbow and its 'buried treasure,' a magnificent 18-hole links course sprawling along the clifftops overlooking mighty Lake Diefenbaker. With the incredible Riverbreaks track only an hour away in Palliser Park, itinerant golfers could do worse than centre a vacation around this area, though accommodation other than at the resorts may be limited and require advance booking. RV and boating enthusiasts will have no problem. It's mind-boggling to find a track of this quality, challenge and scenery in an area some would describe as "being in the middle of nowhere." It's not really true. The three major cities are within 90 minutes drive. Harbor's architecture and views are often breathtaking.

#1 - Par 4.
C: 364 yards
R: 347 yards
F: 329 yards

Pretty opening dogleg left with the lake coming into view in the turn and glimpses of the marina on the left. Ideal tee shot is centre, centre right into turn. That opens up the narrow entrance into green which has sand left and right.

#2 - Par 5.
C: 540 yards
R: 507 yards
F: 434 yards

Reminiscent of Scottish or Irish coast. Tee shot should land just inside sand on the right but beware water beginning just beyond the trees right. That water combined with water further up on the left makes for a very narrow line of approach into the green. Beach right and back left.

#3 - Par 4.
C: 374 yards
R: 348 yards
F: 321 yards

Hard to concentrate on the shot with such outstanding lake views on the right, but tee shot should be struck towards centre away from pond along the first half of the fairway left. Green has traps front left and front right.

#4 - Par 3.
C: 202 yards
R: 175 yards
F: 154 yards

Wow! A wonderful downhill par 3 over trees and shrubs in front with the panorama of Lake Diefenbaker on the left. Most of the trouble is left with sand front left and back left ... and the slope dropping off towards the lake. It's the high handicap hole.

#5 - Par 4.
C: 282 yards
R: 255 yards
F: 211 yards

One good hole deserves another and this one is a real birdie chance. Tee shot has to negotiate trees and gully bang in front to carry to an uphill fairway drifting right. If you look carefully there's a lone tree in the fairway providing a good target line. Yes, the well-trapped green's driveable.

#6 - Par 4.
C: 399 yards
R: 370 yards
F: 345 yards

Aim tee shot just to the left of leftmost grain elevator to land in the turn leaving a comfortable short iron into green trapped left and with two pot bunkers right. More of a slope on this one.

#7 - Par 5.
C: 504 yards
R: 486 yards
F: 445 yards

Trees hug the left side early and then things open up further up. Good tee shot is centre, centre left to provide comfortable approach(es) to green which has water starting short of it on the right side. This green has a marked back-front slope and has sand front left, left, and front right.

#8 - Par 3.
C: 175 yards
R: 151 yards
F: 122 yards

Tricky! Take the high road on this one with water which wanders all along the right and intrudes across the "fairway" halfway. There's beach left and right and a pot bunker dead in front. The water is pretty close back right.

#9 - Par 4.
C: 382 yards
R: 368 yards
F: 325 yards

With trees along the left on this dogleg left, the ideal tee shot target is just inside the fairway sand right. A medium, short iron will take you into a narrow green, major sand front right, mounds and trees crowding left.

#10 - Par 4.
C: 383 yards
R: 367 yards
F: 334 yards

A comfortable start to the back nine, this gentle dogleg right with trees on the right. There's big sand, though, front right and back left.

#11 - Par 3.
C: 162 yards
R: 142 yards
F: 110 yards

Another of this course's fine short holes. This one has a green slightly above tee box level with major sand on the right. Club up? Just maybe. This green undulates dramatically in places.

#12 - Par 4.
C: 362 yards
R: 348 yards
F: 319 yards

A hidden ravine with trees and bushes creeps in from the left about 200 yards out on this testy dogleg left. Why not play safe aiming tee shot centre right into area with plenty of room? Good one will leave short iron or wedge into green guarded by a rightside trap.

#13 - Par 5.
C: 582 yards
R: 550 yards
F: 518 yards

A brute. Coulee left and hidden ravines across the fairway, the first about 150 yards out from the regulars, the second maybe 250. If you skull it pray you're straight. The fairway in the first dip is only steps wide. Bunkers short right could grab your approach and green has traps left and right.

#14 - Par 4.
C: 332 yards
R: 307 yards
F: 286 yards

Just about driveable for long hitters but late dogleg right has major sand trouble on the inside of the turn. A 200-yard iron or wood out into the turn for a wedge on pays better dividends. Rolling green has sand left and right.

#15 - Par 3.
C: 110yards
R: 93 yards
F: 66 yards

Short, stupid and stupendous. The lake views across the 16th tee box left are unforgettable. Delicate shot has to be hit over tree-filled ravine to a shallow green a few paces deep. There's sand behind, front left and front right.

#16 - Par 4.
C: 402 yards
R: 353 yards
F: 333 yards

One of the most spectacular, daunting, tee box views encountered during my summer. Tee shot requires hit about 130-220 yards across tree-filled canyon to land centre on uphill fairway. (If you have a power cart, prepare for a thrill). Good shot leaves mid iron into narrow green guarded left and right by sand.

#17 - Par 4.
C: 361 yards
R: 340 yards
F: 320 yards

Tee shot centre right on this dogleg left is the spot for approach into a green trapped left and right and with a pot bunker dead in front.

#18 - Par 4.
C: 388 yards
R: 370 yards
F: 347 yards

An honest straightaway finisher with dangerous trees lurking in the landing area right and fairway sand left. Ideally, you want to be centre left off the tee for best approach into green which has two traps right and one left.

Elbow, Saskatchewan S0H 1J0
Telephone: (306) 854-2300

The 110-yard, par 3, 15th hole, with Lake Diefenbaker

Maple Creek Golf Club

"Historic town's golfing delight . . ."

Par 36

They say it all began here in 1882 when a group of 22 hardy railway-building souls decided to winter on the banks of the Maple Creek rather than go back east with the others. The following year the town was incorporated and became an important stopover for travellers en route to the North West Mounted Police outpost at Fort Walsh, noted for, among other things, its connections to famous Sioux leader Sitting Bull, 38 miles to the southwest. Nowadays Maple Creek is the "Gateway to Cypress Hills Provincial Park" and so plenty of modern-day travellers pass through. Many of them take advantage of the fine little nine-hole golf course redesigned in 1989 by Franklin Russell. It's links golf on the prairie with breezes adding to the existing challenge of trees, traps and water.

#1 - Par 4.
C: 392 yards
R: 392 yards
F: 353 yards

Pleasant straightaway opener but watch reservoir water in the right landing area around the 150-yard marker if you have a tendency to slice. Centre left is safest for the tee shot. The green in a little chapel of trees has a severe drop-off behind and slopes back to front.

#2 - Par 3.
C: 177 yards
R: 155 yards
F: 155 yards

Lovely short hole with trees both sides and a small fountained pond short left and beware the trap front right. It's small but deep. Hmm. Things could get quite interesting around here.

#3 - Par 5.
C: 511 yards
R: 511 yards
F: 478 yards

Yes indeed. A gorgeous-looking golf hole sweeping left with nothing but open prairie on that side. This is Scottish moorland stuff (sigh). The huge Africa-shaped green has near hidden sand front left, trees right and behind, and a severe slope down to Capetown. It's possible to be on the front of this green and not have a putt to a pin back left.

#4 - Par 4.
C: 390 yards
R: 390 yards
F: 313 yards

After 15 years, I don't get homesick but . . . dogleg right with trees screening the inside but nasty lies await in there if you try to cut the corner. Ideal tee shot is fade hit towards the second telegraph pole from the left. There's a sharp five-foot rise to the hillside green wedged among trees, so club up on approach. A two-foot ridge across green must be the sharpest incline in Saskatchewan.

#5 - Par 4.
C: 416 yards
R: 416 yards
F: 307 yards

Jeez! Are the people of Maple Creek lucky or what? Downhill then uphill dogleg left. Be centre right off the tee for best line of approach into a green tucked away left among the trees. Green has left to right slope. Excellent hole.

#6 - Par 3.
C: 142 yards
R: 142 yards
F: 128 yards

Club down for this downhiller. OB and young trees left and a major grass bunker front left. There are sharp drop-offs behind and right.

#7 - Par 4.
C: 365 yards
R: 365 yards
F: 365 yards

Lovely links-style uphill dogleg right with the green nestling in a basin at the end. Ideal is fade tee shot down centre to swing round the turn. Sets up up nice short iron or wedge approach to avoid massive grass bunker on the right.

#8 - Par 4.
C: 424 yards
R: 424 yards
F: 357 yards

Another beautiful hole sweeping left off the elevated tee box. It's rated the toughest and probably is. Tee shot down left will set up best approach to avoid water starting short right and winding along the right behind the green.

#9 - Par 5.
C: 521 yards
R: 504 yards
F: 454 yards

Longest from the back tees. Hit straight out. Don't try to cut the corner as the reservoir is likely to swallow the ball. Patience the rest of the way.

Maple Creek, Saskatchewan, S0N 1N0
Telephone: (306) 662-2886

The 177-yard, par 3, 2nd hole

Riverbreaks

"A 'Scottish' masterpiece in Saskatchewan..."

Par 36

If, in your mind's eye, you can replace with yellow gorse and heather the sage and choke cherry trees on this wondrous nine-holer hugging the shores of vast Lake Diefenbaker, you are transported to the Scotland's Western Isles or maybe even the legendary Royal Dornoch. Manager Toppy Maisonneuve does tell the story of a Saskatoon doctor of Celtic heritage who makes an annual pilgrimage here to retrace his roots in golf. If you do have any Scots blood in you, it's easy to imagine the plaintive sound of a lone piper's lament drifting across the water. Och aye, it brings a tear to the eye. This course near the prairie hamlet of Riverhurst is in my top five highlights of '95. It's genuine links golf at its best with only two options, fairway or bust. Barr Designs, the architects, have performed a miracle.

#1 - Par 5.
C: 509 yards
R: 458 yards
F: 385 yards

A tee shot landing right of the fairway bunkers left opens up a downhill approach to the green cuddled by the sage. But on the approach watch the sand short front right, a waste bunker and nasty grass pot bunkers casually dotted around. The green has a sharp front end slope.

#2 - Par 4.
C: 304 yards
R: 286 yards
F: 241 yards

Ninety-degree dogleg right. A tee shot carrying at least 240 yards will cut the corner over the heavily-saged hill to land in the fairway. But a steady mid iron to land in the turn right of the fairway sand is the wiser option. That leaves a wedge up to the green surrounded by pots.

#3 - Par 3.
C: 148 yards
R: 149 yards
F: 111 yards

By now you're beginning to realize you've landed in golfer's heaven. Club up one for this shortie with a green perched slightly higher than the tee box. There are four grass pots in the front bank and two behind. Hit the dance floor!

#4 - Par 4.
C: 318 yards
R: 289 yards
F: 240 yards

Down then up with a large inviting landing area. Be careful though. Ideal tee shot should land centre right just inside sand trap. Then it's an uphill approach to a green with a trap wedged front left in the hillside. Several ridges on the green can make for slippery putting.

#5 - Par 4.
C: 322 yards
R: 310 yards
F: 291 yards

Wonderful hole even by Riverbreaks standards. Downhill dogleg right with fairway sand on both sides. The trap on the left is 210 yards out from the tee box and there's also an imposing choke cherry tree right. A good tee shot landing between 'em sets up a wedge approach into green where back right is higher than front left.

#6 - Par 4.
C: 328 yards
R: 308 yards
F: 183 yards

Uphill dogleg left marked by staircase fairway plateaus climbing towards the green. There's sand in the right landing area but near it is where you want to be off the tee. That should leave you a cosy wedge onto a green which has a decided back-front slope.

#7 - Par 3.
C: 130 yards
R: 130 yards
F: 104 yards

What can I say? One of the most spectacular holes I encountered during my summer odyssey. It's 150 feet down to the green at the coulee bottom. Club selection is pure instinct depending on the wind. Enjoy!

#8 - Par 5.
C: 515 yards
R: 499 yards
F: 457 yards

Number seven's a tough act to follow but this super dogleg left gives it a solid try. Tee shot should land left of fairway sand right. The second, or eventual approach, is complicated by a pond eating in short left. Maybe best to land just short of it for chip onto scenic, narrow green.

#9 - Par 4.
C: 424 yards
R: 412 yards
F: 286 yards

Challenging, uphill dogleg left finisher. Tee shot should land somewhere left of the choke cherry bush on the right. Virtually blind approach should be hit just left of the power pole. A lone tree in the middle of the fairway adds to complications caused by sand left and right of the green.

Palliser Park, Riverhurst, Saskatchewan S0H 3P0
Telephone: (306) 353-2065

The stunning 130-yard, par 3, 7th hole

Riverview Golf Club

"Where the golfing outlook is rosy . . . "

Par 36/35

They call the area around the town of Outlook "Saskatchewan's Garden." And it's easy to understand why with the proximity of my old summer friend, the South Saskatchewan River, and the proliferation of irrigation canals snaking through the area. The town's nine-hole course is strung out along the river under some of the oldest elm trees on the continent. The setting is ideal and the course a test with the huge trees threatening fairway edges and overhanging approaches to smallish greens. It was here that what was bound to happen to me some time during the summer did happen. I locked my keys in the car. The banter of friendly members lingering over a coffee more than made up for the inconvenience on a damp Saskatchewan morning.

#1 - Par 4.
R: 357 yards
F: 340 yards

A nice dogleg right along the river complete with views of the mid-stream sandbanks towards the highway bridge. OB right too. Best tee shot is a centre fade on the inside of the large tree. That should set up reasonable mid-iron approach into elevated green with back to front slope.

#2 - Par 5.
R: 526 yards
F: 462 yards

Aim tee shot straight down centre, centre left of this long hole running along the river bank. The undulating fairway could give some unexpected bounces in any direction however. Watch overhitting approach to green nestling in dip.

#3 - Par 4.
R: 363 yards
F: 305 yards

A good looking golf hole with Highway 15 up the embankment on the right and trees along the left side. Drive down the centre makes perfect sense. Watch this green. It is a flat platform back left with the rest dropping right and front. Tricky putts available on request.

#4 - Par 3.
R: 141 yards
F: 122 yards

It should be a straightforward shot but that huge tree immediately back right of the green is an attention-grabber that just might cause concentration problems!

#5 - Par 5/4.
R: 438 yards
F: 415 yards

One pretty golf hole with choke cherry and Saskatoon bushes lining the fairway and a huge elm tree dead centre 200 yards out. Optional, but my way was left of it and it seemed to work for a narrow approach into a trapped green surrounded by bushes and trees. It slopes back to front.

#6 - Par 4.
R: 365 yards
F: 319 yards

A narrow testing dogleg left where you should aim to hit a shot of around 210 yards towards the tallest of the tall trees on the outside of the turn. Cutting the corner's possible but there's ball-devouring shrubbery in there. There's sand front left, front right and behind a green tucked in the trees.

#7 - Par 3.
R: 158 yards
F: 138 yards

Gorgeous short hole. The magnificent elms are the problem. They creep right in on the green, especially one just right of it which creates overhang problems.

#8 - Par 4.
R: 380 yards
F: 337 yards

Yet another challenge. Huge trees travel the left of this narrow fairway and on the right is the bush-filled coulee cliff where a ball can disappear forever. Two large trees straddle the approach route so the more centre the tee shot the better. The green's front end has a sharp slope.

#9 - Par 4.
R: 348 yards
F: 312 yards

Another narrow but attractive hole receding towards the clubhouse. thick trees and bushes threaten both sides, so the message is clear. Be straight!

Box 681
Outlook, Saskatchewan, S0L 2N0
Telephone: (306) 867-8266

The 2nd green and Highway 15 bridge across South Saskatchewan River

Statistical Guide

As stated elsewhere in this book, the author considers each and every golf course to have its merits. What follows below is a statistical guide to inform readers of what to look for in terms of playability, challenge, quality of the experience, value and price.

The official 1995 Course Rating shows to a degree the differential between men's regular tees and front tees and the challenge to be expected.

Gradon's Grading is the author's personal rating. Challenge and playability are assessed on a scale of one to ten. The experience in terms of scenic value and ambience is graded from A to C. An 8C grading, then, would suggest a testing golf course in attractive but unspectacular surroundings. A 10A is the best of both worlds.

CODES: Weekday 18 hole round: $ – $25 and under; $$ – $26-$40; $$$ – Over $40. Montana courses are in US currency. *Special rates for Albertans; N/A Not available at time of publication.

Course	Course Rating		Price Range	Gradon's Grading
	Men	Ladies		
Southern Alberta				
Akokiniskway G.C.	60.2	60.2	$	7B
Balmoral G.C.	67.6	73.6	$	7C
Banff Springs G.C.	71.0	73.0	$$$	10A
Bow Island Jubilee G.C.	67.5	70.0	$	8C
Brooks G.C.	68.7	70.4	$$	8C
Canmore G. & C.C.	67.0	70.3	$$	10A
Connaught G.C.	71.6	73.8	$	8C
Cottonwood Coulee G.C.	66.0	65.0	$	8B
Cottonwood G. & C.C.	70.0	71.5	$$$	9B
Crowsnest Pass G. & C.C.	68.2	70.4	$	8A
D'Arcy Ranch G.C.	70.1	68.3	$$	10C
Dinosaur Trail G. & C.C.	70.0	70.0	$$	9A
Elbow Springs G.C.	69.4	70.3	$$	8C
Fort Macleod G.C.	67.6	69.6	$	7C
Hanna G. & C.C.	69.2	69.0	$	7C
Heatherglen G.C.	68.3	71.7	$$	7C
Henderson Lake G.C.	70.5	73.0	$$	8C
Heritage Pointe G. & C.C.	70.5	70.5	$$$	10B

Highwood G.& C.C.	66.5	64.3	$$	8C
Inglewood G. & C.C.	69.4	72.1	$$	8C
Innisfail G.C.	71.0	71.0	$	10A
Kananaskis Country G.C.				
Mt. Kidd	70.5	68.2	*$$$	10A
Mt. Lorette	72.1	69.8	*$$$	10A
Keho Park G.C.	69.0	67.0	$	7B
Lakeside Greens G. & C.C.	70.5	68.8	$$	8C
Land O Lakes G. & C.C.	68.1	73.1	$	8C
Lee Creek Valley G. & C.C.	71.0	69.5	$	8C
Magrath G.C.	69.3	69.5	$	8C
McKenzie Meadows G.C.	69.6	68.2	$$	8C
Medicine Hat G. & C.C.	69.9	67.6	$	8B
Milk River C.C.	N/A	N/A	$	7C
Nanton G.C.	69.5	69.0	$	8C
Oyen & District G.C.	69.0	71.5	$	7C
Paradise Canyon G. & C.C.	68.3	70.6	$$	9A
Picture Butte G.C.	66.5	67.0	$	7C
Pincher Creek G.C.	69.6	71.9	$	8C
Redwood Meadows G. & C.C.	71.0	74.0	$$	9A
River Bend G.C.	69.4	67.4	$	8C
River's Edge G.C.	65.7	63.6	$	7C
Riverview G.C.	69.5	69.0	$	8B
Rolling Hills G. & C.C.	N/A	N/A	$	7C
Shaw-Nee Slopes G.C.	68.8	72.1	$$	8B
Strathmore G.C.	70.6	69.4	$	8C
Sundre G.C.	68.0	69.0	$	9B
Sylvan Lake G. & C.C.	69.5	71.0	$	8C
Taber G.C.	71.0	71.5	$	8C
Three Hills G.C.	68.2	68.2	$	7C
Water Valley G.C.	N/A	N/A	$	9A
Waterton Lakes G.C.	70.0	74.0	$	9A
Wintergreen G. & C.C.	71.4	69.9	$$	8B
Woodside G.C.	67.0	71.1	$$	7C

Northern Montana

Anaconda Hills G.C.	64.5	68.4	$$	7C
Buffalo Hill G.C.	70.2	70.2	$$	10B
Eagle Bend G.C.	69.3	68.9	$$$	9A
Glacier View G.C.	61.8	61.9	$	7A
Marias Valley G. & C.C.	68.9	68.9	$	8B
Meadow Lake Resort	69.7	69.8	$$	8B
Mission Mountain C.C.	68.7	66.5	$	8A
Polson C.C.	67.9	73.2	$	8B
Signal Point G.C.	70.8	75.2	$	9B
RO Speck G.C.	N/A	N/A	$	6C
Village Greens G.C.	67.0	68.5	$	7C
Whitefish Lake G.C. (North)	68.7	70.1	$$	8A
Whitefish Lake G.C. (South)	69.0	70.3	$$	9A

South-East British Columbia

Cranbrook G.C.	70.9	74.9	$$	9B
Creston G.C.	69.9	72.2	$$	9A
Fairmont Hot Springs Resort	70.0	72.5	$$	9A
Fernie G. & C.C.	69.0	67.0	$$	9A
Golden G. & C.C.	71.0	71.1	$$	10A
Kimberley G.C.	68.6	71.6	$$	9A
Kokanee Springs Golf Resort	70.0	74.0	$$	9A
Mountain Meadows G.C.	70.0	72.0	$	8A
Radium Hot Springs Resort	66.1	69.7	$$	8A
Riverside G. & C.C.	69.2	71.3	$$	9B
Sparwood G.C.	71.0	72.0	$$	9A
The Springs G. & C.C.	71.9	70.8	$$	10B
Trickle Creek Golf Resort	70.6	72.2	$$	10A

South-West Saskatchewan

Chinook G.C.	70.0	72.0	$	8C
Cypress Hills G.C.	N/A	N/A	$	7A
Elmwood G. & C.C.	69.0	71.0	$$	9B
Harbor G.C. & Resort	70.0	68.1	$$	9A
Maple Creek G.C.	72.4	73.0	$	9B
Riverbreaks	N/A	N/A	$	10A
Riverview G.C.	68.0	71.0	$	7C

PRINTED AND BOUND
IN BOUCHERVILLE, QUEBEC, CANADA,
BY MARC VEILLEUX INC.
IN MARCH, 1996